The Early One World Movement

By John Kiang

早期天下一家運動

ONE WORLD MOVEMENT
P.O. BOX 423
NOTRE DAME, INDIANA
U.S.A. 46556

姜 逸 樵 編 著

ONE WORLD PUBLISHING COMPANY

Library of Congress Catalog Card No. 91-68335

ISBN—Soft-0-916301-03-6 $14.95

Published by:

ONE WORLD PUBLISHING
P.O. BOX 423, NOTRE DAME, INDIANA 46556 U.S.A.

Printed by

BOOKMASTERS, INC.
ASHLAND, OHIO 44805

This book is dedicated to

Dr. Linus Pauling

in appreciation of

his great inspiration

to my efforts for

world peace and humanity.

The Author

Preface

After the publication of my *Two Years After* in 1986, comments on my *One World* have still kept coming, reviews on it have appeared here and there, and ideas in relation to it have been exchanged widely. Meanwhile I have extended my try for the unity of all groups that strive for world unity, world government, world federation, world citizens, world peace, humanity, and the like. Consequently documents have been piled up day by day for the last five years. For public information, I am obliged to edit the important ones as up to date supplements to the *Two Years After* which I have also revised, and compile them together as Part One and Part Two of the book under the title of *The Early One World Movement.*

When I started to write the *One World* ten years ago, materials I collected for it had been too enormous and too complicate to manage. In order to facilitate reading for the public, I tried to make the text as terse as possible as a popular manifesto and render all the important references as scholarly annotations. Although the references were carefully selected and strictly applied to support the text with sources, evidence, depth and weight, the annotations grew up almost four times the text, have been the "monumental footnotes" and "at times obscure the flow of the text," as Gary K. Shepherd commented. For this reason Mr. Shepherd and some other friends suggested to issue an additional edition consisting just of the popular manifesto, without the scholarly annotations. I appreciated their suggestion, but preferred to write a new simple book *The Strange World, a Report of the Mission from Moon,* instead. I spent about a year to write the new book, and

1

held its publication for another year, because it mixed up the views of outsiders with those of insiders. Finally I decided to compile the views of insiders as "Our World" to be the Part Three of *The Early One World Movement,* and leave alone the views of outsiders as the basis for rewriting the *Strange World* later when I get time. This is a right arrangement for "Our World", because it presents a part of our efforts for the One World Movement in the early stage.

The distribution of the *One World* has not depended very much on commercial promotion. Many friends have helped it in various ways with enthusiasm. For instance, Dr. Thomas Lee of Santa Monica purchased ten copies as Christmas gifts to his friends; Mrs. Anne W. Morrissey of Chicago purchased six copies for her family members; Mr. Cheung Chiu, a business man in New York, has expressed his interesting again and again to finance its Chinese translation, and Prof. Benjamin B. Ferencz has done many good things for it. For instance, he has recommented it to the United Nations Library and some law libraries, has sent out over a hundred brochures about the book along with his personal letters, has mentioned it often in his lectures, has listed it as a basic reader in the new edition of his famous book *Planethood,* and again in his new book *World Security for the 21st Century.* After his recent trip to Europe he wrote me: "I thought you might be pleased to know that while I was doing some research at the Max Planck Institute for Public International Law at Heidelberg (Germany) I found a copy of *One World* by Kiang on the shelf. You can never tell how far your influence reaches!"

In order to enhance the publicity of the *One World* for approaching its goals of a permanent peace on earth and the general happiness of mankind, some scholars and statesmen nominated it for Nobel Peace Prize in 1986, 1987 and 1988, three times in a row. Unfortunately the Prize authority did not see that a permanent peace on earth is much more important than any temporary or regional peace, and the general happiness of mankind is much more important than any individual or local humanitarian activities.

2

With the failure in Nobel Peace Prize behind, I have treasured much more a personal prize from Mr. Arnold H. Bergier, a philosopher and sculptor of New York. He presented me one of his most beautiful works "in admiration of his scholarship and clear thinking." It is a memorial sculpture of his great friend Albert Einstein with an inscription of his great lesson: "There is no salvation for civilization, or even the human race, other than the creation of a world government."

Finally there is a prize from my daughter Huiping. It is a birthday card she mailed to me several days ago for my 80th birthday. She picked it up from an ordinary store, but it looks like particularly designed to make me happy. In the front there is a picture of mule, a symbol of the hard-working people of my native land—Hunan. The words inside are:

"The world will always need dads like you,
who give so generously,
help so willingly,
care so deeply!
May your birthday be as special as you are!"

John Kiang
May, 1991
South Bend, Ind.

3

Dr. John Kiang

By Dai Cheng-you
March 1991

Contents

Stella Dunn—Lyman Hinckley—Tom
Ehrenzeller and Rick Wicks—Benjamin B.
Ferencz—R. Ward Harrington

PART THREE: OUR WORLD, A SOLID BASE FOR
UNITY

Part One

TWO YEARS AFTER REVISED

A Selection of Comments and Other Documents Pertaining to *One World* in the Two Years after its Publication

問 世 兩 年

I. Foreword

(with Chinese poems as supplement)

There have been two years since the publication of my book *One World*. I am happy to report that the distribution of the book has been going well and its effects have been great and favorable widely, as evidenced by the enormous responses with comments, suggestions and information from all over the world. In order to make these responses available to the public and to reflect how much progress the book and the One World Movement it originated have made in the first two years, I am obliged to publish this collection. It is regretful that a great number of the responses are left out of the compact volume. I like to take this opportunity to express my deep gratitude to all respondents for their interest and encouragement to me. They have indeed done a good service for the great cause.

While under normal conditions the progress of the first two years would be considered as being more than satisfactory, it is far too slow to meet the emergency when mankind and its civilization are in danger of total destruction by a nuclear war which may occur at any minute, and by an array of other crises, including the fast growth of population, the quick depletion of resources, the steady increase of pollution, and the gradual deterioration of the environment. We have to head off the danger by working much harder and acting more quickly. We have to merge all nations into One World for a permanent peace on earth and the general happiness of mankind before it is too late. Time is more important than ever before, and is running out very fast.

It is no surprise that during the first two years, I have experienced various disappointments in my effort and have encountered various obstacles on my way. I have always been able to face adversities with optimism. My faith remains strong, my belief remains firm and my hope remains high. Two more years have added to my advancing age, but I feel even more strengthened and more determined to work for the success of the One World, and to turn my lifetime mission from "impossible" to possible. With this kind of mood and feeling, I wrote early in this year five Chinese classical lyric poems which are reprinted on the following page as a supplement to the foreword. It is almost impossible to translate the tone and style of the Chinese classical poems into English, nor is it necessary since the substance of these poems has more or less spread, and their spirit has permeated here and there, in this message.

John Kiang
October, 1986
South Bend, IN, U.S.A.

春日書懷　姜逸樵

心可放寬氣自和，事留餘地別求奇。
閒門不怕來賓少，繞室敢誇好樹多。名勝
有緣任遊覽，時光無故莫消磨。栽花剪草
忙中樂，過眼煙雲與我何。

學說紛紜費捉摸，客觀應比主觀多。
水平端賴有根底，風格首推無仿摩。好在
靜中看變化，宜從遠處避漩渦。我行我素
不知老，逐浪隨波所爲何？

莫笑空中造樓閣，試爲天下立規模。
搜書萬卷作參考，校稿三年正錯訛。不怕
進行節節慢，祇愁思想框框多。陽春一曲
成高調，瓦釜雷鳴可奈何！

對酒無妨一曲歌，漫言作夢似南柯。
事功有趣百年少，生活無聊半日多。立說
樂於啓後進，著書旨在開先河。鞠躬且盡
耕耘力，莫管收成是幾何！

久涉長途識坎坷，老當益壯別蹉跎。
心無過慮易寧靜，學有未精勤琢磨。願爲
衆生除疾苦，那堪列國酣干戈。移山本是
愚公事，休對人談莫奈何。

一九八六年於南灣之長青軒

II. *A Summary of the* One World

The One World will be realized through the process of group expansion which has been an evolutionary law prevailing everywhere for thousands of years, as shown in the succeeding expansion from the tiny early single family through the primitive community, the small clan and the middle tribe, to the great nation. The expansion has been achieved by merging more smaller groups into less larger ones through various ways step by step. To merge all nations into One World is just one step further, and a necessary consequence of the evolutionary law (Chap. I, a-b).

The utility of the law of group expansion is for our existence, by extending peace within larger and larger groups and by increasing happiness through the division of labor with exchange in wider and wider areas for more and more peoples (Chap. I c).

The size of the group in the several stages of expansion is generally determined by economic life, communication and transportation through tools and energies, and is also effected by weapons. But tools, energies and weapons depend basically on science and technology. Thus, science and technology are the key to the evolutionary law of group expansion (Chap. I d-h).

Now the rapid advance of modern science and technology has, through the conversion of tools and energies into a sophisticated machine, changed our economic life from a locally independent agriculture to a worldwide interdependent industry, and has shrunk our world into a small kingdom in the sense of modern communication and transportation, and into

16

a small tactical theater in the sense of modern weapons. In other words, modern science and technology have gotten all the necessary physical conditions ready for the merging of all nations into One World, as the last step of group expansion (Chap. I i-j).

Actually, the One World has been in the making for quite some time through geographical exploration, popular migration and travel, intellectual dissemination, agricultural dispersal, uniformalization and standardization, social progress, and development in international relations and organizations together with the socialist international movement (Chap. II).

But there are three major blocks remaining in the way to the last step of group expansion and to the making of One World: the independence of the nation, its symbol—national sovereignty, and its agitator—nationalism. The independence of the nation is standing against a world in which all peoples are interdependent, and is standing for the nation which has no big place in the universe and no deep root in history, its time is gone and its value is lost. The national sovereignty is a completely man-made hypothesis like totemism in ancient times. It was originally designed to curb the subversive influence of local rivalries, but has changed from a principle of internal unity and order to a sign of international separation and anarchy. Nationalism has also changed from a force of internal unity to a factor of international disorder. It exploits public sentiment, magnifies local characters, manipulates history, distorts facts, and creates prejudice and hatred. It is a return to tribalism. Unless these three blocks are removed, it will be impossible to merge all nations into One World. So their removal is our primary and most urgent job (Chap. II h-i and Chap. III).

When all nations have merged into One World, they will lose their independent nature with the symbol of sovereignty to wage war, all peoples will become one group, and there will be no other group as an opponent to fight with. Therefore, a permanent peace will exist on the earth. At the moment, however, we and our civilization are in danger of total destruction by a nuclear war which may occur any minute. We have to prevent the catastrophe before it is too late, with urgent measures including: to stand firmly against any kind of war; to disband all armed forces; to stop military conscription and training; to stop making and developing any kind of weapons; and to destroy all weapons already made or convert them into peaceful uses (Chap. IV).

At the moment, we are not only in danger of a nuclear war, but also under the threat of an array of other serious crises including the fast growth of population, the quick depletion of resources, the steady increase of pollution, and the gradual deterioration of the environment. There is no real solution to these crises except to merge all nations into One World with a powerful world government to manage the over-all world business effectively (Chap. V).

In order to manage the overall world business effectively so as to assure the general happiness of mankind, it is necessary to set sound principles for the world government to follow. They include: all natural resources of land, ocean, and space belong to mankind as a whole; all existing economic systems are entitled to operate, compete and adjust by free will; advance through science and technology with respect for humanity and ecosystem; growth with balance; raising living standard in the poorer areas; and controlling population to an optimum size, as priorities; and to save and develop energies, non-fuel materials, forest products, and water, to improve and increase food production, to prevent natural calamities, to protect the environment with conservation, and to unify and equalize the world economy, as the most important measures. The initial financial requirement for managing the overall world business is to transfer all military expenditures of all nations to be the fund for the general happiness of mankind. Annually, these expenditures are about 6 percent of the total world income at the present time (Chap. V).

The World Government will be vested with a supreme authority derived from all peoples, and subordinated to the World Government, are the nations as autonomous or federal components to take good care of their local business. Local culture, economy and government will be respected as much as possible. The World Government will consist of a World Judiciary, a World Administration and a World Council. The

Council is the central organ of the World Government, and will be composed of a House of Commons and a House of Experts. It elects a president who will also serve as the World President in formality. The World Government will have nothing to do with military and foreign affairs, and will be run by experts rather than by politicians (Chap VI).*

Fundamental to the World Government is the World Law, which is superior to any local law, governs the individuals directly, leaves no room for the existence of national sovereignty, and brings an end to international laws. Human rights and obligations will be well respected. A World Constitution as the foundation of World Law will be drafted for adoption. The police will be the only force allowed to exist for law enforcement (Chap. VI).

The One World Movement is a common endeavor of the people who want to work consciously, voluntarily and actively for the merging of all nations into One World for permanent peace on earth and general happiness of mankind. Its membership requires a pledge of loyalty to humanity, of allegiance to mankind, and of devotion to the common cause. It will be a worldwide organization and would like to unite all groups that strive for one world, world government, peace, humanity and the like, into one movement. Its expedient set-up includes a training center—One World University which also serves as the Movement's headquarters. It will launch a world revolution with a campaign for liberation to get rid of the independence of the nation, national sovereignty and nationalism; a campaign for promotion to raise humanity, loyalty to mankind and world patriotism; and a campaign for survival including anti-war activities, protest against the development of weapons, and demand for a total disarmament. But our revolution will not rely on violence, myth or intrigue. We are going to campaign openly with open minds and open policies toward an open world (Chap. VII f-h).

Along with the campaigns, our world revolution calls for the formation of a provisional world government by converting the United Nations, by experiment of the One World Movement with the support initiated by any nation or a group of countries, or by direct action of the people. The main job of

19

the provisional world government is to complete world disarmament, to draft a world constitution and to see it ratified by a World Constituent Assembly and to establish a permanent world government accordingly, and to have important projects prepared for the pursuit of general happiness and to start some most urgent works (Chap. VII i-j).

The fundamental problem of our time is that science and technology have advanced much faster than social adjustment and material developments have left spiritual traditions far behind. There is no solution to this problem except to speed up social adjustment and revitalize spiritual traditions. For the speed-up and revitalization we have to resort to reason, rational and intellect as we did in the Renaissance, and to rely on faith in ourselves and our future as we did with the Enlightenment Movement. With reason, rational, intellect and faith, surely we can work together to merge all nations into One World for a permanent peace and a general Happiness, to establish a World Government to serve all the people, and to advance our civilization to shine the universe, for billions of years to come (Chap. VII k).

III. A Comprehensive Review of the Evolutionary Law of Group Expansion

The evolutionary law of group expansion is the guiding theory of the *One World*. It is an historical and universal law, is not only inevitable but also irresistible, and is the scientific, philosophical and logical foundation for the one world government as well as for the One World Movement. It may be reviewed comprehensively in the following table. For detail, please check throughout the first chapter of the *One World*.

Age	Culminating time	Basic Economic Life	Land needed per person[1] (sq.mi.)	Population[2]	Series	Independent Group Size Expension (Average)		Number reduction
						Population	Territory (sq.mi.)	
Old Stone	30,000 B.C.	Food-gathering	10	5,000,000	Early single family	5	50	1,000,000
Young Stone	10,000 B.C.	Hunting-fishing	5	10,000,000	Primitive community	50	250	200,000
New Stone	5,000 B.C.	Hoe-cultivating	1	15,000,000	Clan	1,500	1,500	10,000
Copper	1,000 B.C.	Animal-raising	$\frac{1}{5}$	155,000,000	Tribe	75,000	15,000	2,000
Iron	1,900 A.D.	Agricultural	$\frac{1}{50}$	1,550,000,000	Nation	8,000,000	150,000	200
Machine	Near future	Industrial	$\frac{1}{150}$	7,500,000,000	One World	All peoples	All lands	1

1. Cf. in general, William G. Sumner and Albert G. Keller, *The Science of Society*, New Haven, 1927, v. 4, p. 17–19, and Clark Wissler, *An Introduction to Social Anthropology*, New York, 1929, p. 28–41, also George H. T. Kimble, *Man and His World*, Morristown, N.J., 1972, p. 292.
2. Based on estimates in *Energy Resources*, a report of the Committee on National Resources of the National Academy of Sciences–National Research Council, by M. King Hubbert, Chairman of the Energy Resources Study, Washington, 1962, p. 15–20; United Nations, *The Future Growth of World Population*, New York, 1958, p. 17; and George H. T. Kimble, *Man and His World*, Morristown, N.J., 1972, p. 185, 186, 218.

IV. Comments Quoted
(with two in Chinese)

"John Kiang has written a plea to the people of all countries on earth to work together to achieve the goal of permanent peace on earth and the achievement of a society in which every person has the opportunity to lead a good life. His argument is presented in detail, and it is supported by many references and footnotes. . . . The principal message is that war has now ruled itself out—a war in which the existing nuclear weapons were used would with little doubt mean the end of our civilization, and possibly the end of the human race. . . . The time has come now for the people of the world to join together in eliminating the evil of war and in building the world of the future. Everyone should read this book and heed its message." **Dr. Linus Pauling, the double Nobel Laureate (U.S.A.).**

"I am very pleased that you sent me your book and I am admiring you for writing such a thoroughgoing discussion of the problem we are all very strongly concerned with." **Dr. Fritz Lipmann, Nobel Laureate (U.S.A.).**

"I share your heartfelt wish for a decrease of nationalistic prejudice and aggressiveness, and also for a decrease of the passionate unreason and violence that stems from dogmas of all kinds, especially from political and religious fundamentalisms." **Dr. Peter Mitchell, Nobel Laureate (England).**

"I am still reading and re-reading parts of your book for which I have much sympathy. I am working on a feeling that world government would come much easier and sooner if we had more common ideologic basis to build on. . . . The time has passed when nations should be allowed to do as they individually wish with regard to global matters, each striving solely in its own interests, with the more powerful now able to destroy all humanity and more. For the common good, we need to frame and abide by a higher system of law and justice, designed with less national, more godlike, perspectives for the preservation and welfare of the biosphere as a whole. The intellectual, scientific and moral foundations are already in sight. Control of nuclear armaments is a logical place to start their implementation." **Dr. Roger W. Sperry, Nobel Laureate (U.S.A.).**

"So thank you for the book, and good luck to all your endeavors to spread as widely as possible, particularly among your fellow-countrymen, the notion that we are all citizens of one world." **Sir John Cornforth, Nobel Laureate (England).**

"Thank you for it (the book *One World*). I have looked through it with interest." **Dr. Ilya M. Frank, Nobel Laureate (U.S.S.R.).**

"An invaluable help to all the peace people workers here." **Dr. Maired Corrigan-Maguire, Nobel Laureate (Ireland).**

"I see your deep devotion to the problem of unifying this world. It has my great sympathy. We scientists all think in this way as we consider our fellow scientists all over the world as one big family." **Manfred Eigen, Nobel Laureate (Germany).**

24

"Thank you for your interesting book, which looks attractive with regard to the presentation and content." **Prof. Werner Arber, Nobel Laureate (Switzerland).**

"I have had the opportunity to read your book, *One World,* and want you to know how much I enjoyed it. The book is a wealth of knowledge and it is quite obvious that you have put much time, research and thought into its creation." **Mr. John Hiler, Member of Congress of the United States (U.S.A.).**

"I stand in awe of your ability to mobilize as much research material as you did . . . your scholarship is titanic." **Dr. Norman Cousins, Chairman of the World Federalists Association (U.S.A.).**

"You are a scholar worthy to walk in the footsteps of Confucius (and) think in global terms." **Dr. Robert Bartlett, prominent historian and Sinologist (U.S.A.).**

"Your book is an apex achievement—a quantum leap for the mankind of earth." **Mr. Luis Ketner, Chairman of the World Habeas Corpus (U.S.A.).**

"John Kiang's proposal for "One World Movement" seems to me nearest to what we all actually need." **Mr. Bruno Micheli,** *Evolution,* **the Press as an Instrument for Peace and World Unity (Italy).**

"I place Dr. Kiang's book *One World* first in order, because his endeavor (to turn people's attention not merely to the imminent threat of one last war into oblivion, but to how we must change our thinking, as Einstein warned, to achieve survival and lasting peace) is the most monumental in coverage and quality. . . . The superiority of the One World Movement outlined in *One World* (over those earlier movements) lies in the endeavor to provide a historical and cultural foundation, namely the substance of the book itself." **Mr. Lyman Hinckley, World-Neighborhood Faith and Law (U.S.A.).**

"You have done a fine job of articulating the position for a democratic federal world government, with which I certainly agree. Beyond this, you have marshalled supporting quotes and comments that are invaluable to those of us working for this cause. The format of your book reminds me of the Confucian Classics as I studied them at Yenching University years ago!" **Dr. Lucile Green, President, World Citizens Assembly (U.S.A.).**

"(Your book) is a truly monumental study of the great One World Movement that is gaining ground through the various NGOs; surging up like a great mist from the sea—which is both visible and at the same time intangible. But clearly, it is rooted in a great spiritual force that is now flowing through the minds of men—if only in somewhat limited numbers at present! And your book must certainly be regarded as the classic reference and academic work of the Movement, and one which should be available in every library throughout the world—particularly in every university." **Ms. Stella Dunn, Hon. Organizer of the Project for Peace (England).**

As you see, your book is very stimulating to me. . . . It is indeed a treasure, and I am sure it will have its due influence to bring us together." **Mr. John Davenport, from Puertito Guimar Tenerife, Islas Canarias (Spain).**

"Thankfully that you read Emery's book and feel inspired by him through those fantastic pages of wisdom. . . . Your title *One World* was so often on Emery's lips. I appreciate it even more." **Wendy, widow of Emery Reves—author of the famous book,** *The Anatomy of Peace.*

"Thank you very much for the copy of your book, *One World.* I find the concepts most interesting, and agree that we must find mechanisms to bring us all closer together." **Dr. Brooke E. Sheldon, Dean of the Texas Woman's University and former President of the American Library Association (U.S.A.).**

"Dr. Kiang has spent his life in pursuit of developing his logical approach to the solution of world problems. One World indeed is an ultimate objective in which, if achieved, all of the petty strife of nationalism, individualism, economic and social turmoil will disappear." **Dr. Jack J. Detzler, Professor, St. Mary's College, Indiana (U.S.A.).**

"Dr. John Kiang has produced an excellent book called *One World,* which is founded on massive research. The work is based on the findings of scholars throughout the ages. It is his thesis that war, disease, the homeless, the starving myriads, the desolation of the environment, among other problems, can only be finally eliminated if we have one world under one government. He finds national sovereignty and nationalism to be destructive to the hopes of people everywhere. There can be peace and harmony for all if the nations of the world can be persuaded to relinquish their claims to independence and join together to form a world government." **Dr. Paul Thomas Welty, Professor Emeritus, Northern Illinois University, Illinois (U.S.A.).**

"I have finally read your book completely through. I misplaced it when I was about half way through. Your book is the most comprehensive, well planned, detailed, researched, and documented book I have ever read. It led logically, step by step, to the One World which can bring world peace and save the human race and the Planet Earth from destruction. Many of our values, attitudes, and beliefs are not too compatible with those needed for One World. Your book should help change them some, but some people will resist because they want to hold onto the advantages they have over their fellow beings under the present system. I hope that I can find time to go and see you and discuss the means of speeding up the movement toward One World." **Dr. Arno Luker, Professor at the University of Northern Colorado (U.S.A.).**

"Dr. Kiang's discovery of the evolutionary law of group expansion is a great contribution to civilization. It is an historical and universal law. Its importance to One World is as much as Isaac Newton's 'Principia' to physics, Jean Jacques Rousseau's 'Social Contract' to democracy, and Karl Marx's 'Class Struggle' to Communism. His finding that the independence of human groups is the root of war is another important contribution to civilization. This finding leads to the conclusion that international war could not be abolished unless the independence of the nation has been eradicated. In other words, no permanent peace could be achieved on the earth until all nations have merged into One World. Also important are the innovations in his project for world government. He plans a central organ of four essential functions in knowledge, opinion, service and justice to replace the traditional three divisions of power, the new democratic centralism, or other kinds of power allocation in the structure of government. He emphasizes technical experts rather than common politicians to run the government. And he eliminates the establishments of military and foreign affairs from the government. These innovations are aimed at changing the nature of the government from ruling to serving the people. It is an application of the principles of democracy in a positive way for a new political system." **Prof. Henry K. O. Wong, a World federalist leader (Canada).**

"Dr. Kiang through nearly 50 years of tireless efforts has produced a comprehensive work, *One World*. He did so by developing a general theory on the evolution of human civilization and by proposing a world system to achieve the ultimate goals of permanent peace and general welfare. Amassing a breath-taking amount of empirical evidence through the course of human civilization to demonstrate the inevitability and necessity of One World, Dr. Kiang has, in his monumental volume with more than 1700 extended, scholarly annotations, evolved the important theory of group expansion through science and technology, laying a firm historical and intellectual foundation for the One World. His volume also contains carefully thought-out guidelines for structuring the One World, complete with concrete steps for its consummation. It is as much as the 1933 Nobel Peace Prize winner Sir Norman Angell's *The Great Illusion* in the interest of pursuing peace, but is more constructive, positive and far-reaching." **Dr. Robert T. L. Lee, Professor at Southern Connecticut State University (U.S.A.).**

"Once in the last century, a famous British sinologist remarked that Chinese used to record their theories and practices in a style of prose without much systematic and thorough treatment for the subject as exemplified by Confucius' works, especially his famous Analects which contains only 11,705 words, in contrast to the Occidental tradition as exemplified by Aristotle's works with voluminous treatises. Lately, Chinese scholars have been joked as retailers of the products of their ancestors. To these criticisms, Dr. John Kiang's *One World* is certainly a strong repudiation. It is the most systematic and thorough treatise on the subject so far, and a new product with the entire world civilization as background.

29

However, Dr. Kiang is a human being, not just a Chinese, and any merit of his book should be attributed to the whole human family, while the success of the One World Movement initiated by the book conceivably requires understanding and supports of all the people. I concur completely with Dr. Pauling's opinion that everyone should read this book and heed its message." **Dr. Y. C. James Yen, the only survivor of the world ten outstanding "Modern Revolutionaries" as honored by the Copernican Quadricentennial Committee in 1943 (China).**

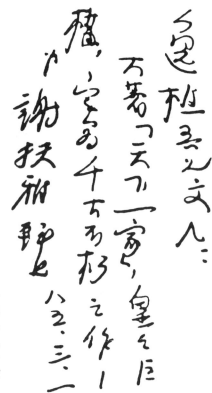

"Your *One World* is indeed a great monumental work which will last forever." **Prof. N. Z. Zia, prominent philosopher and author, at the age of 94 (China).**

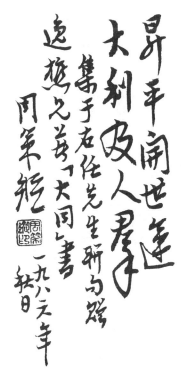

昇平開世運
大利及人群
集于右任先生聯句贈
逸塵之善「大同」書
同年苾
一九八六年
秋日

"In appreciation of your *One World*, I like to present you the symmetrical prophecies of Y. J. Yu that lasting peace will flourish the world and great happiness will bless all peoples." **Dr. T. T. Chow, Prof. of the University of Wisconsin (U.S.A.).**

V. Comments with Complete Letters

From Dr. Ragnar Granit,
Nobel Laureate (Sweden)

November 1st, 1984

Dear Dr. Kiang,

I have but recently had time from travel and other occupations to survey your fascinating and scholarly *One World* for which my sincerest thanks are due.

It is a major study of the background and development of world affairs. One can hardly read any of its sections without getting greatly impressed by the labour and thought laid down by its author.

Its plea shares with many international engagements directed toward the grave issues at stake for humanity but the profound factual knowledge displayed in running annotations and comments is quite unique and should make it an invaluable source of reference for people all over the world.

You have indeed done the cause an immense service because so many people hate to take up a standpoint for lack of knowledge and here, now, by you, it is being provided.

Yours sincerely,

Ragnar Granit

From Mr. Henry Usborne, Joint President
of the Parliamentary Group
for World Government (England)

November 3rd, 1984

Dear Mr. Kiang:

Thank you for sending me your book, *One World*. I have now read it carefully, and with great interest. I must congratulate you on completing what is most certainly a magnum opus. It is essential reading for all would-be peace-makers.

My own conclusions differ somewhat from yours. At the moment, I can see no possibility of either of the two Great Powers, the U.S.A. or the U.S.S.R., giving up their elemental sovereignty to a world federal authority. So I have suggested an alternative solution which, if it were to be accepted, and the UN Security Council of the Great Four were to be created, would, in practice, provide the world with considerable government.

But you could be right; and I could be wrong. The really important thing is that those of us who have spent much time and energy on this subject should publicize our various conclusions. No one can foretell, as yet, exactly how our species will survive. Or even if it will survive much longer.

So I am sending you herewith a copy of my latest m.s. which I hope may soon be published.

I believe that nationalism, and patriotism, are both concepts which can and should be differentiated from what I have called "elemental sovereignty." The first two can well be retained. But elemental sovereignty must be swiftly and finally abolished—or *Homo sapiens* will assuredly soon be extinguished. Evidently you and I both agree on that.

Yours sincerely,

Henry Usborne

From Dr. Frederick Sanger,
Nobel Laureate (England)

November 9, 1984

Dear Dr. Kiang:

Thank you very much for sending me a copy of your book *One World* which I was very interested to see. I am sorry for the delay in acknowledging your generosity, but I had been waiting till I had looked at it in more detail. I must say that I am very much in agreement with what I have read so far. It is encouraging that your detailed studies have come to much the same conclusions as my more casual thoughts, particularly in respect to nationalism as being the main obstacle to progress.

I certainly wish you every success with your "movement," though I feel that the task is formidable in a world where almost all the power is in the hands of those who represent national interests. Let us hope that the message will eventually get through enough people to overcome this. It seems the only way and I admire your efforts towards it.

I enclose a cheque for £25 towards the cost of the book or for the expenses of your movement.

Yours sincerely,

Fred Sanger.

Fred Sanger

From Dr. Gerhard Herzberg,
Nobel Laureate (Canada)

12 October, 1984

Dear Dr. Kiang:

It was very kind of you to send me a copy of your book *One World*. It is good to see such a scholarly work as you have done. I hardly need to say that I am in full accord with your attempt to encourage world government. I believe that the majority of the people in the West would agree with you, provided that a method could be found to encourage the East to participate in this effort.

Thank you again for your most valuable contribution.

Sincerely yours,

G. Herzberg

From Dr. Charles DeBenedetti,
Professor of the University of Toledo (U.S.A.)

March 26, 1985

Dear Dr. Kiang:

My friend, Kuan-chen Fu, was good enough to share with me your excellent study of *One World.* I enjoyed the book very much, and was extremely impressed with your knowledge and erudition.

One of the difficulties of publishing, of course, is to establish access to a wider reading public. I fear that your book might not have this access. Therefore, I'm writing today to suggest that you contact Professor Warren F. Kuehl, director of the Center for Peace Studies at the University of Akron.

Professor Kuehl maintains an excellent newsletter through which the Center advises a national network of teachers and scholars on noteworthy new publications. I think that your work falls within that category, and would urge you to send him a copy along with some information about yourself.

Meanwhile, best wishes in your work. And congratulations—and thanks—for the effort that you invested in this achievement.

Sincerely yours,

Charles DeBenedetti

From Dr. Willy Brandt, Nobel Laureate and former Prime Minister (Germany)

April 22, 1985

Dear Dr. Kiang:

Thank you very much for dedicating me your work *One World.* I have been impressed by the intensity of describing the problems of this world. And thank you for pointing out ways how to solve them. May your ideas help promoting peace and happiness of all man.

Sincerely yours,

Willy Brandt

From Dr. John Brademas, President of New York University (U.S.A.)

May 24, 1985

Dear Dr. Kiang:

Thank you for your note and the copy of *One World.* Your view of social evolution and your vision for the future are certainly worthy of reflection.

Although we may indeed be developing toward the world community you describe, the issues I confronted during my twenty-two years in Congress indicate to me that we, the world, still have a long way to go. I hope and assume that you are a patient man!

With all best wishes.

Sincerely,

John Brademas

From Lord Todd, Nobel Laureate (England)

3 July 1985

Dear Dr. Kiang:

Thank you for sending me a copy of your book, *One World,* which I have been reading with great interest. Your view (which you argue most powerfully) that mankind's only solution is to be found in One World is one with which I and, I believe, most people would certainly agree. After all, mankind's progress has always been in the direction of larger and larger units—from the family to the tribe, from the tribe to the city state then the national and finally the federal state which in one form or another is now prominent in the world. The ultimate is clearly the world state, but I can see many difficulties which will have to be overcome if it is to be realised. The slow forward march of humanity over millennia was rudely destroyed by the industrial revolution which originated in the western world and led to a tremendous and ever accelerating change in material civilization due to scientific and technological advance. Unfortunately, however, social attitudes remain, as ever, very slow to change and it is society's inability to come to terms with rapid technological advance that is the primary source of our present trouble. Not unrelated, too, is the great disparity between not merely wealth but also social development and attitudes in the so-called "third world" countries which have come up against modern technology while still at a "pre-industrial revolution" stage in their development.

While, therefore, I agree with your general thesis (as most thinking people, I believe, would) I fear that a lengthy period will have to elapse before anything like a real world state will be realisable. One can only hope and try to speed the process. I wish you well in your endeavors.

Yours sincerely,

Todd.

Todd

From Dr. N. Bloembergern
Nobel Laureate (formerly Netherlands)

July 23, 1985

Dear Mr. Kiang:

Please accept my apologies for this belated reply. I have received your book, *One world,* in good order several months ago. Thank you very much.

I found the jacket description "A popular manifesto with scholarly annotations" particularly apt and truthful in describing the contents. The text provides food for thought for all concerned, and all of us should be concerned.

Sincerely yours,

N. Bloembergen

N. Bloembergen

From Dr. Dorothy Hodgkin, Nobel Laureate (England)

August 18, 1985

Dear Dr. Kiang:

I do apologise for not having written sooner about your book *One World* which I am very glad to have. I should have written sooner to welcome your contribution—but this summer has been crowded with events and work for me, which I too hope contribute to *One World*.

I must admit I have not had time to read it critically—only to skip through some sections and my immediate future is still crowded. So I had better give you a few comments quickly.

I found it interesting to look at to begin with—its form is so like that of the theses in History that my friends as Oxford used to produce when I was young—and probably still do—a line or two of text per page and the rest supporting footnotes. If I settle down on any page, there is always much to think about—I find myself grudging individual statements—though in general agreeing with your main conclusions and decisions.

In many ways, perhaps more than we realize, we live in One World already. This summer I have been to Geneva and Brazil for international conferences, to France for a holiday with French friends and a Vietnamese boy, returned home for summer visitors, a Chinese professor from Peking, a Zambian friend next week—and this week one from Bulgaria—mixed with my eldest grandson and his newlywed American wife, a lovely and intelligent young doctor. Last night Maria, from Sofia, was delighted to see we had "Shogun" on the TV—she had seen it in Sofia and wanted the repeat. TV is clearly a great link for everyday lives, everywhere. When I went to China in 1965 and brought back Chinese accounts of the synthesis of insulin, I was amazed to find they already had them in New York. Sometimes I think we only have to increase common knowledge of one another, common experience of working together for the barriers to fall and dangers disappear. But still awful things are happening which first have to be stopped.

Constitutions are always difficult—some of the earlier ones work better than the last—it's brave of you to try to set up one for one world. More thanks.

Yours sincerely,

Dorothy Hodgkin

Dorothy Hodgkin

From Dr. Edward Kelly,
Professor of the University of
Northern Colorado

July 14, 1986

Dear John:

I sincerely regret that I didn't get around to thanking you for sending me a copy of your book, *One World*. In reality, I just couldn't put into words the thoughts that ran through my mind as I read it. On the one hand, your thesis seems to be simplicity itself, but when one considers its needs for implementation and its ramifications, the whole concept becomes mind-boggling.

It is my firm belief that although neither you nor I will ever see much of any movement of consequence toward the unification of the world; the powerful blueprint that you have drawn in your book will continue to stimulate loving and thinking people to action toward the ends that you have so clearly described until one day the ultimate goals of a "Permanent Peace on Earth and the General Happiness of Mankind" will be achieved.

May God bless your efforts!

Please tell Susan that Betty and I fondly remember the times that we all shared together.

Most sincerely,

Ed Kelly

Ed Kelly

From Professor Louis B. Sohn, Author of the book, World Peace through World Law *(U.S.A.)*

July 31, 1986

Dear Mr. Kiang:

Thank you for sending me a copy of your book *One World,* which I read with interest. It is a powerful, well-documented brief for liberating mankind from various preconceptions which stand in the way of uniting mankind for common wellness. Perhaps it can stimulate some new thinking, in the same way as the *Anatomy of Peace* energized many young people (like myself) in the 1940s.

The need is clear. Even though the path is strewn with obstacles, the task is not impossible.

Sincerely yours,

Louis B. Sohn

Louis B. Sohn
Woodruff Professor of International Law

From Mr. Francis G. Irwin,
Society of Friends, Philadelphia

August 12, 1986

Dear John Kiang:

Your monumental *One World* arrived to my delighted surprise a short while ago. I was both interested in what you had to propound and the method you chose to do it, after having my appetite whetted by John Davenport's intriguing comments about it.

I found your simple, clear statements reasoned and convincing and your research and annotations most impressive and independently useful. The book's wide dissemination must be highly recommended by every thinking person.

Having made these laudatory comments and expressed my appreciation for the opportunity you so generously gave me to add it to my library, lend it to my friends, etc., I would like to take the opportunity to make some comments, which you might find peripherally useful and pertinent, or at least of some interest.

We humans are of many backgrounds and life experiences and come to "conclusions" with which we can be "comfortable." Truth, reason, logic play much less part in this process than is generally assumed.

People get bombarded daily with innumerable bits of our information-explosion items, tempting them, urging them, threatening them, teaching them, pleading with them, promising them, entertaining them, etc. Partly as a consequence thereof, any ideas which are complicated or abstract or unusual or appear irrelevant are incapable of holding their interest for the time required to fully grasp them.

The movement for world government has not yet been able to present its case so as to overcome this horrendous handicap. Oh, yes, a tiny number of people see the light, but possibly an equal number fall again by the wayside, disillusioned perhaps by the lack of progress they perceive after some years of frusstrating adherence. And when One Worlders, of whatever branch, get together to "recharge their batteries" and plan strategy, you cannot but become aware that each individual has a slightly or considerably different picture of the ultimate goal, of the intermediate steps necessary to achieve it, and of the ways and means envisaged to get us moving in that direction. These facts have to be faced.

John Davenport likes to quote my plaintive "We must be doing something wrong," which at least presupposes that the fault is *not* in the vision—the ultimate goal—but in our method of advocacy. (Don't think for a moment that I claim to have the answer—I'm still actively searching, like many of my peers.) Mostly by trial and error, certain rules have come to be recognized by me and I would like to bring just three to your attention.

The first rule I have come to accept is the urgent need for *simplification,* and would quote as an example the well-thought-out campaign of the Beyond War movement. They say that new institutions will be preceded by appropriate laws and these will automatically follow when popular demand calls for them. Thus they concentrate on attitude change as a prerequisite. How do they attempt this? By explaining that the world has changed—in two statements—each consisting of 3 words (WAR IS OBSOLETE: WE ARE ONE) *Nothing* could be simpler! As international war is unthinkable, we must no longer look at opponents as enemies. Looking down from space, national boundaries are totally absent. Once we change our attitude, it's going to be a totally new ball game. They do not prescribe or even describe what that new world will be. This is their strategy and it remains to be seen how successful it is going to be, or what changes in their methodology they might introduce as they go along. All their work is professionally handled and first-class. I watch their progress (and even assist them on occasions) with much interest.

The second rule I have come to believe in is that soundness and rationality alone will not carry the day for us. Logic and common sense must be supplemented by *appeals to emotion.*

Humans are often swayed and deeply affected by their feelings. They frequently justify their beliefs and actions based mostly on sentiment and "gut feeling."

I think that Joy Sitz, a member from Iowa of the WFA, is on the right track when she states: " . . . we believe that a global consciousness is required before people will begin to seriously accept the concept of world federalism. . . . How do you instill global consciousness? The same way you instill national consciousness . . . through the use of symbols: banners, anthems, logos, colors, pledges, etc. We have all at one time or another experienced a surge of national pride on seeing the flag go by, having the "Battle Hymn of the Republic" rousingly played, reciting the pledge of allegiance, etc. They all have a unifying effect. Yet there is nothing to symbolize our unity as planetary citizens. . . . " (She proposed an international contest for a Global Anthem.) My own feeling is that, in addition to her idea, we should also follow the pledge route—perhaps a solemn affirmation of consideration, protection and care for our whole fragile planet and all its diverse inhabitants.

The third rule we have to follow, if we want to succeed, is in my opinion the absolute *necessity of widest exposure*. And due to our small numbers, imaginative steps, even possibly some extreme measures, are called for. IF WE ARE NOT KNOWN, OUR IDEAS WILL BE IGNORED. If we get in the news, repeatedly and increasingly, people will become interested, take sides, discuss some pros and cons, resulting in more momentum being established. *Visibility* is the name of the game; controversy will follow—no doubt about that—but opposition is by far preferable to remaining unknown and totally ignored. Once opposition becomes vocal, we will be able to put our case and give people a chance to judge for themselves.

Each one of us One Worlders should be imbued with a sense of urgency, a compelling mission which precludes an attitude of "business as usual." You, dear John Kiang, have provided one of the classic pieces of literature for our cause, the record of which will remain, when you have long gone. But this is only half the battle. An inspiring and well qualified teacher is wasted, if there are no pupils and we don't know how to get them in the classroom and make them listen. That is the next great challenge.

My warmest appreciation and regards to you,

Francis G. Irwin

VI. Sir Martin Ryle's Last Testament

Sir Martin Ryle, Nobel Laureate (England), died on Oct. 14, 1984. His widow, Rowena, kindly sent his "Last Testament" in lieu of comment on One World. *Originally, the "Last Testament" is a letter arising form a request by Professor Carlos Chagas, the president of the Pontifical Academy of Sciences, for topics to be discussed at a meeting entitled "Science for Peace."*

24 February, 1983

Dear Professor Chagas:

You ask a very difficult question in seeking topics which should be discussed in considering the contribution which scientists may (should) make towards peace.

I am afraid that I can only express my own views and hope that out of them some topics may emerge. I think one cannot separate science from the political/military/historical background, and perhaps I should summarise my personal views here first. Inevitably I see through British eyes, but I think the view might have been similar if I had spent my life in any European Country.

1. *Political.* The USSR exists, the US exists, they must either learn to live together, or die together.

The political system of the USSR is appalling, but those who suffer under it—and have little freedom to influence it—are those who will die. (In World War I some 5 percent of casualties were innocent civilians; in World War II about 50 percent; in a nuclear war it would be perhaps 95 percent.)

One cannot change the Russian system from outside— only annihilate it and the innocent with it. Change must come from within and will be slow. (Our Western systems are not perfect—the ever-increasing gap between rich and poor; the increasing power of the multinational companies, inadequate contribution to the Third World; Vietnam and the destabilising of Chile, Central America, and so on.)

There are great asymmetries; for European Russia, strategic and theatre weapons are the same. The effects on the two super-powers of World War II were very different. In the USSR, seven million combatants and 12 million civilians were killed; in the United States, 400,000 combatants were killed (in all the theatres of war put together), and no civilians. Two million square kilometres of the Soviet Union were occupied and severely damaged, but not even a square metre of the United States.

The effects of these historical facts on post-war attitude cannot be ignored.

We, in Europe, whose experience (by being fought over, occupied or bombed) falls between [these extremes], have the responsibility of appreciating both attitudes.

2. *Military.* Present nuclear arsenals are so large that if even a few percent were launched, much of Northern Hemisphere civilisation would be destroyed. In these circumstances, "Balance of power" and "Negotiation from strength" are meaningless. Either East or West could dismantle 10, 20 or 50 percent of its weapons with no military disadvantage.

Yet the Pentagon has urged the development of "Third-generation" weapons, and shortly before his death, President Breshnev stated that USSR would match every US weapons development.

3. *Proliferation.* The eagerness of nuclear countries to export "research" and "power" reactors to non-nuclear nations—with the know-how, fuel, etc.—constitutes the only politically respectable route for the acquisition of

weapons-grade plutonium. It is the route which was used by practically every new nuclear weapons and near-nuclear weapons state.

The construction of even a few warheads to "settle" a long-standing situation may now be the most likely trigger for the Final world war. In much of the Third World, nuclear power provides no solution to the low-density energy needs.

4. *What could science/scientists do?* Sadly, some 40 percent of professional engineers and probably a higher proportion of physicists in the UK are engaged in devising new ways of killing people; the US figures are I think much the same. Although there are plenty of jobs available in these areas, it is practically impossible for a young graduate of PhD to find a socially-useful job. What do I say when young men and women come and ask my advice?

One can lay the blame on the government for distorting the distribution of expenditure and the powerful commercial pressures put upon them, but sadly that is not the whole story, the lure of challenging problems, high technology and unlimited funds seduces young physicists/engineers. This is not necessarily limited to *nuclear* weapons. With tanks, aircraft, rocket launchers and others which have kept going the 130 wars in the Middle East, Africa and South America since 1945—until the international arms trade is banned—this is where the money lies. The young seem able to work on, say, an anti-aircraft missile without regard for the consequences. They have never seen an aircraft shot down, nor felt the identity of its crew—whether hostile or friendly—which came from having flown in military aircraft. To so many, it is simply an intriguing scientific problem; the morality and responsibility are pushed aside—the politicians make the decisions.

5. *The universities.* While most of these supremely unnecessary developments are made in the defence establishments and in the industries working for them, the reduction in state support for the universities has meant that science and engineering departments rely more and more on contracts—and this today means "defence" contracts.

It raises the whole question: should the universities try and retain the original status of an "association of independent scholars"—or should they become cheap research establishments for the state? In the UK, we have had a long history of royal commissions, board of inquiry in which the impartial voices of university members have been very important; the possibility of impartiality is fast disappearing.

6. *The individual scientist.* Besides his own narrow field of research, I believe that the scientist has a particular social responsibility in being aware of what is going on—and saying when he feels it to be wrong. Some, when challenged, would agree with what I was arguing, but would not commit themselves openly, for example, as signatories to a letter to the *Times.*

I do not think this irresponsibility is limited to Cambridge.

Most scientists simply do not want to think about these things—and like most of the public believe—or accept—that "the experts know best."

7. *Fundamental research.* Much of university research is, of course, still aimed at increasing our knowledge of the natural world. But can one ever foresee how such work might be misapplied? (Rutherford counting alpha-particles.)

At the end of World War II, I decided that never again would I use my scientific knowledge for military purposes: astronomy seemed about as far removed as possible.

But in succeeding years, we developed new techniques for making very powerful radio telescopes; these techniques have been perverted for improving radar and sonar systems. A sadly large proportion of the PhD students we have trained have taken the skills they have learnt in these and other areas into the field of defence. I am left at the end of my scientific life with the feeling that it would have been better to have become a farmer in 1946. One can, of course, argue that somebody else would have done it anyway, and so we must face the most fundamental of questions.

Should fundamental science (in some areas now, others will emerge later) be stopped?

It seems that in some areas, the resulting evil now outweighs the good. (We do not *have* to understand the evolution of galaxies, or the sub-atomic particles with those expensive machines at CERN.)

The benefits of medical research are real—but so are the potential horrors of genetic engineering and embryo manipulation. We devise heart transplants, but do little for the 15 million who die annually of malnutrition and related diseases.

Our cleverness has grown prodigiously—but not our wisdom.

Yours sincerely,
Sir Martin Ryle

VII. A Letter to the Best Sellers

October 15, 1984

Atten: Mr. Edward Gannon, Editor

Thank you for sending me two copies of your *Bookreview,* Vol. 44, No. 6, Sept., 1984 containing Mr. Paul T. Majkut's comment on my book *One World.* But I wonder if Mr. Majkut had actually tried to read the book and understand it. His comment is based completely on his imagination and prejudice.

1. My book has nothing to do with the "second-rate Catholic universities, where political science and theology perform unnatural or supernatural acts." I had the idea of One World and started to work for it early in China. Although I happened to live in South Bend close to the University of Notre Dame, I have done my business and writing independently for more than twenty years, without any affiliation with that Catholic university. I am not a Catholic either. Besides, if there is any "crackpot mystico-religious politics" in the "cracked heart" of the book, please point out clearly where and how.

2. In order to facilitate reading for the general reader, I have tried to make the text of the manifesto as terse as possible, and render all supporting materials as annotations which are more extensive in scope and much richer in content than the ordinary footnotes. It is a new attempt and a new style. Its merit has yet to be evaluated. The new style is unique and strange at the moment, just like the first appearance of the footnote system not too long ago. It may take some time for the general reader to get acquainted, but should not be too "staggering" for the scholars who are used to check source, origins, authority, etc. up and down and back and forth.

51

3. As a result of the separation of supporting materials from the text, the text just "occupies a narrow band at the top of each page," as arranged by the printer to keep the text and its related annotations as close as possible. But its contents are certainly not so narrow. It runs to approximately 80,000 words, five times more than the text of the famous Communist Manifesto. It is probably the longest manifesto ever written so far.

4. The point of the manifesto is not "equally narrow" either. But it is quite different with that "although we are all different, we should be nice to each other and respect each other and shun nasty nationalism" as Mr. Majkut assumed. I started *One World* with the point that "the merging process which has converted enormous groups into a small number of nations will eventually bring all the nations into One World," as Mr. Majkut has noticed in my Preface. I have stood with and worked for this point all the way. It is an historical investigation and a scientific approach. It is not a plea for goodwill or good behavior. No one would miss this point if only checking through the first chapter.

5. My studying in library science has indeed helped me technically to do my research. Unfortunately, I did not have much time to stay with a library job, as Mr. Majkut indicated. Since I tried to invent a machine and got the first patent for it in 1959, I have been too busy to run the business with an international market. I did not actually do the research and writing of the book until 1975 when I quit the profitable business completely. Since then I spent all my time and energy to check over thousands of books and other materials. This was how the "relentless documentations" were brought about. I made this clear in my Preface which Mr. Majkut checked evidently. Yet he ignored the fact and developed a false account instead.

6. Actually, the "relentless documentations" are just a portion of my collection as a result of carefully selecting and editing. They have been employed, not "willy-nilly," but necessarily to support the text with evidence, depth and weight. In this regard, Professor Norman Cousins commented that "I stand in awe of your ability to mobilize as much research material as you did. . . . Your scholarship is titanic."

7. As a resident of South Bend for more than twenty years, I know quite well that people in this area are very friendly. I love South Bend, since it is my second hometown. But I have not realized that I was so lucky to have found my "way to South Bend, a place more compatible to universal brotherhood and Dewey-like One Worldism" as told by Mr. Majkut. I do not know the exact meaning of the "Dewey-like One Worldism" either.

8. In contrast to Mr. Majkut's imagination and prejudice, I want to stress that my *One World* is a scientific work. It has tried to stand with facts and stay away from mystery, superstition, illusion, vague ideas, wishful thinking and elusive talking. It is a systematic and penetrating study of the subject, based on the development of history on the one hand and the achievements of science and technology on the other. There are in it a good number of discoveries and innovations important to social evolution, world government, peace and the happiness of mankind. Actually it is a manifesto of revolution for world unity with the evolutionary law of group expansion as a guiding theory, major symptoms of the nation as primary targets, permanent peace and general happiness as ultimate objectives, together with a blueprint for world government and a practical program for actions. This is a simple summary of the contents which Mr. Majkut's review did not touch at all. The proof copy of the book is still with you. Please check over and find out the truth. Copies of the book may be furnished at your request.

9. In his last passages, Mr. Majkut sees One World as remote as "the Milky Way," at the same time, as real as "the problem of one China, isn't one of the goal but of answering whose?" "The sun dominates and dwarfs its planets." This kind of contradiction and attitude proves only that he has tried every way to dump my *One World,* with his imagination and prejudice.

10. Thus, Mr. Majkut has, by his sheer imagination and prejudice with obvious arrogance and malice, seriously distorted the true picture of my book *One World* and thwarted its selling, and also seriously hurt my integrity, prestige, image, honor, and my efforts for the great course of One World. For

these reasons, while reserving all my legal rights in the matter, I, as an academic man, first write directly to you, as an academic book reviewer, and ask you to take appropriate measures immediately, to restore the true picture of the book, and compensate for my losses.

Sincerely,
John Kiang, the Author of *One World*

The foregoing is the letter I sent to the Best Sellers on Oct. 15, 1984, with only a few words changed. In addition, I like to point out that the Chinese inscription on the title page of my One World *is a traditional phrase coming down from two thousand years ago. It is not taken from Sun Yat-sen, as Mr. Majkut asserted. Its meaning is subject to various interpretations. I use it simply as the equivalent to the English title. My letter to the Best Sellers is a protest against its book review by Paul T. Majkut on the proof copy of* One World. *It appears in its Vol. 44, No. 6, Sept., 1984, p. 224. It is the only comment with an irresponsible attitude toward my* One World *as far as I know since its publication, and is reprinted below for reference:*

Kiang, John
One World
One World Publishing (P. O. Box 423, Notre Dame, IN, 46556), 648 p., $24.95

On the surface, *One World,* subtitled, ''The Approach to Permanent Peace on Earth and the General Happiness of Mankind, A Popular Manifesto with Scholarly Annotations,'' appears to be that kind of crackpot mystico-religious politics that is typical of second-rate Catholic universities, where political science and theology perform unnatural or supernatural acts, depending on your skew, in public. But a careful reading of *One World* shows that its imbecility is not only on the surface, but deep in its cracked heart.

The Chinese inscription, taken from Sun Yat-sen, may be taken as the theme of the book, roughly translated: ''All under heaven belong to one family. This is the way to secure world peace and the welfare of all humanity forever.''

54

The documentation of the "manifesto" is staggering. Every one of its 648 pages is at least two-thirds annotation, small print statistical information, explanatory quotations from anthropologists, sociologists, historians, economists, *et al.* The manifesto, *One World,* occupies a narrow band at the top of each page. Its point is equally narrow—that although we're all different, we should be nice to each other and respect each other and shun nasty nationalism.

Kiang left China after WWII because he wanted to further this message that "the merging process which has converted enormous groups into a small number of nations will eventually bring all nations into One World." He had written a thesis at Hunan University, *An Introduction to One World,* but his mentors at the University of Nebraska wisely disappointed him, saying his topic was "too broad and too unrealistic" to pursue. So he became a librarian, which accounts for the relentless documentation employed willy-nilly throughout the book, and eventually found his way to South Bend, a place more compatible to universal brotherhood and Dewey-like One Worldism.

One World is a must for people who like almanacs, miscellanies and print-outs, the kind of book to thumb through just before going to sleep or on a lazy Sunday morning. "The Milky Way is a nebulous band of faint stars, extending entirely around the celestial sphere."

The problem of one world, like the problem of one China, isn't one of the goal, but of answering *whose?* "The sun dominates and dwarfs its planets."

Paul T. Majkut, San Diego, California

VIII. An Antecedent Letter

March 25, 1975

Dear Patrons:

We are glad to report to you that we have agreed to sell our business in catalog card duplicators and supplies to Gaylord Bros., Inc. As you all know, Gaylord Bros. is the leading firm in library supplies with a fine historical background and a wide service system, and their new president, Mr. Walter W. Curley, a prominent librarian, has been eagerly looking for new ideas and better products for you. We are sure they will keep up all we have achieved in the service and serve you well. We will do business as usual until May 1, 1975, which has been set as a closing date for the transaction, and then Gaylord Bros. will be in charge. Please send your orders to Gaylord Bros. after the closing date, but remit your payment directly to us for all orders filled by us before.

As the episode of our 15 years business is coming to the last page, we like to take this opportunity to express our deepest gratitude to you for your patronage and cooperation in the past and to wish you good luck with Gaylord Bros. in the future.

Maybe you like to ask why I want to quit a well-established business. At the moment, I can just tell you that I have had, for more than 30 years, an idea to unite all the peoples in the world together for a real peace forever and a great happiness of all. I need more and more time first to write out my idea for publication with a pre-assigned Call Number as you might have noticed in my duplicator trade mark: 321.04 K531w, and then to launch a One World Movement of which a round

56

symbol also is seen in the trade mark. I hope someday I will be in contact with you again for the new adventure of One World Movement.

Very truly yours
John Kiang, Manager
Chiang Small Duplicators

Nine years later when I presented copies of my One World *to the American Library Association, I told my former patrons through a letter to the President of the Association:*

"Now I am glad to report that my idea has been written out in this book and am making contact for the new adventure of One World Movement. It is an adventure much more important than the duplicator business and worth much more support, for it is not a private enterprise, but a great campaign for world peace and humanity; and it strives for no personal benefit, but for the happiness of all the peoples.

"From technical point of view, the pre-assigned Call Number may not quite fit this book because the title has been changed from World Commonwealth to One World. But I keep it as an original sign for both the book and the Movement. I believe all librarians would be interested in carrying this library profession-mind sign to the world all over in order to achieve the ultimate goals of the library profession."

IX. Letters for Starting

Letters for starting the work are many, including those to Dr. Norman Cousins, Chairman of the World Federalist Association; Dr. Armand Hammer, famous industrialist with interest in world peace; and Mr. Pierre Elliott Trudeau, former Prime Minister of Canada. Seven typical ones only are presented here.

To Mr. Philip Isely,
Secretary General, World Constitution and Parliament Association (U.S.A.)

June 14, 1984

Dear Philip:

Thank you for your letters of May 8 and 30, 1984. The returned manuscript has been received.

I like to tell you that my book has been printed with an introduction by Dr. Linus Pauling who urges: "Everyone should read this book and heed its message." It will be available for the public next week. I will present a copy to you later. It is somewhat different with the manuscript you previewed, but the essentials are the same:

First of all, it tries to lay down an historical, philosophical and scientific foundation; or to formulate a basic theory, for the unity of the world (Chap. I & II).

Secondly, it tries to set up two ultimate objectives for the unity of the world: permanent peace on earth and the general happiness of mankind (Chap. IV & V).

Third, it tries to sweep up the three major obstacles: the independence of the nation, national sovereignty and nationalism, as a primary mission to open the way for the unity of the world (Mainly Chap. III).

And fourth, it tries to launch a world revolution to achieve the unity of the world with three great campaigns: campaign for liberation to get rid of the independence of the nation, national sovereignty and nationalism; campaign for promotion to raise humanity, loyalty to mankind and world patriotism; and campaign for survival, including anti-war activities, protest against the development of weapons and demand for total disarmament. The world revolution will be directed by the One World Movement as the center of the program drafted in the last chapter of my book.

As regarding world government, my book makes only an outline in chapter VI, leaving the rest open, in order to avoid unnecessary and premature controversies. If the world revolution succeeds, there will be little trouble to work out a world constitution and a world government will be automatically formed.

At the beginning, one of the major jobs for the One World Movement is to unite all groups that strive for one world, world government, peace, humanity and the like into a solid force for the world revolution. There are in existence hundreds of this kind of groups with millions of members in the world. We believe our ultimate goal is the same. If we remain separate to stress certain differences, no one can accomplish much, and if we stand together as one revolutionary force, nobody can stop us. The time requires us to unite together more urgently than ever before. Let us put the unity of the world ahead of anything else. Let us unite now. To unite ourselves is an initial step to unite the world. This is an appeal excerpted from my book. You might have noticed it in its manuscript.

There are in these groups prominent ones, such as yours and the World Federalists Association. But the One World Movement is the very one suitable to be the common agency, because its simple title is common enough for all to share, its basic theory is common enough for all to follow, its ultimate objectives are common enough for all to pursue, its primary mission is common enough for all to carry, and its revolutionary campaigns are common enough for all to take part. These are the main reasons for me to sponsor the One World Movement. It is not to start an organization with a slightly different idea. It is a necessary action for our common course, a heavy duty to take, and a great challenge for response.

As you know, I have been watching what you have done for almost twenty years, and I have admired you personally all the time for your sincere devotion and infatigable efforts. I like to take this opportunity to urge you again to join the One World Movement and provide a leadership for it. This does not necessarily mean that you have to give up your own project. It would be wonderful if your project can develop a world provisional government for the common course. But I cannot note the possibility in my book until the second edition.

If there is anything I can be of your assistance in the inauguration of the Graduate School of World Problem, please let me know. I will do as much as my time allows.

I do not know Wang An, the Chinese industrialist of Boston, personally. I have planned to enlist him into the One World Movement, but nothing has been done. I do not know if I can be of any help in obtaining some funding from him.

Very sincerely yours,
John Kiang

To Mr. Henry Usborne, Joint President of the Parliamentary Group for World Government (England)

November 27, 1984

Dear Mr. Usborne:

Thank you for your letter of Nov. 3, 1984 together with your manuscript of "Prescription for Peace." I appreciate very much your giving me the privilege to preview the manuscript which, after a quick study, has been sent back to you via mail. Your long experience and intimate knowledge in the struggle for world government and peace are, indeed, invaluable.

It is obvious that your Minifed, Fourth Power, and Middle World are different to my One World. But I believe that they are your expedient design for avoiding nuclear war, and are not your ultimate goal which is world government and for which you have worked since your early years by leading the Parliamentary Group for World Government with a Crusade. Hence, I believe that there is no difference in our ultimate goal, and for this reason, I want to urge you to join in the One World Movement and provide a leadership for it.

The One World Movement is expounded in my book *One World* with the revolutionary law of group expansion as a guiding theory, symptoms of the nation as primary targets, permanent peace and general happiness of mankind as ultimate objectives, together with a blueprint for world government and a practical program for actions.

Actions include: 1. to build up the Movement to be a world revolutionary force and to unite all groups that strive for world government, peace, humanity and the like into the Movement; 2. to establish a world university as a training and working center; 3. to set up a worldwide information system; 4. to launch a world revolution with campaigns for liberating all peoples from the national independence, national sovereignty, and nationalism; for promoting humanity, loyalty to mankind, and world patriotism; and for survival, such as anti-war activities, protest against the development of weapons, and demand for total disarmament; 5. to get financial and other supports from public and private sources; and 6. to develop a provisional world government and to work out a constitution for a permanent world government.

Along with these actions, a Minifed may be worked out if it is feasible and practical to develop into a provisional world government. Thus, I urge you again to join the Movement with a leadership, and start to act for it with your friends in your area—the great European area and the wide Common-wealth area. It is an historical challenge to you.

With highest respects
John Kiang

To Senator Richard G. Lugar, Chairman of the Committee for Foreign Relations, United States Senate (U.S.A.)

May 5, 22, 1985

Thank you very much for your letter of April 18, 1985.

I guess my book *One World* might have reminded you of the same title written 40 years ago by another Hoosier, Mr. Wendell Willkie, with broad view and open mind. But this time, I believe, the chance for extending the Hoosier tradition to the world through Washington is much better, because we have a great Senator who is holding a key position in foreign relations in the Capitol.

I think, I believe you would agree with me that the U.S. foreign policies should not be formed completely in pragmatic ways and the American leadership in the world cannot depend entirely on military strength and economic power. It is necessary to do something dynamic with open mind and bold action, and to go ahead with some idea high and some deal noble. For these reasons, I believe that the Hoosier tradition of the One World idea can play a vital role in stimulating the U.S. foreign policies and in reenforcing the American leadership in the world; and for these reasons, I am imploring you to urge the U.S. government:

1. to support the One World Movement morally and financially, even just with some gestures for the beginning;

2. to recognize with a special act the One World Movement as a non-profit, tax-deductible organization.

In this regard my appeal to the American people in my book *One World* is copied herewith for your review. Your help

62

to the One World Movement will be a great service to the peace of the world and happiness of mankind.

Highest respects,
John Kiang

To Mr. Robert J. Hawke, Prime Minister (Australia)

July 20, 1985

Dear Mr. Hawke:

Two years ago, you referred Wendell Willkie's *One World* very strongly in a speech to the National Press Club in Washington, D.C. Now I am presenting you under separate cover a copy of my *One World* with compliments for your review. It was written and published in the home state of Wendell Willkie. I believe you will find it much more ground for your thesis as you told to the Club that ''the interdependence of all nations, all people is the stark choice before us all, a choice never before faced by humanity, a choice between survival and extinction.'' Your comment on my book will be highly appreciated.

Highest respects
John Kiang

To leaders of all groups that strive for world unity, world government, world federation, world citizenship, world peace, humanity, and the like

April 26, 1985

Dear leaders:

Please allow me, as one of your fellow men, first to applaud your noble efforts for a better world and a brighter future of mankind, and secondly, to urge you earnestly to unite into one party, and to work as one team, under common guidelines for common objectives, and with common policies. We now have in the world some hundred groups with probably millions of members striving for the same ultimate goal. If we remain separate to stress certain minor differences, no one can accomplish much; but if we stand together as one revolutionary force, nobody can stop us. The time requires us to unite into one party more urgently than ever before. Let us put our unity ahead of anything else. Let us unite now. To unite ourselves is the initial step toward uniting the world.

In order to unite us into one party, I propose that we have a world conference to work out for the party, a statute, an organ, and a working program. Is this proposal desirable and adoptable? What is your suggestion? Do you like to be a sponsor of the conference and can you help it financially? Your opinions will be carefully studied for action.

With respects,
John Kiang

To Great Peace Marchers

August 23, 1986

Greetings to all great Peace marchers.

Since you started the March, our hearts have been going along with you all the way.

As you have marched almost three thousand miles, you know well how long and how rough is the road to peace.

The road to a real and permanent world peace is even much longer and rougher, for there will be no real world peace until the world is one, and there will be no permanent world peace until we have a world government.

Let us join together to strive for a real world peace through the world unity. Let us join together to strive for a permanent world peace through a world government.

Let us join force in the One World Movement.

You are welcomed wholeheartedly.

Sincerely yours,
John Kiang

To Mr. Michael J. Jackson, famous musician (U.S.A.)

May 12, 1986

Dear Michael:

Two months ago in the 28th annual Grammy Awards you said, ''I wanted to write a song the world could sing.'' We have been very much impressed with your noble idea and wonder if you would like to write a World Anthem or a song for the One World Movement, for all peoples to sing. Whether you will do it alone, or to work it out with your friends such as Lionel Richie, Bruce Springsteen and Kenny Rogers, it would be the best way for you to fulfill your wish and a great contribution to world peace and humanity.

Under separate cover, I am sending you a copy of my new book *One World* with compliments. The title may remind you of a Hoosier tradition of your hometown since Wendell Willkie. Please check and see if the song on page 152 can be a basis for you to write the great song. We are very anxious to look forward to hearing from you.

For world peace and humanity.
Sincerely yours,
John Kiang

The song mentioned above on the page 152 of One World *is the popular song "It's a Small World," with the last sentence "Let us join together for peace forever and happiness*

everywhere,'' I add to it. Let us repeat it here as a temporary
World Anthem:

> It's a world of laughter, a world of tears;
> It's a world of hopes and a world of fears.
> There is so much that we share, it is time we are aware:
> It's a small world after all. Let us join together,
> For peace forever and happiness everywhere.

X. Design for the World Flag

See cover page of this book

1. White round ring stands for the earth, "W" for its geographic figuration, and together for One World.
2. Green stands for young, rich land, healthy environment, green revolution, to go ahead, etc.

XI. A Multiple Reply

August 14, 1986

To: Mr. John Davenport
    Mr. Lyman Hinckley
    Mrs. Stella Dunn
    Dr. Doug Everingham
    Mr. Bruno Micheli
    Mrs. Elizabeth R. Dana
    Mrs. Georgia Lloyd
    Dr. Lucile W. Green
    and a great many other friends

First of all, I want to thank you very much for your thoughtful letters, of which a good number contain thousands of words. I appreciate all your remarks, suggestions, information and comments on my book *One World,* and your opinions on my call for unity of leaders of all groups striving for world government, world peace, humanity, and the like, but I apologize deeply for the delay in replying to them, Now, please allow me to write you collectively some answers and items of common concern somehow.

Let's begin with Mr. John Davenport's "gadfly" inquiry: "The 2000-year-old Roman Catholic Church is the most skillful and best-organized political institution on Earth. . . . Thus the mere fact of your geographical contiguity to the University of Notre Dame, together with your 'paradoxical' non-Christian background, rouses intense curiosity in me. May I be permitted to ask, for example, who or what organization is bankrolling the publication of your book?" For answering this inquiry from a Roman Catholic land—Spain, I like just to quote my reply to a vicious book review earlier:

"My book has nothing to do with the 'second-rate Catholic universities, where political science and theology perform unnatural or supernatural acts.' I had the idea of One World and started to work for it early in China. Although I happened to live in South Bend close to the University of Notre Dame, I have done my business and writing independently for more than twenty years, without any affiliation with that Catholic university. I am not a Catholic either. Besides, if there is any 'crackpot mystico-religious politics' in the 'cracked heart' of the book, please point out clearly where and how." However, I must admit, I am a Notre Dame football fan.

Who is responsible financially for the publication of my book? I am glad to make known that it is myself who has founded the One World Publishing Co. just like twenty years ago I organized a firm to manufacture and market the card duplicating machine which I invented with three U.S. patents. My experience in the duplicating business is a story of success. I started it with almost nothing, but made it growing up in ten years steadily with patrons from more than eighty countries. Then in 1975 I quit the profitable business completely in order to devote all my time and energy to writing the book *One World*. The money I made in the business is enough for my simple living with a small amount for the start of the One World Movement.

As regards religion, my stand is with the principle of "right to freedom of thought, conscience and religion" as included in the section of Human Rights and Obligations in my book. At the present time we are urging all religions to help the common cause of peace and humanity through world government, to serve for a god of universal love, and not to work for any nationalist fetish.

I thank Mr. Davenport for his "nit-picker" remarks, and appreciated more for his comment: "It is indeed a treasure, and I am sure it will have its due influence to bring us together in one world." Although he was somewhat confused with the "romantic approach" of the Urgent Appeals in my book, he made a big notice: "As you see, your book is very stimulating to me." Obviously for this reason as well as for the "irrational

reaction'' as described by himself, he sent me three long letters in two weeks with a beautiful post card followed up.

Mr. Lyman Hinckley of the World Neighborhood Faith
and Law sent me two even longer letters. One to me along
with ten leading persons "each is engaged in a comprehensive
endeavor to turn people's attention not merely to the imminent
threat of one last war into oblivion, but to how we must
change our thinking (as Einstein warned) to achieve survival
and lasting peace." He compared all our efforts with comments; and the other letter begins with a review of each chapter of my book. I admire very much his wide knowledge and
experience in our common endeavor and his consistent plea
for his neighborhood approach. While I cannot agree with his
opinion that there is something disturbing in my proposal that
all natural resources belong to mankind and all economic systems are entitled to operate; and that it is better to maintain
experts as advisors to politicians rather than to have them
serving the people by running the government directly, I do
appreciate a number of his remarks, especially that "the superiority of the One World Movement outlined in *One World*
(over those earlier movements) lies in the endeavor to provide
an historical and cultural foundation, namely the substance of
the book itself." This is a very important remark which
should not be ignored by anybody. I believe that a world government cannot be established unless there is a firm philosophical foundation for it. To lay down such a foundation is a
main job for our great cause. It is, as Mr. Hinckley rightly put
it, "the substance of the book itself." Its importance to the
world government is as much as the theory of "Principia" to
physics and the doctrine of "Social Contract" to modern democracy, according to Mr. Henry Wong in a review.

Mrs. Stella Dunn of the Project for Peace, London, sent
me three letters with much more documents. She began with a
stimulating comment on my book, and followed by intimate
information and experience in the attempt to unite federalists
into a party. Much of her information and experience is invaluable and educational. Her opinion on nationalism and
about the merging of all nations into One World is somewhat
different with mine. I think it is better to discuss these topics

later, because she had not had time to read my book in detail as she indicated when she wrote me. But I like to make one point clear at the moment, that the human group merging has been a process over some million years, and all facts in this process have to be viewed in the long run comprehensively, and should not be observed or evaluated in short terms or by any particular case.

From Dr. Doug Everingham of Australia is a letter of more than four thousand words, beginning with a favorable response to the call for One World Movement membership, and commenting on my book along with some famous works such as Sir Normal Angell's *The Great Illusion,* then telling his personal contacts with Tom Liggett of the World Peace News and Howard Kurtz of the War Control Planners. He found Philip Isely of the World Constitution and Parliament Association "such a forceful personality with zeal which put him in jail as a conscientious objector still burning strongly." I wonder if he can find words other than these to sketch Garry Davis of the World Government of World Citizens. "There is only a couple of fathoms between a crank and a pioneer. The first is a fathom above ground. He becomes the second when he is a fathom below." Dr. Everingham quoted the dictum of Charles Bliss. I admire even cranks for the great cause, although I am a practical man with a firm belief in science.

After reviewing the principles of the Minifed of Henry Usborne, the English pioneer in world government, Dr. Everingham went into details of the Penrose Voting Formula. To my surprise, it is a project very close to the proposal I made in my book, Chapter VI, note 55, pp. 532–3.

Among other information given by Dr. Everingham, most striking is about the rapid development of international drug industry. "the drug empire is too big for single governments and was described by a recent article in *The Rationalist* (an Australian magazine) as possibly more threatening than the arms race."

Finally, Dr. Everingham indicates that he will have three articles published this year in the new journal, *Medicine and War,* and that he has made a copy of his letter to me for his friend, the Prime Minister of Australia, Hon. R. J. Hawke, and has urged him to look into my book. Dr. Everingham has indeed worked very hard and considered everything for the great cause.

From Mr. Bruno Micheli of Italy is a cordial letter with four lovely volumes of *Evolution* published in the last eight years. *Evolution* is a collection of articles, documents and other writings which appeared in *Europe-Universe, European Evolution, World Evolution* and *Evolution*. It is "an instrument for peace and world unity." Its "evolution" means "non-violent, progressive improvement." "Starting at the individual . . . up to the world level, where it ought to be coordinated and harmonized by the world government, so many of us are auspicating." It is interesting to note that the word "evolution" also is the base of the theory expounded in my book, but it is specified as the law of social evolution, and is a necessary product of economic development led by science and technology. It has made human groups expanding from the early single family, through the primitive community, clan, tribe, to the nation, through a process of merging more smaller groups into less larger ones, in the same way everywhere. Thus it, as a law with such a long history of validity and such an universal application, will eventually bring all nations into One World. This is the meaning of "evolution" implied in my book, and explored especially in its long first Chapter. It is necessary to stress that, however, while we are relying on the social evolutionary law in order to establish a strong belief in the approach of One World and world government, we are not allowed to wait for any eventuality when we and our civilization are in danger of total destruction by a nuclear war which may occur at any minute, and by an array of other serious crises, including the fast growth of the population, the quick depletion of resources, the steady increase of pollution, and the gradual deterioration of the environment. We have to head off the danger by pushing the process of merging all nations into One World in every way, and by realizing the world government before it is too late.

Now, since this letter has been going too long for reading, I am obliged to hold my discussion on the correspondence from other friends, such as Mrs. Elizabeth R. Dana of the Federalist Caucus, who has indicated to have my book reviewed in their annual report, Mrs. Georgia Lloyd of the Campaign for World Government, whose latest letter to me is with two meaningful statements: "Global Peril. What Can We Do" and "How to Combat Terrorism," and Dr. Lucile Green of the World Citizens Assembly, who remarked that "the format of your book reminds me of the Confucian Classics as I studied them at Yenching University years ago," and informed me that a Summit Meeting sponsored by WGOC is scheduled for Friday, Sept. 12, 1986, in Milwaukee, and that the issue of a party for world government is on its agenda. This is good news because it is an important step forward to our unity.

As regards our unity, I have emphasized in my book: "If we remain separate to stress minor differences, no one can accomplish much, but if we stand together as one revolutionary force, nobody can stop us. The time requires us to unite together more urgently than ever before. Let us put the One World ahead of anything else. Let us unite now. To unite ourselves is an initial step toward uniting the world."

A calling for unity is also found in the front pages of the *Evolution:* "Persons of good will of the whole world: Let us unite and build together peace and harmony on truth, honesty, justice and love." In addition, Mr. Micheli remarked in his letter of April 15, 1985 to Mrs. Dunn: "As to the establishment of a non-violent, world-wide, evolutionary political force, no matter how it will finally be called, I am of the opinion that it does not particularly matter whether it takes place in Israel, Canada, or elsewhere, provided it is not delayed until when it might turn out to be too late."

Why this kind of calling has been much ignored by our leaders? Mr. Davenport is of the opinion that "leaders as a character type are singularly intractable to teamwork that does not feed their egos." If this is a common weakness, we have to overcome it before we start to unite us for teamwork.

Regarding the issue of a party for world government, I hope the Summit meeting will not spend much time to discuss the desirability or necessity of such a party, but to concentrate on the topic of how to establish it, including its:

1. Name; such as World Government party, World Unity Campaign, One World Movement, etc.

2. Organ: Temporarily, my proposal is: a council, a president, several vice-presidents—one at large, one for organization, one for information, one for world peace, one for mankind happiness, and one for finance, with a secretary-general.

3. Program for actions including I. to build the party to be a world revolutionary force; II. to set up a worldwide information system; III. to establish a world university as a training and working center; IV. to campaign for liberating all peoples from the national independence, national sovereignty and nationalism; and for promoting humanity and world patriotism; V. to strive for world peace, such as anti-war activities and demand for total disarmament; VI. to plan for happiness of all peoples in respect to resources, population, environment, science and technology, etc.; VII. to get financial and other supports from public and private sources; and VIII. to develop a provisional world government and to work out a world constitution for a permanent world government.

After all we need a statute or bylaw for its organization, and a declaration to make clear its thesis or fundamental theory, its objectives, its program for actions and its statute. If this Summit Meeting cannot do all or any of these documents, a committee may be set to make drafts for adoption, and a date and place for its inauguration also have to be decided right now. In addition, I like to suggest to set up two special committees, one to look for a world anthem and one to work out a world flag. I have tried to contact some musicians, such as Thom Gambino, Kenny Rogers and Michael Jackson, for a world anthem, without success. I have also had something in my mind for a world flag.

As a conclusion of this letter, I like to quote the comment on my book I just received from Professor Louis B. Sohn who, as you all know, is the author of the famous book *World Peace through World Law*. I believe all of us would agree particularly with the last paragraph of his comment:

"Thank you for sending me a copy of your book *One World* which I read with interest. It is a powerful, well-

documented brief for liberating mankind from various preconceptions which stand in the way of uniting mankind for
common wellness. Perhaps it can stimulate some new thinking, in the same way as the Anatomy of Peace energized many
young people (like myself) in the 1940s."

"The need is clear. Even though the path is strewn with
obstacles, the task is not impossible."

For peace, humanity through world government.

Sincerely yours,
John Kiang

XII. Declaration of the One World Movement

*(Revised text
of Chapter VII of the* One World*)*

Principles

WE HAVE LEARNED:

—That mankind has continued to expand its group life in social evolution for thousands of years by merging smaller groups into larger ones, from the early single family, through the primitive community, clan, and tribe to the nation; and now a last step is being taken to merge all nations into one world. This step is a consequence of the long process of group expansion which prevails everywhere as a social evolutionary law. It is an historical necessity, not only desirable but also logical and not just anticipated but even inevitable.

—That the great utility of group expansion is to achieve peace and to pursue happiness. Success has been made in this respect step by step. Now it is quite possible for it to attain its ultimate goals: a permanent peace on earth and a general happiness for mankind, through the merging of all nations into one world as the last step.

—That the group expansion, although at work all the time everywhere, is subject to physical conditions developed primarily by science and technology with tools and energies to make changes and improvements in economic life, transportation and communications, and weapons. The rapid advance of modern science and technology has now made all physical conditions ready for the merging of all nations into one world: the economic life of locally independent agriculture has been replaced by one of world-wide interdependent industry; the fast transportation and communications have swept away all national border lines, leaving no room for national territorial integrity, and have shrunk the vast world into a small kingdom for a world government to take care of it easily, and finally there has been on the earth no place where deadly weapons cannot reach within minutes to destroy everything, reducing the entire world to merely a small standing tactical theater, and everybody a permanent hostage. Hence, clearly the time is ripe for the merging of all nations into one world.

—That, along with the rapid advance of modern science and technology, the One World has actually been in the making through the contributions of geographical exploration, migration, travel, intellectual dissemination, agricultural dispersal, uniformity and standardization, social progress, and developments in international relations and organizations, together with the socialist international movement. Any single one of these contributions in a short period of time may be of little importance, but all together and in the long run, they have laid down a broad foundation for the One World.

It is based on these known facts that we have a deep conviction for the future of mankind in One World, and it is based on such conviction that we commit ourselves to work for the merging of all nations into One World.

This work is very urgent for us, because mankind and its civilization are in danger of total destruction by a nuclear war which may occur at any minute, and by an array of other serious crises, including the fast growth of population, the quick depletion of resources, the steady increase of pollution, and the gradual deterioration of the environment. We have to head off the danger by working hard and acting quickly, and we have to get the job done before it is too late. Time is a factor more important than ever before and is running out fast.

Primary Mission

SINCE THE MERGING OF ALL NATIONS INTO ONE
world is an historical development and a social evolution,
what we have to do first at the critical time is to release it from
the interference of nationalist forces, which have raged since
late last century in reaction to the general trend of civilization
led by the rapid advance of science and technology. The nationalist forces stem from three original evils: the independence of the nation, national sovereignty, and nationalism.
These evils have not only slowed down, but have even tried to
hold back the historical development and social evolution in
various ways.

The independence of the nation is standing against a world
in which all peoples are interdependent and geographical isolation no longer exists; and is standing for the nation, which
has no big place in the universe and no deep root in history,
and its time is gone and its value is lost. In short, the independence of the nation is standing against the real world and
for an outmoded political body. And finally, it is the root of
war between nations.

National sovereignty is a completely man-made hypothesis, just like totemism in ancient times. It was originally designed to curb the subversive influence of local rivalries by
strengthening a national government. It has done an enormous
disservice to mankind since its change from a principle of internal unity and order to a symbol of international separation
and anarchy.

Nationalism has also developed from a force of internal
unity to a factor of international disorder in modern times. It
originated from barbarism and tribalism. It commands a paramount loyalty and duty to one's own nation, leading to rivalry and hostility with other nations. It wants one's own
nation to be militarily stronger, leading to strategical struggles
against other nations, and it asserts one's own national interests emphatically, leading to economic egoism in dealing with
other nations. It always exploits public sentiment, manipulates

78

history and distort facts for its own interests. It is the aggressive force for imperialism and also the conservative elements for isolationism. And necessarily it is the strongest agitator of the independence of the nation and national sovereignty.

The independence of the nation, national sovereignty, and nationalism are the main stumbling blocks on the way to the merging of all nations into One World. This is why we are determined to uproot them as our primary mission. To be sure their elimination would be followed by other obstacles which originate from them, such as the "national liberation" which is an echo of the independence of the nation, the "national self-determination" which is a shadow of the national sovereignty, and the notorious imperialism which is an outgrowth of nationalism.

Objective 1:
Permanent Peace

IT IS ONLY THROUGH THE SUCCESS OF OUR PRImary mission can the merging of all nations into One World be accomplished right away, and only through the accomplishment of the merging of all nations into One World can our objectives be achieved at once. Our objectives are the ultimate goals of group expansion: permanent peace on earth and general happiness for mankind.

While war has been getting bigger and worse in recent centuries, the methods for maintaining peace have become less and less effective: the conventional ones, such as the balance of power, collective security, and disarmament have been able to do very little and the new ones, such as deterrence, detente, non-proliferation and SALTs do not make much sense either. Consequently, with nuclear and chemical weapons, computer guidance and space techniques, war has been threatening mankind with a total destruction at any minute. There is no way to escape the catastrophe unless war is completely abolished, and there is no way to abolish war completely until the nation no longer remains in independence which is the root of war. This is why the merging of all nations into One World is the only way to achieve a permanent peace over the whole world.

Since we are under the threat of total destruction by an imminent war, urgent measures must be taken right away to prevent the catastrophe before the completion of the merging process. These measures include:

1. Standing firmly against any kind of war;

2. Disbanding all armed forces except the police, and stopping military conscription and training; and

3. Stopping the making and development of any weapons, and destroying all stockpiles; or converting them into peaceful use.

Objective 2:
General Happiness

IN RESPECT TO THE OBJECTIVE OF GENERAL HAPpiness, there is a necessary condition, which is the elimination of all war costs forever, and an indispensable means, which is the transfer of all military expenditures to finance the general happiness. The prerequisite for both the condition and the means is the abolition of war through the merging of all nations into One World. Thus, the merging of all nations into One World is also crucial for the pursuit of general happiness for all peoples.

The program for pursuing the general happiness includes two propositions, two themes, two priorities and five important measures. The two propositions are:

1. All natural resources of land, ocean, and space belong to mankind as a whole, and

2. All existing economic systems are entitled to operate, complete and adjust by free will.

The two themes are:

1. Advance through science and technology with humanity and the ecosystem; and

2. Growth with balance.

The two priorities are:

1. Raising of the living standards in the poorer areas through the improvement and development of agriculture, industry, transportation and education, and

2. Control of the population to an optimum size in relation to food and other natural resources.

The five important measures are:

1. Saving and developing energies, non-fuel minerals, forest products, and water;

2. Improving and increasing food production;

3. Preventing and reducing natural calamities;

4. Protecting the environment with conservation by minimizing the destruction of natural resources, holding down pollutions and relieving urban overcrowding with a pattern of small towns; and

5. Unifying and equalizing the economy with a world bank and world monetary system, universal income and inheritance taxes, and social security for all; by removing any barrier to trade and travel; and by stabilizing price and employment.

Sketch of World Government

IN ORDER TO PERFORM ALL THESE TASKS, IT IS obvious that the establishment of an effective World Government is urgently needed.

Vested in the World Government is a supreme authority derived from all peoples as a whole, and subordinated to be World Government are the nations as autonomous local units.

Under the World Government human rights and obligations will be well respected without any distinction as to race, sex, language or religion.

The World Government will consist of a World Judiciary, a World Administration and a World Council. Judiciary will be independent. Administration will consist of various service units, but no military unit, nor any unit for foreign affairs. The World Council will be the central organ of the World Government, and will be composed of a House of Commons and a House of Experts. Its President, elected by itself, will serve as the World President in formality and ceremony.

There are four essences contained in the World Government: justice, service, opinion and knowledge. Justice will be upheld by the World Judiciary, service done by the World Administration, opinion expressed by the House of Commons, and knowledge furnished by the House of Experts. To coordinate the functions of the four essences there will be a World presidium with an integrative complex.

Accompanying the four essences is an important feature: to run the government by experts rather than by politicians, and to serve rather than to rule the people. This is to apply the democratic conception of ''for the people, by the people and of the people'' in a a positive way.

Finally, it is necessary to note the importance of the World Law, which is superior to any local law. It will govern the individual directly, leaving no room for the existence of national sovereignty and bringing an end to international law.

Of the World Law, most important is a World Constitution, of course. Based on the fundamentals thus projected for the World Government along with the world structure, a practical World Constitution will be drafted for adoption.

Expedient Setup of the Movement

STARTING WITH A PRACTICAL WORLD CONSTITUtion, there will be a much brighter world in the future. This is an unshakeable belief of the One World Movement (Abbreviated as OWM hereafter).

The OWM is a common endeavor of the people who want to work consciously, voluntarily and actively for the merging of all nations into One World with the principles, the primary mission, the objectives, and the scheme of government, as summarized above. It is an endeavor for all people of the world. Thus, everyone everywhere is urged to join in the cause.

First of all, we want to expand our membership as fast as possible. Membership requires a pledge of loyalty to humanity, of allagience to mankind, and of devotion to One World with peace and happiness for all. A small sum for annual membership dues is also required.

The warmest welcome is extended to those who would like to become members consciously, to recruit voluntarily good men and women to be members, and to organize our members in an area into local units, and members of a country into a political party, while at the same time remaining as a chapter or a section of a chapter of the OWM. As a chapter or a section, the group is obliged to carry out all assignments of the OWM and is responsible to it; and being a political party of the country, it is appropriate and convenient to exert political influences, to sway public opinion, and to campaign for power in order to lead the country into One World.

Meanwhile, we would like to invite all groups that strive for one world, world government, peace, humanity, and the like to unite with us into one movement. There are in existence hundreds of such groups will millions of members in the world. We believe that our ultimate goal is the same and that the OWM can represent all of us as a whole. If we remain separate to stress certain differences, no one can accomplish much, but if we stand together as one movement, nobody can stop us. The time has come that we need to unite together more urgently than ever before. Let us put the One World ahead of anything else. Let us unite now. To unite ourselves is an initial step toward uniting the world.

Along with the development of our organization, we have to establish an effective information system in every important area throughout the world, with necessary instruments such as newspapers, magazines, radio and television networks. We cannot carry out mass educational campaigns to rouse the world public without an effective information system. We cannot make our voice heard without the necessary instruments.

Needless to say, the most urgent work before us at the moment is to prevent and abolish war. We have to have a task force to handle this extremely important job. Since the early days of this century, war has been developed by modern science and technology to a point where its real meaning and actual effects can be understood by nobody else better than the scientists themselves. This is why Kapitsa and Sakharov consciously refused to work for it any longer and Linus Pauling has worked vigorously against it for years. We urge brilliant scientists to provide us with a strong leadership for the task force.

A team of experts is also needed to work out practical and detailed plans on every important subject for pursuing the general happiness of mankind. The draft of a World Constitution and other important laws, and bylaws for the OWM is their responsibility, too.

Finally, we need a group of business leaders to raise money for a One World Fund and guide its use in the best interest of peace and humanity. It is obviously impossible for us to carry out extensive programs without a huge fund.

We plead with all foundations to channel, all governments to appropriate, and all rich people and groups to contribute as much money as possible to help us. No money is needed more urgently than for our effort to save the world from total destruction, and no money could be used more meaningfully than by our seeking a bright future for mankind. We believe no one else can serve the purpose better than we can for foundations such as the Carnegie Foundation for International Peace and we believe we are the best place for great philanthropists to realize noble dreams.

Further, it is important to note that in the long history of civilization there has never been a cause as great as One World. The opportunity to support the greatest cause is unique. It has not appeared before, and may disappear very soon. Please take this unique opportunity to support the greatest cause by making generous donations right now.

Thus far, we have projected five working groups: organization, information, peace, planning and finance. Each group will have a standing committee headed by a chairman. In order to guide and coordinate the work of the various groups, there will be an executive council, composed of the chairmen of the standing committees, together with a president, one or more vice presidents, and a secretary-general. In addition, there will be a world university as the center of activities.

One World University

THERE HAVE BEEN SOME UNIVERSITIES UNDER the title of world, and there are also many plans for new ones, with the emphasis on intercultural understanding. Actually, that is not a reason good enough to create a world university, because such an emphasis has to be common for all universities.

The university in our plan will not offer regular academic courses, which other universities can do well. It will concentrate on developing a solid nucleus of disciplined personnel with firm principles, to do the job of eliminating the independence of the nation, national sovereignty, and nationalism for the permanent peace and general happiness of mankind, through the merging of all nations into One World.

Students will be recruited from all countries. They must have good academic qualifications and a high interest in working for mankind. They will be sent back to staff the chapters or local units of the OWM, after graduation.

Most of the faculty members are the leading staff members of the OWM in organization, information, peace, planning and finance. They will study and discuss theories, problems, policies and strategies with the students, thus making the university a workshop of the OWM.

85

The faculty members will also work together as the general staff of the OWM to provide guidance and coordination for all its activities throughout the world. They stand ready to help the establishment of a provisional world government.

With the World University as the center of activities, the setup of the OWM so sketched is indeed of an expedient nature. As soon as our membership is growing significantly, our local units and chapters are developing close to maturity, and other friend groups are uniting with us into one movement, a world congress will be convened to adopt bylaws and to adjust our structure accordingly. Until then, owing to the extreme urgency and necessity for peace and humanity, we must in the name of mankind start and continue to work with the expedient setup to the best of our ability, and carry out our strategies as far as possible.

Strategies

OUR STRATEGIES CALL FIRST FOR A CAMPAIGN for liberation: to get rid of the independence of the nation which keeps mankind in separate prisons; to discard national sovereignty, which is merely a dead duck; and to eradicate nationalism, which is a revival of tribalism.

The campaign for liberation necessarily includes the release of mankind from the heavy burden of nationalized histories, from the serious bondage of nationalized traditions, and from the strong persuasive influence of nationalized education. In other words, we have to get out of a small fabricated world and not regard our own nation as the center of the universe anymore; and we must no longer linger over yesterday's flower or hesitate to cut down any evil fruit tree.

Coupled with the campaign for liberation is a campaign for promotion: to raise humanity, to build up an ultimate allegiance and a supreme loyalty to mankind, and to develop a world patriotism to replace the old, narrow and blind sentiment.

A third campaign is one for survival, which is the prerequisite to liberation, promotion and anything else. This campaign includes various anti-war activities; refusal of military conscription; protest against the manufacture, development and sale of weapons, whether nuclear, chemical or conventional, with further actions to destroy them or convert them into peaceful uses; and the disbanding of the armed forces.

The three campaigns will amount to a real world revolution, for they will be carried out everywhere with the determination to bring forth a fundamental change in the social, political and economic systems of the whole world. But they differ from conventional revolutions in one important aspect: they do not rely upon violence. This is not only a necessary demonstration of our sincere efforts for peace, but also a logical application of our deep belief that reason and conscience are the essence of humanity. Non-violence is our principle, and we observe it strictly, even in the strikes which we may have to call for under certain circumstances. We also adopt a practice of non-violent resistance as our tactics.

Admittedly, there are in human nature some viruses which make violence a part of human behavior as it is in other animals. But this is just what we have to purge from us rather than to live with, in order to perfect our spiritual civilization.

In the intensity of violence, terrorism ranks only next to war. Although by no means a new phenomenon in the political arena, terrorism has become more active in recent years, and has endangered more innocent people as in the skyjackings. Consequently, the image of terrorists has turned from bad to worse in the public mind. Yet they are dedicated and smart people. We believe, that if only they knew what they do debases their goal, they would give up their violent way at once; and that if they decide to join us, they will be able to make a significant contribution to the cause of One World which is much greater and more urgent than any causes that have raised their enthusiasm and devotion.

Under the principle of non-violence, our campaigns may not be so sensational and so exciting as to induce an impulsive public response. But what we seek for is public judgment rather than public sensation. We believe that mankind has grown mature enough to see what and where its real interest is and to know how to act appropriately, if only we can fully present to the public all the undeniable facts and truths.

For this very reason, we will campaign openly with open minds and open policies toward an open world, and we will campaign with common sense and straight actions. We have nothing to hide, we do not pretend mystery, and we go along with no superstitions.

It would be an unforgivable mistake to think that our peaceful, open and plain campaigns are an easy way to the success of world revolution. On the contrary, it is the most difficult approach, especially during the early stages when we have not obtained sufficient instruments and developed them to do the job efficiently, while we have excluded the use of the old methods of revolution, such as bloodshed, myth and intrigue.

The instruments we need include television, radio, newspapers, magazines, movies, art, song, dance, sports, and so on. They are nothing new. But we need them in sufficient quantities to carry out our campaigns everywhere and to develop their effectiveness to the fullest in our service. Meanwhile, we want to enlist the service as much as possible of all such instruments now in private or public hands the world over. If only half of them come to help us positively, the world revolution may succeed suddenly at any moment. We believe that no single one of them is not interested in peace and humanity. We urge all of them to do their best for the cause of One World, not to stay away at the critical time, and at least not to spread any nationalist curses under any circumstances.

With all the instruments available, we will bring our campaigns directly to all people, and like to have them spread and discussed in homes, farms, factories, universities, and other schools. We want to see a chain reaction set in motion by the people and to get the initiatives and demands of the people reflected throughout villages and townships, to county, province and state levels, and finally up to their national governments. The major goal of our campaigns is to convince all national governments, through persuasion and pressure, mainly by voice and voting of their people, to give up their independent status and join in a world government.

Provisional World Government

NATURALLY, THE IDEAL SOLUTION WOULD BE IF all nations were convinced simultaneously. But such a development can hardly be counted on. We have to get the process of merging the nations going at the earliest possible moment, even with a minimum of two nations. For this reason, our strategies call for the starting of a provisional world government as the second step of the world revolution. The beginning of this step may be very arduous, but breakthroughs will come as no surprise once it sets foot on the ground and gets going.

The main job of the provisional world government includes: 1. to complete world disarmament; 2. to draft a World Constitution and see it ratified by a World Constituent Assembly or through some other process; 3. to establish a permanent world government in accordance with the World Constitution; and 4. to prepare important projects for the pursuit of general happiness, and to start some most urgent works.

Since the operation of the provisional world government will concentrate on only a few activities for a short transitional period, it is not necessary to organize a fully fledged government. The sketches projected earlier for the World Government and the OWM may serve as a guidance, and expedient plans and personnel assistance will be provided by the OWM to meet any exigency.

There are three ways possible to form a provisional world government: by converting the United Nations, by the experiment of the OWM with support initiated by any nation or a group of countries, or by direct action of the people with the assistance of the OWM.

If most of the members of the United Nations, including the permanent members of its Security Council, could be convinced to give up their position as its masters by dropping national sovereignty and other related principles from the Charter, there would be little difficulty in converting the world organization into a provisional world government. This is a practical approach and deserves to be tried by all means.

Meanwhile, the OWM should try to form a provisional world government as soon as possible, because the conversion of the United Nations may not proceed fast enough to meet the urgency. Of course, the OWM will no longer need to maintain a separate government if the conversion succeeds in time.

To form a provisional world government, the OWM needs the following supports from every nation: 1. moral and financial assistance; 2. pledges of allegiance to mankind for permanent peace and the general happiness, and not to press for capitalism or communism; 3. denouncement of the independence of the nation, national sovereignty and nationalism; and 4. preparation for destroying its own weapons and disbanding its own armed forces. These are also the common requirements for all nations to pursue the great cause of One World. In addition, a suitable site and adequate facilities for the operation of the provisional world government is sought as a special support.

The crucial problem now is which nation would take the lead in rendering such supports. There is no doubt that if any nation, especially a great nation or a group of countries should, at the most critical moment in history, take the initiative, many others would follow suit immediately. Such initiative is indeed a great challenge for response.

The American people are in an excellent position for meeting the challenge. They are highly advanced in science and technology, are richly composed of all kinds of racial origins and cultural varieties, and are often respected for their tradition of generosity. They know that the world is one and they cannot withdraw their responsibility away from it as clearly expressed forty years ago by Wendell Willkie, one of their many openminded and far-sighted leaders.

The Russian people are also in an excellent position to meet the challenge. We have faith in them, and we believe that

90

they are interested in the "creation of secure peace and tranquility for all mankind" with "full readiness for common effort," as their scientists have expressed.

China can meet the challenge with one quarter of the world's voices. India can do it with strong voices, too.

As a pioneer of the World State, H. G. Wells started to urge not only the British people, but all peoples of the world to take action eighty years ago. Harold J. Laski made a similar effort in the years over the two world wars. And in the late 1940s, more than 100 members of British Parliament banded together to advance a Crusade for World Government. With such a great background, we cannot see how the British people will not stand up to meet the challenge today.

Rejuvenated after the terrible disaster of World War II, the Germans and Japanese can meet the challenge with much painful memory and new vigor.

There are countries which historically or geographically are in an important position to meet the challenge, such as France, Australia, Mexico, Pakistan and Nigeria.

Undoubtedly more ready to meet the challenge are the countries where a humanitarian spirit has traditionally permeated, such as Canada, Switzerland, Sweden, and the other Scandinavian countries.

The Scandinavians would be in an even stronger position if they met the challenge together as a group.

The European Community has indeed established a strong position to meet the challenge. Also in a strong position to meet the challenge are groups such as the Pan American Union, the League of Arab States and the Organization of African Unity.

The strongest position for meeting the challenge is held by the Third World as a group. This is a unique opportunity for it to lead the divided world into an integrated one.

Finally, we want to emphasize that to meet this challenge is a privilege belonging to every nation and every group of countries, not just to the ones listed above; that to pursue the great cause of One World is an obligation of all nations and all groups of countries, not just of any one that takes the initiative; and that this great cause is something for which everyone has to do the best right away, and is not something on which one can wait and see how the others act and react.

When people are convinced to apply persuasion and pressure on their governments by voice and voting, but their governments are still stubbornly controlled by die-hard reactionaries and refuse to join in the great cause, it is time for the people to take direct action either to support the provisional world government formed or to be formed by the OWM, or to form one through a world convention by their representatives. If the latter is the case, the OWM will do as much as possible to help them achieve their goal, but refrains at the moment from prescribing what action they should take. They have the right and wisdom to do what they deem necessary.

The formation of a provisional world government is only a step, not a goal, of the world revolution. The goal of the world revolution is the establishment of a permanent world government. Until this goal is achieved, no success can be claimed for the world revolution.

Urgent Appeals

THE ROAD OF THE WORLD REVOLUTION FROM its starting point to success is unequivocally rough and precipitous. But we are marching on courageously without any hesitation and regardless of sacrifice. We are sure we can overcome all difficulties encountered when more and more people join the march and more and more supports come from those to whom we direct our urgent appeal:

To begin with the common people among them, there exist the moral virtues in the greatest purity. We urge you not to remain as a "silent majority" anymore. Speak out loudly against, and never vote for, those who do not work truly for humanity and peace.

Leading the common people are those who work hard on farms and in factories. We urge you not to provide for military establishments or activities with your products, and to refuse to make or transport weapons.

''As one-half of the human race, women must take on their share of helping to improve it world wide.'' You, the peaceful half of the human race, can contribute even more to solving the problems that spell life or death for all families. We urge you particularly to persuade your husbands and sons not to take part in killing and in getting killed.

A key position is held by the younger generations of today to work for a better world of tomorrow which belongs to them. Start to do whatever you can for your future right now. Reject to any call for, and get rid of, military services; and work vigorously for the cause of One World, in the tradition of examples set thirty years ago by young Carry Davis, the World Student Federalists, and the students who started to form a World Republic.

Naturally, one of the most important concerns of young people is the choice of study and subsequently profession. If the chance presents itself, we suggest that you study science, which is the foundation of civilization, and emulate those scientists from whose activities flow the currents of real history.

The value of science, as the foundation of civilization, lies not only in its usefulness, but also in its nature, which transcends national boundaries, races and creeds. The contributions of scientists, as the origin of real history, include not only their discovery of the laws of nature, but also the increase of their interest in humanity. In this respect, modern examples, in addition to those referred to earlier, such as Linus Pauling, Andrei Sakharov and Pyotr Kapitsa, may be found in Bertrand Russell, Albert Einstein, Alfred Kastler and many other Nobel Laureates.

At the present time, however, the increase of their interest in humanity has not been generated into a force strong enough to head off the threat of a total destruction of mankind by nuclear war. In spite of their efforts in warning the public and their governments, this threat is growing greater and greater. It is a deadly challenge to civilization itself. For an effective

93

response, all scientists are urged to work actively for the cause of One World as pioneered by the Emergency Committee of Atomic Scientists, and at least not to take part in developing and making nuclear weapons and other armaments or in planning military strategies and tactics.

Science in its proper sense includes both the natural and social sciences together with their technologies. Needless to say, the responsibility of the social scientists is as important as that of the natural scientists. In addition, social scientists are urged to serve the cause of One World by giving due regard to the similarities of cultures, and by not exaggerating indulgently the differences in ideologies.

Equally important is the responsibility of philosophers, educators, writers, artists, actors, musicians, athletes, and other professionals. All of you are urged, each in your own position and in your own way, to do your best for the cause of One World in the pursuit of humanity and peace, as Emery Reves did with his famous work *Anatomy of Peace,* and as Norman Cousins has done for world federation.

Originally, the pursuit of humanity and peace for one world is a common objective of the major religions, especially the monotheistic creeds including Judaism, Christianity and Islam. It is tragic that this objective has been largely subordinated to nationalism in the individual countries. In order to save civilization, of which religion is an important factor, all the leaders of the major religions are urged to preach their holy objectives rather than to pray to nationalist fetishes.

Blessed by nationalist fetishes are the military and political leaders portrayed as the "third type of man" who cares only for power, but they are only a very small number in the world. And they are human beings, too. And as human beings, you leaders are urged to change your outmoded concepts and methods in steering your ships, and to work for a permanent peace and general happiness instead of leading your people to the slaughterhouse and pushing your countries into hell. Your leadership would enable you to make extraordinary contributions to the cause of One World. The opportunity is unique for each of you to be a hero to all the peoples of the world.

94

Common Destination

FINALLY, IT IS NECESSARY TO EMPHASIZE THAT no one is without responsibility for taking the necessary actions at the time of the greatest crisis in history.

The most serious symptom of this crisis is the threat of a total destruction of mankind and its civilization by a nuclear war. In origin, however, it stems out of two great gaps: science and technology have advanced much faster than social adjustment, and material developments have left spiritual traditions far behind. Obviously, there is no sure way to close the two gaps except to speed up social adjustments and revitalize spiritual traditions; and there is no one who can do the speeding up and revitalizing jobs except man himself. Man is his own salvation.

Undoubtedly, the merging of all nations into One World is the fast means of speeding up social adjustments, and the pursuit of permanent peace and general happiness is the effective method of revitalizing spiritual traditions; and both the merging and the pursuit will eventually be achieved. But we cannot afford to wait when our survival is at stake. We have to push them through by all means before it is too late. Here again, man is his own salvation.

To be our own salvation, we must first resort to reason and the natural law for readjusting ourselves as rational beings to face the great changes of the world. In other words, we have to rely on intellect which is like light, illuminating ancient Greece and Asia Minor, early China, and lately, the Renaissance. Now let the light once again illuminate our time with new sources of scientific knowledge.

And second, we must have faith in ourselves and our future along the lines started by the Enlightenment Movement. While sailing in a great stream of historical forces, we have always held the rudder of the ship in our own hands. We have always responded to great challenges with unprecedented efforts. We have never given up our struggle for survival and the betterment of life, and have proved to be one of the toughest, most tenacious, and most adaptable creatures. There is nothing which has been impossible for us to achieve. We have made the old dream of flying come true and have even flown to the moon. There is no reason why we cannot make another old dream, that of One World, come true. We have been able to control nature very well, and there is no reason why we should not be able to readjust ourselves to our own salvation.

Further, it is necessary to emphasize that if we should fail to be our own salvation, it would mean not only the destruction of ourselves, but also the destruction of a history of thousands of generations in the past, and the future of millions of generations to come; and it would mean the destruction of a proud civilization which is the only one known to us in the infinite universe, has been built for millions of years by the hard work of our ancestors, and can soon be advanced to a much higher degree for the benefit of ourselves and our posterity.

When we realize how important the task is and how heavy the duty is for us, as our own salvation, to carry out, we see clearly that there is no way for us to retreat at all. We have to seek nothing less than a full triumph and we have to accomplish nothing short of a complete success.

For a full triumph and a complete success, we have to march together with a great courage, the utmost determination and above all, an unshakable faith. We have to work hard and act quickly. We can not wait for any favorable eventuality nor for any helpful miracle. Time is running out very fast.

Let us march together, work hard and act quickly to merge all nations into One World for permanent peace on earth and general happiness of mankind; to establish a World Government to serve all the people, and to advance our civilization to shine the whole universe, for billions of years to come.

Let us march together, work hard and act quickly to achieve the greatest mission of all times for our glorious common destination.

Part Two

SUPPLEMENTS TO TWO YEARS AFTER

Up to 1991

I. Comments Quoted

From Capt. TOM HUDGENS,
President of the World Citizens Assembly

January 26, 1987

"I met you in Milwaukee last September at the WGOCC meeting and have since read your book ONE WORLD. . . . It is a scholarly review of the necessity of world government, and I concur "yes" to it.

I believe also with you that we must unite all the world federation organizations into one world movement. I would like to meet with you at some time convenient to you to discuss how this might be brought about. I would be happy to travel to South Bend to meet you there or wherever you suggest.

I am also enclosing a copy of my book LET'S ABOLISH WAR for your information and comments. I wish I had known of your book at the time I wrote mine so I could have included mention of yours."

From Dr. GEORGE P. JAN,
Professor of Political Science,
Chairman of Asian Studies of
the University of Toledo

April 28, 1987

"In ONE WORLD Dr. Kiang meticulously and systematically analyzed the development of international relations and the main causes of world conflicts. He prescribed the proper course of action to achieve his goal of one harmonious world where mankind can live in long lasting peace. . . . In the final analysis, world peace can be achieved only through the common efforts of the people of the world, especially the people at the grass roots level. Dr. Kiang's tireless work for world peace is certainly an inspiration to people of the world.''

From Mr. TSU SUNG CHIU, Chairman of China Television Company

May 26, 1987

''I hardly need to say that I am in full accord with your attempt to encourage world government which is also the ultimate idea of Confucianism. It is no doubt that, as shown by the warm responses published in your book, the majority of the people in the world would agree with you. May your great ideas help promote peace and happiness of all mankind.

With my best wishes for your success in your effort.''

From Mr. YORK E. LANGTON, Board member of the United Nations Association—USA

May 29, 1987

''Mr. Kiang, this is the most important cause in the world that you are working on. There has to be a structure to maintain peace with justice. There are many organizations working for peace, making protests of all kinds, which should be encouraged but for the most part they are not realizing that there must be a structure to bring about cooperation, law, justice and peace. They are primarily protesters who help to bring about a favorable climate. They have not thought through the subject as you have in ONE WORLD.''

From Dr. ALFRED M. LILIENTHAL,
Prominent lawyer and author of
"Which Way to World Government?"

June 24, 1987

"In a world in which Western Civilization, as we have known it, is being threatened on so many fronts, One World seems more unattainable than ever. . . . But it is at such a low point in history that John Kiang's outline for the future takes on more meaning. Idealistic it may be, but the unity with the world must come about on a voluntary basis or we will have no world at all.

Increasing Nationalism on the governmental level, along with the all-too prevailing individual me-me-meism poses the grave present danger in our atomic infested world.

This invaluable book points the way out of the present global morass."

From Dr. CHARLES W. MEISTER,
Famous author and former President
of Eastern New Mexico University

June 28, 1987

"ONE WORLD has an incredible amount of scholarship on one of the world's most pressing problems. This book is encyclopedic in scope, containing a vast amount of statistical information and other material. Your material is arranged logically, making your argument quite impressive. Throughout your work one feels your love of mankind and your sincere effort to serve its best needs.

A couple of examples stand out. On p. 268 you point out that as recently as 400 years ago, ⅘ of the world's land had no nations, and that nearly half of all modern nations have come into existence since World War II. Also, on p. 378 you remind

101

us that under the current balance of terror foreign policy, obtaining additional allies may actually decrease a nation's security.

TWO YEARS AFTER provides interesting comments from world leaders on your One World program. Thank you again for sending me these books. I want to wish you success in giving leadership to a world badly in need of a lasting peace.''

From Arnold Henry Bergier, a philosopher and sculptor of New York, with a sculpture of Albert Einstein, actually an award more meaningful than any other prizes for world peace and government, along with a "citation" as follows:

February 6, 1989
(Chinese New Year's Day)

''Presented to Dr. John Kiang, in admiration of his scholarship and clear thinking, and with the hope that together with others of our persuasion, we can help to save this beautiful green and blue planet from ultimate doom caused by the depredations of the power-hungry, greedy, paranoid fools who usually dominate human affairs.''

From Mr. Jeffrey D. S. Liang, a business leader

August 22, 1989

''Though many people, including myself, have occasionally cherished similar ideas, I did not expect to find a huge book of such caliber on the subject, nor did I expect to see so much evidence presented so systematically and eloquently to point out the direction that the human race must follow to avoid self-destruction. My belated congratulation to you on a difficult job well done. When one day the coming generations can enjoy life as world citizens, they should be thankful for the leading role you have been playing in the movement.''

II. Comments with Complete Letters

From Mr. Eng. Reinhart Ruge, Mexico, President of the World Constitution and Parliament Association

February 26, 1988

Dear Mr. John Kiang:

With the best thanks and greatest appreciation, I acknowledge and welcome your wonderful book ONE WORLD together with the booklet TWO YEARS AFTER.-

We both have one thing in common: our lives are dedicated to obtain peace on planet Earth, by uniting all countries and thus making war impossible.- Today the Human race will only have a chance of survival if we can effectively abolish war.- It is only when we abolish war, that we will be able to disarm and get rid of the monstrous weapons of collective suicide which stupid and short sighted scientists, technicians and politicians have developed in order to protect their empires of National Sovereignty, National independences and Patriotism.-

I hope that we will be successful in our endeavours, before it is too late.- How to go about forming a ONE WORLD? It will be only possible through a new organism: The World Parliament—a Democratic Federal Non-Military World Government, as designed and conceived in the Federations of Earth through an appropriate Constitution.- (I suppose that Mr. Philip Isely, our Secretary General has sent you all the pertinent literature.)

The World Constitution and Parliament Association has now worked intensively for more than 30 years to obtain the Constitution for the Federation of Earth through 3 World Constituent Assemblies, at Interlaken, Switzerland and Wolfach, Germany in 1968, at Innsbruck, Austria, 1977 and Colombo, Sri Lanka 1980.- With the WCPA as an agent, three provisional World Parliaments have been in session: at Brighton, England 1982, at New Delhi, India 1985 and at Miami Beach, Florida 1987. We consider this work and these sessions as very real and conducive towards a new World Organization, that will be able to solve our ever increasing World problems.- We do not believe the United Nations can be changed into something useful. 43 Years of experience with the United Nations has demonstrated the contrary.- As you quote from one of our former proclamations, correctly in your book: page 588: "If the Governments of the World have not the wisdom to unite for the good of man, then we the people must unite! We must arm ourselves to the hilt with every bit of wisdom, understanding and love we can find in ourselves . . . and the victory we will win will not mean the defeat of one man by another. It will be a victory for all men.—"

I hope that we will soon have an opportunity to meet, and continue further discussion. Certainly I personally would welcome it very much, if you would be able to reproduce much of our work in the next edition of your book, since I consider this essential for a positive approach towards a common survival in an era, when most of the efforts are oriented to produce more arms, create greater pollution and waste endless recourses in stupid and unnecessary, often harmful projects, with the result that the rich are getting richer every day and the poorer are getting poorer every day.- Of course this created dangerous social conditions.

With all my best wishes,

FOR PEACE AND HUMANITY

Reinhart Ruge

Ing. Reinhart Ruge, Sc. M.
President

From Dr. Benjamin B. Ferencz, Counselor at Law, Adjunct Professor, Pace Law School

July 16, 1988

Dear John: (I feel I can call you by your first name since we are kindred spirits and brothers in the search for peace.)

May I thank you most sincerely for sending me a copy of ONE WORLD and your brief report TWO YEARS AFTER. I have read them both—although I have not yet been able to give them the detailed study they richly deserve. I think you have made a remarkable contribution. I am impressed, grateful, and a little ashamed that your encyclopedic book had escaped my attention.

What more can I say? I was delighted to find that there was someone else out there who, coming from a completely different background, was treading the same paths I had walked for years and was coming to very similar conclusions.

I felt a bit like a scientist who, working alone in his laboratory, makes a discovery which is published at about the same time by another unknown scholar working independently in another part of the world. Not that I think we have invented something completely new (our quest is an ancient one that has attracted many fine minds,) but we have both addressed the same contemporary audience with almost identical pleas for a more rational approach to world order.

Because of my training, I have tended to approach the problems from a legal perspective. I soon realized that producing six heavy tomes (See brochure attached) was not enough. The message had to reach the minds of those who influence the decision-makers. So I wrote A COMMON SENSE GUIDE TO WORLD PEACE (Inscribed copy attached.) That attracted the attention (and admiration) of Ken Keyes Jr. who asked permission to reprint it and make it attractive for popular consumption.

I had never met Ken and didn't even know where Coos Bay was. We collaborated by mail and phone and PLANET-

HOOD was the result. Then Ken and his wife came to visit me here in New Rochelle. He was in a wheelchair, completely paralyzed from the waist down—a victim of polio for the last 40 years. I took him to my class at law school, to the United Nations and he addressed a group of diplomats. His overwhelming spirit of love for humankind, optimism and enthusiasm was inspiring to all.

A few weeks ago, he called to ask if I wanted any revisions in the text—the first 100,000 copies was about gone and he was about to print another 100,000! He is a man without funds. Most of the books are given away free. Whatever money is received is used completely to produce and circulate additional copies. I am moved and flabbergasted by the entire experience.

I mention this only because it relates to my comment about your ONE WORLD. As I have indicated, I think it is a very fine book—worthy of great distribution. Yet, I checked and found that it was not in the U.N. library. [I immediately recommended to them that it be acquired. I have also arranged to have it ordered by the Pace law library.] I was saddened by the thought that such a scholarly and worthwhile compendium of wisdom and knowledge has probably had very little recognition or support.

Scholars, unfortunately, are little appreciated in our society and we must communicate in terms that the public is willing to hear and able to comprehend. PLANETHOOD (thanks to Ken Keyes) has already reached more readers than all of my other books combined. I therefore particularly admire the determination, patience and skill that must have gone into the preparation of your wonderful book and the broad vision which is there to reward the reader.

What can I do to help spread the message?

I assume that the International Institute for Peace Studies which has recently been established at Notre Dame (thanks to a $6 million grant from Mrs. Kroc) is aware of the jewel they have in its own back yard. I hope they may be helpful in disseminating copies of your book to a wide audience and to libraries everywhere.

Should you be in this area at any time please do me the honor of phoning and we shall certainly meet. I look forward to getting to know you personally and to an exchange of views.

With cordial greetings,

Ben

From Mr. S. L. Gandhi, Secretary, ANUVRAT Global Organization—India

Feb. 6, 1989

Dear Mr. Kiang,

Thank you for your letter of October 10, 1988 and for the two books 'One World' and 'Two Years Later' which you so kindly sent to me along with it. I fully endorse your theory that the resolution of the conflict that stems from narrow nationalism and religious fundamentalism lies in the abolition of separate entities of nations which are responsible for causing divisions in mankind. May your dream of 'one world' be realized soon and may the world escape being annihilated by a nuclear war.

I have been highly impressed by your dedication to this noble cause of eradicating violence from this globe. Needless to say that your book will go a long way in uniting the peoples of the world into one family. In India the ancient sages and seers uttered the same truth thousands of years ago. They said 'VASUDHEV (Entire World) KUTUMBKAM' (is one family).

One great saint of India realized forty years ago that the potential threat to mankind stems from our being unethical and selfish. He threw off the yoke of sectarianism and launched the ANUVRAT MOVEMENT which secures individual commitment to basic human values responsible for this chaotic situation. His name is His Holiness Acharya Tulsi, head of a jain sect and a great champion of world friendship and world peace. His approach to peace differs in that he seeks peace asking individuals to accept small (anu) vows (vrat) not to indulge in violence and hatred. He feels that virtually no efforts have been made to unite forces of peace and nonviolence which are in a state of disarray today. He has long been dreaming of one world and has been promoting the idea in his own way.

In fact I find his ANUVRAT MOVEMENT and Your One World Movement almost identical.

The international conference on peace and nonviolent action which I organized at Ladnun under his auspices from 5th to 7th December, 1988 was a small step towards the unity of peace lovers who alone can be instrumental in ushering in an era of one world.

It was a great success as it attracted more than 80 overseas participants to Ladnun—a small desert town in Rajasthan. The delegates issued a joint action plan to eradicate violence from this world which includes the popularization of the concept of one world.

My organization will introduce your book and will extend active support to your movement. Both these movements have many things to share. Let us work together and do let me know of your activities.

I once again express my gratitude to you for the precious gift i.e. your book entitled 'One World' and look forward to hearing from you.

Yours sincerely,

SL Gandhi

(S. L. GANDHI)

III. Reviews

By Dr. John Roberts,
Editor of the WORLD FEDERALIST,
Institute of Mundialist Studies, England

Bulletin No. 4, 1987

This very remarkable book is two things—a scholarly tome and a 'Popular Manifesto'. As such it is a unique addition to the literature on the achievement of world government. It is the life-work of an exceptional man, a Chinese librarian turned inventor and businessman who cherished an ambition from his childhood to work for human unity. A quite extraordinary collection of facts, comment and analysis is the impressive result.

It is not complete, of course, for no one man can hope to comprehend so vast an undertaking as the sources of that evolving unity which is already absorbing the industry and imagination of thousands of people. And, like all books dealing with the present and future, its references began to be outdated as soon as they were collated. But it is a marvelous example of what will be done, once scholars turn from their fruitless obsessions with explaining and excusing the follies of mankind and instead begin to look for the beginnings of the creation of a united world. We can only urge our readers to get a copy, or at very least to order one from their local library.

This volume is an enterprise of the greatest value in showing how to weld together the opinion-makers of the academic world, who have an unfulfilled duty to lead their lesser colleagues towards the sense of unity. John Kiang has read omnivorously, has thought deeply and has written cogently. Upon the publication of this book, he dispatched copies to Nobel Laureates and other eminent scholars across the world. Their vastly laudatory reactions, often revealing, and in general very encouraging, are printed on the dust-jacket and in a paper-back 'Two Years After.' As they say: "Don't miss it!"

Read John Kiang's "theories, principles, objectives and programs" in a future issue.

Bulletin No. 1, 1988

Further perusal of this intrepid work reveals the prodigious reading that was necessary for such an undertaking by John Kiang. (Details in previous issue.)

This is a very thorough and painstaking consideration of many, many things, with a wealth of example and analogy. The spread of cultivated plants is just one illuminating episode in the story. The Section 'One World in the Making' has some fascinating reflections upon the remarkable convergence of legal systems. It also provokes the thought that the 'South Bend Tribune', not widely considered one of the world's great newspapers, has served Mr. Kiang very well indeed on many occasions.

Points may be questioned e.g., English nationalism (p 309); language is not seen as, but may well be (p 373 etc.), essential to nationalism; was China ever a 'nation' in the European sense, rather than a world on its own? one might even cavil at 'Cold War' p 241 as a main cause of . . . And perhaps only a librarian could call the greatest publicist for one world of our century 'Herbert G.' Wells, although he was sometimes known as Herbert George!

John Kiang traces merging of peoples as a social, evolutionary, historical and universal law "The law of group expansion is not made by human beings, yet it is an iron rule for our existence." "To merge all nations into One World is the last step in the long process of group expansion, as an historical, universal and social evolutionary. It is not only desirable, but logical, not only expected, but inevitable."

All in all, let us reiterate that this is a book to marvel at and to publicise.

Here we are again! A book to remember and to be proud of. Mr. Kiang is a scholar whom the world federalists should honour—one of a handful of dedicated students of the new discipline of mundialism. This volume is a creation of the first importance and, as Henry Usborne has said "It is essential reading for all peace-makers."

The Prelude of the book has some interesting and little-known quotations, all to the point and its final section is about 'the One World movement'. The other sections are headed 'Group Expansion', 'One World in the Making', 'Anatomy of the Nation', 'Permanent Peace', 'General Happiness' and 'Structure of the One World' but such a list gives no idea of the depth of reading and the wealth of apposite quotation that here gives the clue to it.

Mr. Kiang, as pertinacious as he is able, sent his book to a large number of Nobel Laureates and other prominent thinkers. Their enthusiastic tributes to the quality of the book decorate the wrapper. They are eminently believable. And there John Kiang has also a complementary volume printed two years after the original publication which prints these and details the reception of the first volume.

The comments on 'the nation-state' and on 'national sovereignty' are themselves of particular value, the first for their strong condemnation and insights, the latter for a condensed historical survey. To read the book carefully is an education in itself.

By Mr. Gary K. Shepherd,
Editor of the UNITED WORLD,
Vol. 2, No. 4, July-Aug. 1989

At long last, someone has finally done it; someone has finally used the world "revolution" to describe the unification of the world. It's about time.

I believe that sometimes those of us who believe in a United World, in our effort to avoid offending or frightening people, tend to de-emphasize the important and drastic nature of the changes that world unification will represent. We seem eager to state that the change will be relatively easy and painless. This is in fact, pure misrepresentation; the world unification will likely be very painful and disturbing to the lives of the vast majority of people. That is, paradoxically, one of its primary benefits.

I believe we are doing the people of the world a disservice when we try to sell the world unification as being one that will not require sacrifices of them. The nationalists know that the vast majority of people have the innate nobility to sacrifice themselves for the welfare of the common good. We denigrate them by expecting anything less.

There can be absolutely no doubt what is required to being the people of the world together is a real revolution. John Kiang, in his *ONE WORLD: The Approach to Permanent Peace on Earth and the General Happiness of Mankind*, seems to be one of the few who have recognized this fact. "The formation of a provisional world government is only a step, not a goal of the world revolution," he writes. "The goal of the world revolution is the establishment of a permanent world government." He also says, "The road of the world revolution from its starting point to success is unequivocally rough and precipitous. But we are marching on it courageously, without any hesitation and regardless of sacrifices."

Unfortunately, Kiang undercuts his own arguments in the earlier part of his book, when he speaks of his "law of group expansion." This expansion, he claims, shows a steady increase over time in the size of political entities. And a decrease in the total number of them. He even provides a table which demonstrates how there has been a gradual expansion from single families, through clans, tribes, and nations, culminating in the creation of one world, which includes everyone.

There is obviously considerable truth in all this. However, I am sure not even Mr. Kiang believes it really is all that simple. There is little historical evidence to suggest that

113

increasing size of political entities leads inexorably to world unity. History has shown that nationalism and its related philosophies can be divisive as well as unifying. The progression is not as neat and tidy as Mr. Kiang's tables indicate.

And there is another danger to such thinking. The danger that if we begin to believe that "history is on our side" we will sit back and wait for history to do our job for us. We cannot afford that kind of thinking. In any case, one thing is certain; the change from a great many tribal divisions to a small number of national divisions is basically just a quantitative change; while the change from a world of divisions to one of no divisions, is a qualitative change. As Kiang himself points out, "it (nationalism) will strive to remain in force as a root of imperialism, a curse to universal humanity, and individual freedom, and a reactionary force against the general trend of modern civilization, unless some drastic action is taken to eradicate it completely."

Whatever its defects, the book remains a powerful presentation of the case for world unification. It is filled with keen political insight, and an awesome amount of documentation. Indeed, this last strength is also something of a weakness, for Kiang's monumental footnotes at times obscure the flow of the text. It might be useful if Kiang could be prevailed upon to issue two editions of his work; one as it is, and another consisting just of the Popular Manifesto, without the scholarly annotations, which might tend to scare off readers of less scholarly bent. In such a format it could be reduced to a small paperback booklet that would be cheaper to produce and could enjoy a wider distribution.

Kiang included with his reviewer's copy a copy of a smaller pamphlet called *Two Years After,* which consists primarily of a summary of the larger book and the reactions of those who have read *One World.* These letters heap praise on the book from a great variety of individuals, including Linus Pauling. Without attempting to join that chorus, I can honestly say that I found his book impressive. It remains the most realistic and far-reaching discussion of the idea of attaining world unity to have been published in recent years, and certainly deserves comparison to books such as Wells' *Open Conspiracy,* and Reves' *Anatomy of Peace.*

One minor quibble; in his book *Two Years After,* Kiang shows his concept of one world flag. Basically it consists of white circle on a green field with a large letter *W,* for *world,* inscribed. I think the green circle and white field are good and powerful symbols, but the *W* is a mistake. It would be meaningless to non-English speakers. I'm surprised Kiang, as a non-native English speaker, didn't think of that first.

IV. Exchange Of Ideas

With Mrs. Elizabeth R. Dana,
Secretary of the Federalist Caucus

April 7, 1987, from Elizabeth

The copy of "Two Years After" arrived yesterday, and I have already read large portions of it hastily. So many good friends are mentioned, both those I have known personally and those known only through correspondence, but reasonably well despite the distance of being continents apart, that it was like our tradition of "Old Home Day," back in New Hampshire, when so many who have moved away return to their respective towns to celebrate old times, with long-time friends!

I continue to marvel at the clarity of your thinking, exposition and goals. You are making a great contribution, and I hope you will continue to be able to work closely with others in leadership positions within the overall movement, for I think a number are beginning to realize the importance of "getting our act together" across organizational lines. We suffer from our own brand of "nationalism" and sometimes seem just as "hung-up" by organizational "sovereignty" as do the nations, themselves! We seem to forget that the key to making federalism workable was the idea of vesting sovereignty in the INDIVIDUAL, thus providing each one with full privileges of citizenship at EACH level of governance to which he/she has, by representation, delegated a portion of such sovereign power.

Unfortunately—and here I believe I must include the OWM in my criticism, but am sure you will not be surprised at that, given the tenor of some of my earlier remarks—our organizations also seem not to take into adequate account the entirely different POLITICAL situation today, from that of the days of Willkie and Reves. (Incidentally, on page 50, in re "I do not know the exact meaning of the 'Dewey-like One World-ism' either": I believe Mr. Majkut was inadvertently reveal-ing, once again, his utter inadequacy as a reviewer of your book; that is, that he recalled the title "One World" and as-sociated it correctly with a presidential candidate of the '40's, but erroneously with Dewey, rather than Willkie.) In my own view, Parliamentarians Global Action, itself, is FUNCTION-ING like a transnational political party for genuine peace and greater economic justice, even though it is not one, officially. Nor do I believe it can BECOME one until vast numbers of voters individually indicate their desire to be represented by them with respect to these transnational goals—the easiest means of doing which, today, is by becoming part of the Fed-eralist Caucus, which exists for that primary purpose. In this regard it is wholly unlike any of our dues-based organizations, but simply supplements their non-governmental capabilities by enabling their MEMBERS, individually, to become part of this transnational political partnership with these legislators, directly—much as party affiliation does in the sphere of do-mestic policy-making. In other words, today this extraordi-nary POTENTIAL for political unity exists—which did not exist 45 years ago—yet it is being all but totally ignored by our established world government organizations. So PGA is forced to forge ahead WITHOUT the substantial base of known voter support that it both deserves and needs to be suc-cessful, or even for its individual members not to have to run undue risk of defeat at the polls because of the very well-organized opposition to them that has always characterized the efforts of the "other side"—those who would like to see an even greater dependence on military might than we now endure.

Perhaps the most dramatic example of the discontinuity that exists between GROUPS that say they want peace, and their reluctance to inform their members about the importance of affiliating themselves in association with these legislators, occurred during the last year. You may recall that a major U.S. citizen group gave the six heads of government who have been working with PGA a Peace Award, whose presentation was broadcast live from eight points around the world simultaneously, via satellite, so even people with "dishes" could view it from their own living-rooms. In effect, they were applauding these heads of state for having accepted PGA's invitation to help secure a nuclear-weapons-free world. Yet, there was no interest whatever in letting their members know how each of THEM could, in effect, accept the same invitation personally, by becoming part of the constituency back in each legislator's home District, and so help to provide the political base necessary to continue on this path. And just recently, PGA itself has just been awarded the first annual Indira Gandhi Peace Prize, whose financial benefit is comparable to that of the Nobel Prizes. Of course, such recognition is extremely valuable in its own right. But, ultimately, it cannot SUBSTITUTE for direct constituent support, politically.

The question I think we need to address is, How can we resolve this wide-spread problem? What can we do to overcome the resistance of our own groups (many of which are not political at all, that is, they are organized as tax-deductible groups, barred from playing any significant political role AS ORGANIZATIONS) to encourage their MEMBERS to add this type of political action to the other things they may already do (letter-writing, demonstrating, etc.)? My own feeling is that, for any NEW group coming on the scene to work for peace, to leave this component out of its program is to start out with a 45-year handicap in the race for potential adherents. I really believe we are very close to being in a situation almost directly analogous to that of the abolition-of-slavery movement in the 1850's. At the time, the Democratic Party was a regional party in the South and the Whigs a regional one in the North, at least to a large degree. But, especially on the western frontier, where people were, perhaps, a bit more immediately aware that the U.S. would soon be a CONTINENTAL nation, an incipient Republican Party was forming that would be not only the first one of national scope, but was also beginning to perceive slavery as a national—not just state—issue. And, as it gained in strength, leading up to its first presidential success in 1860, all the little private abolitionist societies which had laid the groundwork for that goal's achievement, began to disappear, as all their former members had to do was join the Republicans. Of course, this in no way meant that private efforts to secure full rights for blacks would no longer be necessary. But the basic CONTEXT was altered by the outcome of the War, so the primary goals of the earlier groups had, over time, to be transformed; and then, the same kinds of PEOPLE who had joined the earlier groups began to organize such groups as the NAACP, the Urban League, etc., to address those problems not resolved by simply achieving an end to slavery, per se. In similar fashion, I do not believe achieving an end to WAR (partly by building a huge constituency to support legislators already committed to that top priority) will eliminate the need for citizen groups whose primary goal is peace—but it WOULD change the present context within which they operate, to the extent that their now-subsidiary goals would still require considerable private energy. Is there any chance of the OWM becoming a leader in helping ALL of us see the need for our own transformational strategies, and so perhaps overcome the hesitancy outlined above? I shall welcome any comments or ideas you care to make—and also enclose a check for your wonderful new book.

April 16, 1987, to Elizabeth

Thank you for your thoughtful letter of April 7, 1987 and the check for the book TWO YEARS AFTER, but I have to return you the check, because the book was sent to you with my compliments. I appreciate and agree in general with your broad view over the situation of the organizations for world government. In my opinion, the only way for us to overcome our common weakness, or say, to get out of the jungle, is to unite all of us into one party. This is the goal I have pursued for years, have urged in sections IX and XI of the TWO YEARS AFTER, and have strongly appealed in its last section—Declaration of the One World Movement, with proposals for a World Anthem and a World Flag. Your cooperation in this effort will do a great service to the great cause.

With Mr. Dieter Heinrich, President, World Federalists of Canada

May, 1987, from Dieter

I would be grateful if you would send me a review copy of your book "One World." We are preparing a literature list for the World Federalists of Canada (3,000 members and supporters) who would be informed about your book. If you cannot send a review copy free please suggest what you would like me to pay to cover your costs.

I would like to enclose for your comment a draft of a book I'm writing for the World Association of World Federalists. I'd be pleased if you could send any suggestions by July 1, 1987 for the final draft.

Are you planning to attend the WAWF Congress in Philadelphia by the way?

I look forward to hearing from you.

May 28, 1987, to Dieter

I am very pleased to have your letter today. I have tried to contact with your Federalists of Canada in the last three years by writing letters and sending information and books, but I don't know why there has been no response.

Thanks for the copy of your draft "The Common Security Alternative". Under separate cover I am sending you one copy each of my books ONE WORLD and TWO YEARS AFTER with compliments. You comment and introducing them to your federalists and the public will be highly appreciated.

I don't know at the moment I will be able to go to Philadelphia, August, to observe the WAWF Congress. But I will go to Miami late next month to be a cheerleader for the World

Constitutional and Parlimentary Association conference. Hope to meet you if you happen to be there.

With Mr. Tom Ehrenzeller, Program Director, Association to Unite the Democracies

June 17, 1987, from Tom

Thank you for sending us **One World** and its supplement. The Association to Unite the Democracies is interested in studying and discussing all serious proposals for building toward a democratic world government.

Most plans for world union have a single "first step" which must happen before any other progress can be made toward the ultimate goal. Your plan has the merit that its first step, the overcoming of nationalism, is a general rather than a specific act, so that many things may be done which may achieve diverse worthwhile aims and yet all can be seen as building toward One World if they dilute, disperse or otherwise loosen the bonds of nationalism. This of course raises the question of whether you have a specific program or plan, either tentative or firm, for a course of action to get the world from where it is to where we all want to be.

AUD is interested in working with other peace and federalist organizations dedicated to the ultimate goal of world democracy. We would be very interested in learning about the organization being developed around the book **One World.** If you have any sort of public events, I help edit the **World Democracy News** which reports on events of world peace and unity organizations as well as news of events around the world effecting the growth and unity of democracy. I would be happy to list any upcoming events of the One World Movement in the newsletter if you would let me know about them ahead of time.

I have not read **One World** thoroughly, but I have looked through it and found it very interesting. The endless footnotes are an immense scholarly resource in themselves. There are two points about it, one general and one more specific, which I would like clarified. Firstly, there is a general attitude in the book that in it lies the final answer. In other words, all the world has to do is read this book, follow its directions, and we will have one world. There have been many books in the past which have offered what their authors considered **the** answer to the problems of the world. Is it overstating the case to say that you consider **One World** to be the one and only answer to the problems of the world, or is it offered as **an** answer which may supplement other works and be itself developed upon as time goes by? There seems to be something of a didactic tone to it, as if it were telling the world not only how things could be or should be, but how they will be. If this impression is mistaken, as well it may be from quickly looking through the book, please correct me.

The more specific point I wonder about is where it is stated that the One World Government will be run by experts rather than politicians. While politicians can be annoying, they are a necessary evil to democratic government unless you propose direct democracy in which government decisions are made directly by popular vote. Since I gather it is not direct world democracy which you are advocating, and you disclaim governing through politicians, that is, representative democracy, there seems to be some question whether it is democratic government at all that is being advocated. Government can be, and to a large degree must be operated by experts, but when choices have to be made and basic issues decided, then the democratic voice must be the deciding one.

If the One World plan does provide for democratic decision making, or has an extremely good reason why not, please clarify this point for me. I have long been of the opinion that, once the twin perils of nationalism and nuclearism are overcome, once a system of democratic world governance adequate to global problems is in place and just systems exist for human governance at all levels, that much of the popular interest in politicians and issues will probably fade. Issues, to the extent that there are any, will be decided one way or the other, either by the legislature or by referendum, and then the regular citizenry will go about their business. Unfortunately, there is a large measure of this attitude even today when crucial issues have to be decided and are being ignored instead. The biggest issue, which no national government or citizenry has even looked at seriously yet, is the one dealt with in innumerable works from Union Now to One World: nationalism versus the survival of humanity. However, once this and the connected major issues of the era are decided, and the leaders of the USA and USSR no longer have the supreme power to destroy the world in their hands, politics may lose much of its popular interest.

A positive offshoot of this may be that voters will elect trained professionals to run their government rather than popular personalities. Thus, your suggestion that the political system will be run by experts is well taken. But, if it is to be democratic, as to my mind it must be, then the decision-making "experts" must be elected.

Your thesis that overcoming nationalism is the key to uniting the world is of immense interest to me personally. A few years ago I wrote a book **Solar Man,** a copy of which I enclose, which attempts to answer this problem. The solution I offer is that we give humanity a new security blanket as we wean it from the one called nationalism. The new security blanket I suggest is the Solar System. Unlike the Earth alone, which we have already carved up into states and counties and private plots, the Solar System is an as yet undivided common heritage of all mankind. If we can explore it together as united world citizens and come to identify with our planet, our star and our region of the universe, we can then discard the worn-out and dangerous toy called nationalism which we have clung to into what is now our tempestuous adolescence as a species. We can thus build a united Solar Nation inclusive of all mankind.

I would appreciate any comments you might have concerning either the book or the concept of **Solar Man.** I have long been developing ideas for another book tentatively entitled **World Democracy** which I hope to put together in the next year or so. It will develop upon **Solar Man,** drawing upon my experience as a World Federalist and staff member of AUD, the many other organizations and interested individual point of view I have encountered, and scholarly works on the subject of world union of which **One World** is one of the most impressive.

July 26, 1987, to Tom

Many thanks for your letter of June 17, 1987 and the publication "A Foreign Policy for the United States." But I did not find your book SOLAR MAN in the envelope and I do hope to have a chance to read it, because I am going to write a book THE STRANGE WORLD; a report of the mission from moon. I will appreciate it if you will make some notes in your WORLD DEMOCRACY NEWS about my books ONE WORLD and TWO YEARS AFTER.

Now let me answer your two thoughtful questions very briefly. First to your general question: Your impression is correct. My book is a manifesto of revolution for world unity with the evolutionary law of group expansion as a guiding theory; national independence, national sovereignty and nationalism as primay targets, permanent peace and general happiness of mankind as ultimate objectives, together with a blueprint for world government and a practical program for actions. Is it something completely new? No. There have been some far-sighted people who suggested some theories, proposed some programs or projected some actions, here and there. But I have not seen any publication which put all or most of them together in a systematic and scientific way. This is what I have tried to do with more discoveries and innovations as features. I have written with affirmative tone and definite terms, because I believe they are truth. I think we need practical action rather than academic discussion now, and I feel we cannot afford to lose time anymore. But my theory, programs and projects are up for free acceptance and adoption, and are subject to criticism and challenges. They are not "didactic".

As regards your specific question, I like to point out first that in my project the future world government is democratic, but is not in the form of traditional democracy, nor in the sense of "new" democracy. It is a positive democracy based on the division of four functions—opinion, knowledge, service and justice to serve the people, rather than to rule by check and balance of power in legislative, executive and judicial branches, as explained in the text and annotations of my book p. 534–539. Secondly when the military and foreign affairs have been eliminated from the business of world government, "government can be, and to a large degree must be operated by experts" and "much of the popular interest in politicians and issues will probably fade" as you have envisaged. Therefore, the problem is how to entrust the experts while the voice of the people can still be heard. In this respect my project calls for a House of Experts and a House of Commons with some designs for their respective duties and elections as outlined in the text and annotations of my book p. 530–533. You are kindly urged to check over these pages (p. 530–539) for more clarification.

My wife and I will fly to Philadelphia on the tenth of next month for the constitution bicentennial occasion, then proceed to Washington for another meeting. I hope to have a chance to meet you someway.

With Mrs. Stella Dunn, Hon. Organizer, Project for Peace, England

June 9, 1987, from Stella

Many thanks for sending me a copy of your interesting follow-up book entitled *"Two Years After"*, which I have just received; and in which I note the mention of our previous correspondence.

Unfortunately, I cannot write to you fully at the present time, as I am having to cope with pressure of work on all sides. But I am, however, enclosing copies of some recent correspondence with Mrs. Elizabeth ("Betsy") Dana, Secretary-Treasurer of the Federalist Caucus in Portland, Oregon, with whom I know you are also in direct contact. And the attached correspondence broadly indicates the lines on which I am now working.

I also note with interest that we still seem to be working on somewhat similar lines. But if these efforts to create a more United World are to develop realistically, I think you might agree on the need to create a closer NGO working link between East and West.

But at the same time, however, one must bear in mind that Members of the Soviet Communist Party in particular, seem to be *more* consciously aware of their national ideological identity, than World Citizens in most other parts of the world would appear to be. And bearing in mind the strong missionary zeal of that particular party, to impose their ideology on others, it is unlikely that they would wish to support any other International Party, Movement, Parliament or World Government, which is likely to weaken or submerge their Communist identity and particular brand of Communism.

And as this is a political fact of life which has to be taken into account, when seeking to create World Unity, surely the only way in which to overcome this problem would be through an International Three-Party system, in which the main opposing sides would be able to retain their existing identities; but with a slight compromising modification?

Also, this would then enable China to support such a Movement. And you will no doubt agree that a country which has a quarter of the world's population can hardly be excluded from a One World Movement of *any* kind. But with a certain amount of compromise on all sides, however, there would seem to be no valid reason why NGOs in both Russia and China would not wish, and be able, to join the International political structure we both envisage.

With regard, however, to the Three-Party ideological set-up which I have proposed—in relation to an International Peoples' Parliament at a midway meeting point between East and West—I do, of course, realize that this would still be somewhat divisive; even though it would be a positive step towards greater working cooperation and Unity.

And although I would certainly admit that such a system might not be regarded as ideal by Utopian standards, I would nevertheless like to point out that a system based on political Diversity within the call for Unity, fits in with the old Greek theory of the relationship of opposites. For this presents a situation in which *one* extreme can serve to *complement* (rather than conflict with) its opposite counterpart. And this, it seems, is sometimes the pattern of nature and life itself—as, for instance, in the case of the opposite sexes, light and darkness, happiness and unhappiness, life and death, etc.

Would it not, therefore, seem that everything which relates to politically constructive development, can have a useful and harmonious part to play in integrating the main streams of political ideology?

But I do not, however, see how the widely established World Federalist Movement—with its affiliated branches in many parts of the world—can be expected, at this stage, to change its name altogether, and adopt a new identity: such as "World Government Party", "World Unity Campaign", or "One World Movement", which you suggest.

Alternatively, therefore, I wondered if it would not be possible for the World Federalist Movement, the One World Movement and other kindred NGOs, to cooperate in becoming the spearhead of a World Federalist Democratic Party, as part of the Three-Party Peoples' International Parliamentary system (as hereto proposed)?

For would this not help to *protect* the World Federalist element in an International Peoples' Parliament, from any kind of Communist subversion—whilst at the same time helping to promote constructive interaction between the two sides? And with your invaluable Chinese-American background, would it not be possible for you to contact Peking University, for a Professorial and Student reaction in this matter (particularly as you would be able to do so in the Chinese language)? And perhaps it would also be possible for you to send them a copy of *"One World"* and your latest book (*"Two Years After"*)?

But on a more personal level, however, I am sorry to tell you the sad news of the death of my old friend Professor

James Liu, of Stanford University and formerly of Peking, who I mentioned in previous correspondence. I was informed about this last Christmas, by his daughter, Sarah Liu (a former student at Yale, now studying medicine at Stanford), who I met many years ago, when she visited London as a small child. And she told me (in her message last Christmas about her father) that she cabled her aunt in Peking about this. And as Professor Liu's eldest sister, her Aunt was able to get a visa to go to Stanford. So it seems that the situation in China must now be getting a little easier toward the West.

With all best wishes for the continuing success of your wide-reaching enterprise and publications.

Sept. 8, 1987, to Stella

Before I left for Philadelphia, your letter of June 9, 1987 reached me, and after I returned home, your letter of July 18, 1987 arrived. Thank you very much for letting me know your three-party project and all information concerned.

The Philadelphia events included: The International Bicentennial Symposium, August 6–8, 1987, conducted by the World Federalists Association, a public Rally in the evening of August 9, 1987, and the Congress of the World Association of World Federalists, August 10–13, 1987.

In the morning of August 11, 1987, a meeting of the World Government Organization Coalition was held as an interjection of the federalists programs. It was chaired by Dr. Lucile Green, with participants more than expected, proceeding longer than scheduled, and debates hotter than usual. But as usual, it accomplished very little. "Is it not, therefore, time for the world federalist movement and other kindred organizations to unite in seeking pastures new, if they are to start moving forward politically to their goal of world federation and the promotion of world government, as a means of bringing about peace and a better organized world?" So mindfully you asked in your Memo to the NEC and Council of AWF/UK and Others with a significant title: TIME FOR POLITICIZATION. Unfortunately there are still not many people who like to listen to this kind of voice. They still prefer divided rather than united, even among the world federalists themselves with two confusing associations and a number of other entities. For the very reason my proposal to unite all groups that strive for world unity, world government, world citizenship, world peace, humanity, and the like, into a single political party, did not get much support in the Coalition meeting. A copy of my proposal is enclosed here for your review. I should tell you, however, that I met with Mrs. Elizabeth Dana there. She had a great courage to stand out for the political unity idea, although with different approach.

I do not know how much attention did your three-party project draw and who would have spoken for you in the WAWF Congress where it is supposed to be the right place to air out your view. I left Philadelphia early for Washington to attend another important conference and did very little observation on the WAWF Congress.

As regards the International Bicentennial Symposium, its slogan is "strengthening the United Nations" culminating with "The Declaration of Philadelphia". A copy of the declaration also is enclosed here for your review. The declaration stresses "imagination" rather than reality and demands for "imaginative action" rather than to do something real. It wants to strengthen the United Nations, but gives no clear reasons why the strengthening is needed, nor tells how to do the job practically and effectively. It is a good declaration, but actually, good for nothing, or in your words "barking up the wrong tree".

Why we have to strengthen the United Nations? Because it is too weak to fulfill its noble purposes. Why it is so weak? fundamentally it was established as an association of its member nations, and its member nations are its real masters with a dominant position fortified by its Charter such as "sovereign equality" in Part 1 of Article 2, "equal right and self-determination" in Part 2 of Article 1 and Article 55, "territorial integrity and political independence" in Part 4 of Article 2, "domestic jurisdiction" in Part 7 of Article 2, "self-defense" in Article 51, "regional arrangements" in Part 1 of Article 52, and the veto rule in Parts 2 and 3 of Article 27. It is the dominant position of its member nations that makes the United Nations so weak. This is a reality which can not be evaded unless there are some ways to change the dominant position of the member nations. But the dominant position of the member nations is fortified by the Charter of the United Nations itself, and cannot be changed unless such fortification is removed. It is clear, therefore, that the most important step to strengthen the United Nations so as to bring it close to a real world government is to remove such fortification from the Charter of the United Nations. This also is the main job of restructuring the United Nations.

Furthermore, the dominant position of the member nations of the United Nations and its fortification in the Charter are not something built just in the air. They have a wide ground in the independence of the nation, its symbol—national sovereignty, and its agitator—nationalism. It would be very difficult to change the dominant position and remove its fortification if their wide ground is not demolished. In other words, the work for strengthening the United Nations should begin with the elimination of the independence of the nation, national sovereignty and nationalism.

There was a great number of people who wore a button of "Let's Abolish War". This motto is the title of a book by Captain Tom A. Hudgens who is a true worker and leader for the great cause. But the question is how to abolish war. It is an age-old question, and there has been no definite answer until lately the root of war is found in the independence of human groups. This finding leads to the conclusion that international war can be abolished if the independence of the nation, its symbol—national sovereignty, and its agitator—nationalism are eliminated. In other words, the work of abolishing war should also begin with the elimination of the independence of the nation, national sovereignty and nationalism. Details in this respect may be found in pages 395–415 of my book ONE WORLD.

It is true that the independence of the nation was a great image with a great value two hundred years ago when the American Founding Fathers made the famous "Declaration of Independence" in Philadelphia. Since then the world situation has changed drastically along with the rapid advance of modern science and technology. Our world now is a small kingdom and all peoples are closely interdependent. The image of the independence of the nation has been shaking and its value has been diminishing. ''What Philadelphia 1787 Has to Say to the World of 1987?'' Dr. Norman Cousins, Chairman of the International Bicentennial Symposium, wondered with an opening speech. To this question my answer is: the great leaders of 1787 Philadelphia would make a ''Declaration of Interdependence'' denouncing the independence of the nation as the main block on the road to world peace through world government, its symbol—national sovereignty as modern totem, and its agitator—nationalism as new tribalism. As a matter of fact, there has been a ''Declaration of Interdependence'' of which a copy also is enclosed for your reference. It was sponsored by the American Movement for World Government under the leadership of Captain William H. D. Cox, and is more meaningful than the declaration for strengthening the United Nations.

Oct. 18, 1987, from Stella

I apologize for the delay in writing to thank you for your nice long letter of 8th September; and I was most interested to read your account of the World Federalist Congress in Philadelphia.

Of course I fully agree with you about the weakness of the United Nations. But in no way do I think there is the slightest chance of being able to restructure it on the lines which you indicate. For as you will know only too well, it is not possible for any political developments of this kind to take place at the UN, unless they are officially initiated by the Government of a Member State and supported by the General Assembly. And I certainly cannot envisage any of the political leaders—and particularly those of the Nuclear Powers—being willing to give up any part of their national sovereignty at the present time.

131

For they clearly intend to cling to this with all their might. And I therefore think that when World Government eventually *does* come, it will have to come from another direction—and for reasons other than those which are now being pursued by the "SUN" (Strengthen the United Nations) Brigade.

In the meantime, therefore, I think we must pause and ask ourselves the most urgent question of the moment—which is surely "What can the NGOs do, on an immediate and practical basis, to improve the state of the world—and its millions of starving, tortured and oppressed inhabitants—at the present time?" And does this not lead us to the age-old concept that "the meek shall inherit the earth?"

However, for reasons given in the attached "Follow-Up Memo" to Mr. Henk van der Most (Development Officer of WAWF), it seems that this is more likely to be brought about through activities in Amsterdam and Jerusalem, than in Philadelphia or New York. Or in any other city, for that matter.

Also, with regard to the subject of Unity (which you, yourself, so enthusiastically expound), you may be interested in the attached article entitled *"PEACE UNION*—A World Organization of Peace Societies" by Professor Archie Bahm (Professor of Philosophy Emeritus at the University of New Mexico, Albuquerque, USA), which seems to have been published in China. For his views on the need for Peace Organizations to unite, seem very similar to your own.

But I am also enclosing a copy of the comments on this article. For although you will see (from Dr. Suter's reply to the Professor) that he considers the "Peace Union" proposal to be a "very worthy idea", he does not think it would be possible to bring this about in practice, for the reasons given in his correspondence with Professor Bahm.

And as I think that Dr. Suter's advice is both sound and practical, you will see that my short-term proposals in the attached "follow-up memo" are based on the less formal concept of co-operation—geared to a spectacular and dramatic World Peace Event in Jerusalem, and an NGO World representative "Committee of Ten" in Amsterdam—rather than the more formal kind of "Peace Union" which Professor Bahm advocates; and which politicization of the relevant

NGOs and wider section of the World Community would also involve. But which could only be regarded as a long-term policy.

In the meantime, however, I think you might agree that what the world now needs is an International Call for Peace—at both the higher and lower levels—on which the eyes and ears of the world will be centred. But which is clearly not likely to take place at the United Nations at the present time.

Incidentally, you will see that I have received a very encouraging letter from the Rt. Hon. Peter Archer, Q. C., M. P., in the House of Commons—who is a leading Member of the Parliamentary Group for World Government and President of AWF/UK, as well as being an Honorary Vice-President of WAWF. And you will note that he seems to think ''there may be hope for the Middle East initiative, but that it may have to wait until after the next Election'' (which I think is due to take place in Israel next year).

I therefore hope to continue working in this direction during the coming months.

Nov. 18, 1987, to Stella

Thanks for your letter of Oct. 18, 1987 and the related documents. To them my response may be briefly stated as follows:

First, your proposal of a Jerusalem conference is indeed a well thought-out design for a peace show. What is the reaction from Mr. Henk van der Most? Incidentally I appreciate your referring to Mr. Most my letter to you on the observation of the Philadelphia occasion of last August, but I apologize that there are some errors found later in that letter. The big error is the missing two letters ''in'' from the word ''independence'' in the first sentence of the last paragraph of the second page. This passage should read as ''It is true that the independence of the nation . . . '' and not ''that the dependence of the nation . . . ''. It is a typing error, but is an unforgiving one.

Second, I concur with the statement made by Dr. Everett L. Millard that ''Our purpose is not merely disarmament, or human rights, or population control, or protection of the ecology, or a new order of economics. Our central purpose is to build a world political structure of peace. Our other concerns are parts of this single major goal. Our other interests are important to us, and we are important to them, as aims which humanity can achieve only by organizing a more effective world political structure." This statement "set out our case very well" as introduced by Dr. Keith D. Suter in his Report to Members of the Australian Branch of the World Federalists. I do not know the World Federalists have ever accepted Dr. Millard's statement as their official policy. If not, I urge them to do it right away. By the way, do you know Dr. Millard's recent address?

Third, I agree with Dr. Suter's comment in principle on Prof. Archie J. Bahm's article "Peace Union" which was published in the *Journal of Peace Studies* of Kyung Hee University, South Korea, not in China. Bahm's idea of Peace Union is quite different with my proposal to unite all groups concerned into a world political party for action. His idea is of high academic value, but serves little practical purpose at a time when our world is in danger of a total destruction and mankind is on the verge of extinction any minutes in a nuclear war.

Finally I like to take this opportunity to reiterate and stress the policy of the One World Movement in respect to the problem of war and peace: We stand against any kind of war and strive to abolish war from our civilization. In other words, we strive for a permanent peace on earth. We believe that this can be achieved only through a world government as signified out in the title of your organization, by eliminating the independence of the nation, its symbol—national sovereignty, and its agitator—nationalism, since the root of war, as revealed by history of thousands of years, is the independence of human groups such as the clan and tribe in the past, and the nation in modern times. There will be no real peace until the independence of the nation as the root of war has been eliminated. We warn that only a real peace which is global in scope and permanent in nature can save mankind from an imminent extinction and promote its happiness to a much higher level.

134

With Mr. John H. Davenport,
Secretary, Popular Initiative and
Referandum Committee, Spain

Dec. 6, 1987, from John

Well, since I wrote you last April the editors of the *World Policy* Journal have read my 90-page (!) ms—including my footnote reference to "John Kiang's exhaustive and depressingly 'rational' arguments for ONE WORLD (Notre Dame, Indiana, 1984)"—so at least you've gotten a bit more publicity for the book. They turned down my ms., though—as I had expected, so I'm now leisurely looking for a somewhat more adventurous publisher. I've sent a "letter of inquiry" to the Friends General Conference Publications Dept., for example. But I'm sure that—in its present style!—it would "curl the hair" of most of my staid Quaker friends despite—or maybe precisely because of!—my references to that revolutionary "One Worlder"—Jesus Christ, whom I consider was a real, live, historical hero.

I am debating in my mind right now about letting you read the ms. You do publish things, after all! Including one item that I have somehow overlooked—until just last night when I was searching *One World* for quite another purpose, namely, to see if you had picked up on *Leopold Kohr's* book, since it was originally published in 1957—and ignored by everybody! So had you!

What I found was at the tail-end of your footnote No 77 on p. 542:

"To this list I would like to add my own doctoral thesis, *Conditions for Federation,* at the University of Nebraska, Lincoln, Nebraska, 1956."

Bless your humble heart! They say that humility is a Chinese character trait, but I don't believe in "national characteristics"—but now I believe in your *personal* trait!

The amazing thing is that—from your analysis of the "problem" of federation—it would seem, even without my

135

reading that thesis, that you and Kohr are in basic agreement on the "conditions."

However, I must absolutely insist that you read this new 1986 edition of the *Breakdown of Nations* and tell me what you think. The alternative is to beg, borrow or steal—surely you would not force a poor pensioner like me to buy?—a copy of your treatise. (Incidentally, Lilienthal never responded to your request to him for a fotocopy of his pamphlet, *Which Way to Peace*—but never mind).

Kohr is as pessimistic as you about creating "the essential thing . . . that most of [the members of a federation] should belong to a middle-sized class" (your fn. 85, p. 544).

But I am an incurable optimist—didn't you know that? And he has unwittingly provided me a key—despite his pessimism—to a possible solution. It would be interesting to know if this key is as new and bright and shiny to you as it was to me when I found it in Kohr.

Since I don't have access at the moment to a fotocopy machine—I broke my left leg 3 weeks ago and I'm in a cast until New Year Eve!—I am going to use my time to copy his description of the key—which *he* thinks will not be used, but which *I* see can be used as a sledge-hammer if it's no good as a key. Let me quote, beginning at page 190 of the 1986 edition. He has previously said that the great powers must be broken down into small states if a world federation is to be at all possible.

Now he proceeds:
Can it Be Done? . . .

1. Division through Proportional Representation.

The *conventional* federal principle of government grants an equal number of votes to each participating *sovereign unit of a federation* irrespective of the size of its population. This is quite reasonable since international law does not distinguish amongst sovereigns, and does not make the degree of sovereignty dependent on quantitative considerations. France, with 45 million inhabitants, is not more sovereign than Liechtenstein whose population is less than 13,000. While she has more *might* than Liechtenstein, she does not have more *right* than that miniature principality. Nor does she have more of a physical existence.

For this reason, large member states of international organizations are always clamoring for proportional rather than state representation so that their numerical strength might be brought into play in a more realistic manner. But as long as the law of nations considers every sovereign state the coequal of every other, the great powers have no chance of gratifying their passionate desire to be considered not only bulkier than small states, but greater, and endowed with more rights as well.

This unsatisfied desire is *the key* with which the great powers can be tricked into accepting gracefully their own liquidation. They shall be given what they so sorely want—but with a string attached. Let us illustrate this with the example of the *European Council.* [Remember, he wrote this in 1957!] . . . composed of 4 large powers, Great Britain, France, Germany and Italy, and a number of small states such as Belgium, Luxembourg, Denmark or the Netherlands. Its principal problem of survival is the division of in [sic] four self-centered and thus basically uncooperative great powers.

France—to illustrate the technique of division on a country clinging with particular tenacity to power and glory concepts—would never agree to be split up into her original historic regions.

I interrupt here to call your attention to the paradox, the sharp, almost contradictory contrast between Kiang's and Kohr's basic theses: one emphasizes growth by accretion, the other by mitosis and federation of the divided parts; one aims at centralization and solidification of sovereignty, the other at decentralization!

But she would certainly not object to the invitation to sit in the representative bodies of the European Council with, let us say, 20 voting delegates compared with, let us say, 1 delegate from Luxembourg, 3 delegates from Denmark, and 5 delegates each from Belgium and the Netherlands.

137

However, while France—and the equally favoured Great Britain or Germany would naturally be agreeable to such a redistribution of votes, Luxembourg, Denmark or the Netherlands would not, for the simple reason that it would leave the great-power domination of the European Council unchanged [and] make and unpleasant actual condition legal as well. But the smaller countries would raise few objections if

—here comes the trick!—

the 20 members of the French delegation were elected, not nationally but regionally and were, consequently, to be entrusted only with *regional* responsibilities, and *regional* representation. Such a shift in the source of delegation would alter the entire picture in an imperceptible, yet radical and fundamental manner.

It is this that would bring about the eventual dissolution of France. Why?

France, [in the same way] as she effected her subdivision into more than 90 *departements* for reasons of internal administration, would now, in oder to benefit from the increase in her voting strength, have to divide herself into 20 federal districts in the administrative interest of the European Council. . . . Thus the 20 members elected in the various districts of France would not appear in the federal assemblies as a unit, but as 20 individual members representing not one but 20 electorates and not one common but 20 different regions. These members would serve only two political organisms—their district and the European Council, as the Swiss serves only . . . his canton and the overall Swiss federation. And . . . just as Switzerland recognizes no . . . sub-federation of German or French cantons to act as a disruptive intermediary . . . so the European Council would recognize no . . . sub-union of French districts. From a federal point of view France—as also Great Britain, German and Italy—would therefore cease to exist as a component part of a European union.

However, the mere division of France into European-Council districts would not be enough. France is a tightly centralized state and . . . as long as centralization exists, great power exists, and any division under these circumstances would be but fiction.

To make division effective, the great powers would have to . . . transform their present centralized systems into decentralized federations. . . .

And he answers this question, "Can It Be Done?" with a convincing "Yes!" But the next chapter, the shortest in the book and perhaps in any book ever written, entitled, "But Will It Be Done?" consists of only one word:

"No!"

So, as I say, he shares your pessimism, John. And as I say, I do not.

This is not the place for an extended defense of my optimism. Maybe if you coax me, I shall put them into a small book form and you can publish them! In brief summary, though, they are:—

1) It doesn't cost any more to be an optimist than to be a pessimist;
2) it makes people feel better to be around you;
3) it makes you feel better to see them feel better—unless you are a real Scrooge type!
4) When people feel better, and soak up a bit of your optimism, they *tend to* feel better about themselves and their own sovereign power to act freely in their own—not their country's or their race's or their religious leaders'—interests;
5) Nor, I should add especially for your benefit, in the interests of "humanity". This is not the "Enlightenment" of your Manifesto (601, n.145,146) but I refer rather more to the Einstein quotation you put in 600n140 and—typically, my dear John! understood only in part. You got "the minds" but you missed the words I here underline for you:

"Science has brought forth this danger, but the real problem is in the minds *and hearts* of men. We will not change the *hearts* of other men by mechanism, but by changing *our hearts* and speaking *bravely*."

(*NYT Magazine,* 23 June 1946)

6) When men—and women, and children—feel free to act on the *heart's* reasons, "bravely," and optimistically without being able to predict the consequences of their acts, then those consequences will *tend to be*—statistically, in accord with the mathematical laws of queueing theory—happier than those of actions—or inaction—based on pessimism.
7) Psychologists have labelled this effect "the self-fulfilling prophecy."
8) It has been long known to politicians as "the bandwagon effect."
9) And a brasilian folksong—with which I lead off my essay; I wonder, should I send it to you at least if only to "look at"?—puts it this way:

"When you dream alone, it's only a dream.
When you dream together, it's reality."

The title of my (90-page!) article is "*Making* Our Dreams Come True." If you want to read it, ask Dr. Robert B. McFarland, M.D., (2660 13th Street, Boulder, Colorado 80302) to sent it to you.

Jan. 6, 1988, to John

I have read your letter of Dec. 6, 1987, with even more interest than before, because of the new style of two-column layout, and your "incurable" optimism. Of course, I like to read your article "Making Our Dreams Come True", but not in the ms form which is prepared for publication. I cannot publish it, because I have not set an effective selling system yet.

To your surprise, the conclusion of my doctoral thesis "Conditions for Federation" at the University of Nebraska, 1956 is different with that of Leopold Kohr's "Breakdown of Nations." It is neither pessimistic, nor optimistic. It is neutral or nothing. For this reason, I rejected a request for publication later. The reason for me to stress in my book the essential that most of the members of a federation should belong to a middle-sized class is to remind the world federalists of the actual big difficulty they have to face. It seems to me, as a man who have studied the theory and practice of federation for a long time including almost two years exclusively for a doctoral thesis, there is hardly a way to overcome such a difficulty if the old principles of federation are held tightly, blindly and emotionally. This is why, as you may have noticed in my book, I did not count very much on the federal way toward a world government. Instead I have pursued a course of merging all nations through the elimination of the national independence, national sovereignty, and nationalism, into One World in which there is only one sovereignty that belongs to the whole people of the world and is vested in the world government. All nations are respected as autonomous units with self-ruling governments to take good care of their local business, but they are not sovereign states any more and no longer have equal right for representation in the world government. It is possible, therefore, to construct the world government on a real democratic and rational basis, as I suggested In Chapter VI of my book, especially on pages 530–542, including a kind of "breakdown of nations" in the last part of note 55.

As regards Lilienthal's photo copy, he did told me that the small book has been with his other papers at the archives at Stanford and it is difficult for him to make a copy until he get a chance to go there from Washington.

With Dr. Claude E. Forkner, Originator, President, The Medical Passport Foundation

Feb. 24, 1988, to Claude

Thank you very much for your letter of Feb. 9, 1988 and the paper "A Global Referendum for Human Destiny." I have read the paper through with great interesting, and will note your proposal of global referendum in the future edition of my book ONE WORLD, of which a copy is being sent to you together with a supplement TWO YEARS AFTER, under separate cover, for your review. Your comment will be appreciated.

I admire you very highly for your sincere effort to initiate a global referendum as a means to get rid of the threat of nuclear weapons. But I wonder if it is practical when most people are still ignoring the real danger of nuclear war, and are still unable to act beyond the philosophies, laws and policies of their national governments. How to transfer the nuclear threat into a simple question of "do you want to live or do you want to die" for common people to vote, and how to get common people out of the control of their national governments to vote independently, freely and consciously, are big problems for a referendum for human destiny.

There is no doubt that a global referendum is better than any measures, such as freezes of limitations on nuclear weapons, or promises not to use them first, as you rightly explained. But how much better is a problem even it is to be carried out and implemented through to destroy the existing nuclear weapons all at once, because they can be reproduced easily and quickly with advanced techniques when demanded by great and bitter wars for desperate use by warmongers or fanatic zealots. It is impossible to free mankind from the threat of nuclear and other devastating weapons completely until war is abolished as a means to settle international disputes.

But there is no practical way to abolish war as long as the nations remain as independent states to watch each other as rivals even enemies. Hence the elimination of the independence of the nations, together with its symbol—national sovereignty and its agitator—nationalism, holds the key to a lasting peace of the world.

Actually the elimination of the national independence, national sovereignty and nationalism holds the key not only to a lasting peace of the world, but also to the merger of all nations into One World, because they are still the main obstacles on the way to such a merger, although modern science and technology have made all physical conditions ready for it. This is why our One World Movement has set their elimination as its primary mission.

142

So, I hope someday, your genuine proposal of A Global Referendum for Human Destiny will be extended to vote for an elimination of the national independence, national sovereignty and nationalism, so as to abolish international war for a permanent peace on earth and to clear the way for the merger of all nations into One World in order to assure a general happiness of mankind.

March 3, 1988, from Claude

Your letter of 24 February is greatly appreciated. It seems to me that your project of ONE WORLD and our project of a REFERENDUM FOR HUMAN DESTINY are in the same direction. The ultimate aim of each is PEACE. The means by which this can be implemented also, it seems to me, are the same. The only possible exception is that the Referendum by-passes nationalism, partisanship and political representatives.

The RFHD substitutes the concept of HUMANITY as the motive, as the inspiration, as the guidelines, as the symbol for a better world. Humanity has no national boundaries, has no religious, ethical or political boundaries.

If we are to reach the innermost souls, the hearts of people, if we are to win in the quest for ONE WORLD, elimination of nuclear weapons, "peace on earth to men of good will" it is imperative that we reach out, appeal to a set of exceedingly high values. These values such as spiritual, devotional, consecrated, forgiving, friendly, tolerant, humbleness are embodied in the word HUMANITY. In every heart, even in the most primitive peoples, these values exist to some degree albeit often latent. We must reach out to these human aspirations and release human beings from their bondage of nationalism, boundaries, partisanship, aggressiveness, unquenchable thirst for power. Governments, politicians, are in a sense so dominated by fear, distrust, security, aggressiveness, selfrighteousness that they are blinded to the philosophical, religious, spiritual values.

Your ONE WORLD project and our REFERENDUM FOR HUMAN DESTINY cannot succeed if we deal with governments. It seems to me that the people of the world are

143

becoming disenchanged with politics as practiced, with the failures of nation-to-nation negotiations, with the drift of the United Nations toward power blocks threatening each other. This gives us the opportunity to reach for a better solution to the dreams of all people, not in trying to influence politicians to do what they cannot do, to change their colors. An excellent example of this has been, and still is, in Jimmy Yen's International Institute of Rural Reconstruction. Since its inception it has answered the basic needs of people—set an example of the power of HUMANITY rather than that of governments. It is the greatest social study ever done.

I am looking forward to receiving your book "One World" together with the supplement "Two Years Later".

I think it is well for us to keep the HOT LINE open since we seem to be on, or near, the same wavelength.

With Dr. Everett L. Millard, World Congress of Organizations for a Peaceful Earth

Jan. 16, 1988, from Everett

Your concern for the survival of humanity is an inspiration to all of us who are working toward a more effective control of our destiny. I enclose the *Prospectus* for a project, with which you may be familiar, to serve and secure our future.

We invite you to join us in the formation of the Planning Council which will guide the development of a World Congress of Peace and of an Assembly of Peoples in an advisory and eventually a participatory role at the United Nations. I enclose also a list of the initial members of the Planning Council.

"COPE" is a way to put into action the principles we talk about. So great an undertaking urgently needs the wisdom and the leadership of persons such as yourself who foresee the needs of human society in the coming age. Please let us have your reply to the invitation we extend to you in this letter.

Your advice will be welcome and valuable to those of us who are engaging in the development of the project the *Prospectus* describes. To the greatest degree, your influence as a member of the Planning Council can help to advance its cause.

Jan. 28, 1988, to Everett

Thank you for your letter of Jan. 16, 1988, the Prospectus and the Planning Council list of your COPE. I am honored by your invitation to join the Council. I like to accept it with some prompt observation as follows:

1. As you know, there has been a World Government Organizations Coalition initiated by Dr. Lucile Green with a number of participants appearing in your Council list, for somewhat similar purpose. I cannot see the reason for two coalitions existing side by side. Why not try to combine the two coalitions into one at the early stage?

2. While the idea of coalition sounds good, I do believe it is only the first step to move the like-organizations closer for talking and talking, not really for action. For real action, it is necessary to unite all into a solid organization, with fundamental principles for all to fellow, clear objectives for all to pursue, practical programs for all to work, and a common structure for all to struggle for.

3. What is the common structure for all to struggle for? It is a structure which should be able to ensure a lasting peace of the world, to advance the quality of life of mankind, and to conserve the resources of the earth. There has been no one other than a world government, since the development of history and the achievement of science and technology have brought all peoples into a inseparable world. The nation cannot be regarded as the basis of a common structure anymore, because it has outlived its time as an independent institute. The United Nations cannot be considered as a substitute for a common structure either, because it is merely a toy of the member nations as its masters.

4. In this connection I like to quote your own words from Dr. Keith Suter who said that you "set our case very well" as fellows: "Our purpose is not merely disarmament, or human

145

rights, or population control, or protection of the ecology, or a new order of economics. Our central purpose is to build a world political structure of peace. Our other concerns are parts of this single major goal. Our other interests are important to us, and we are important to them, as aims which humanity can achieve only by organizing a more effective world political structure.'' Is it not that you mean to unite all of us into a strong organization to struggle for a world government?

5. Finally I like to take this opportunity to tell you that I have been trying for years to urge the leaders of the like-organizations to unite into a political party for the realization of a world government. I think our unity is more important than anything else in the pursuance of our common goal. I have set to work for the unity as the first job of my One World Movement. I will go along with any strong leadership all the way in this direction, and will submit the identity and fund of the One World Movement to a really united party without any hesitation. Our cause is too great for any of us to remain separate for minor differences or particular identities.

With Dr. Bennet Skewes-Cox, President of The Academy of World Studies

Oct. 3, 1988, from Bennet

Your proposals will be referred to our Academy's Board of Directors at our next meeting, and they in turn will transmit their considerations to whoever represents us at the November meeting of the W.G.O.C. which I unfortunately will be unable to attend.

Under separate cover I am sending as a gift for your library a copy of my 1964 book, *The United Nations from League to Government* based on my original study of 1947. This was the first such analysis of the U.N. Charter, article by article, as to the practicability of using the amending process to give *the U.N. governmental powers.*

Unlike the later work, *World Peace through World Law* by Grenville Clark and Louis Sohn (with the former I had a long-term correspondence and with the latter I've enjoyed a long-time acquaintance), I had concluded that *a league and a government are so different that any future world government would probably be the result not of amending the U.N. but starting at scratch. . . . the same conclusion reached by the drafters of the U.S. federal constitution.* They simply scrapped the old Articles of Confederation and drafted an entirely new instrument at Philadelphia. It is to be noted, however, that the federal structure they created did not eliminate the states, did not abolish certain states "rights" and did not do away with pride in one's own state. Thus must the role of nations be preserved in any future global federation.

Our Academy (see pamphlet enclosed) is considered to have one of the world's most complete research libraries—books, periodicals, articles, file cards, clippings, correspondence, memoranda, etc—on the subject of world government (and barriers to it!) and we encourage its use by scholars. An issue of the Academy's publication, *Worldview Perspective,* is also enclosed for your information. Your book is of course a part of our collection.

Oct. 31, 1988, to Bennet

Thank you very much for your letter of 3rd Oct. 1988, and the special gift of your outstanding study on the United Nations' charter, article by article. Your conclusion is very close to my opinion that the reform of the United Nations should begin with the change of its nature from a looser than confederation to a real world government. Yet there are some world federalists who know nothing even the difference between a league, confederation and federation, but cry for the United Nations "Don't throw out the baby with the dirty bathwater."

In addition to your invaluable view, there have been a good number of letters I received from other concerning leaders, but are still not enough for me to make an appropriate assessment. For this reason and also for a minor personal trouble, I have tell Dr. Lucile Green not to present my proposal for

147

a world unity party formally in the coming Nov. 9 and 10 meetings of the new World Citizens Assembly in New York.

With Dr. Mac Truong, Attorney at Law

April 7, 1989, from Mac

Thank your for having shared with me your book "One World." I admire your great courage and inspiration which have motivated you to devote so much time and energy in a cause which is supposed to be so worthy of every man's effort: the future of mankind in a new brighter era for all.

I have been very excited about it. Had there been one hundred people like you on earth, we should be able to make of it a better place of living and build a great new civilization for all mankind.

I share one hundred per cent all your ideas. You rightly state that "modern science and technology have gotten all the necessary physical conditions ready for the merging of all nations into One World, as the last step of group expansion." I wrote: "History shows that men have tried and succeeded in building larger and larger systems of communication bringing in together more and more people . . . If isolated human beings have succeeded in building small communities and if from these smaller communities they have succeeded in building larger ones as nations and groups of nations, there is no theoretical reason why a universal system of communication cannot be built for all mankind. (TOGETHER WE BUILD THE WORLD, pp. 356 & 357)

Had there been an established World Government, you would be deserving to receive a World Peace Prize for having raised human consciousness to the greatest human problem: our unity or our extinction.

Dear Professor Kiang, I think it's time for us to act together in a universal partnership spirit and devote our time and effort to the common cause. It's time for us to meet each other and design a common plan for our joint action. Action is what we need to bring our dream to reality. Unity and cooperation are what we must reach to achieve our common goal.

I wish that you, as an expert in the matter of World Government, will be kind enough to *write a foreword* for the next edition of TOGETHER WE BUILD THE WORLD. Your foreword will be an important contribution to our cause and greatly appreciated. I am also open to *any suggestion* you may have so that we could combine our plans of action in the benefit of what has always been closest to our respective hearts: the universal republic or the world government.

Dear Professor Kiang, if by good fortune you can come to New York, I would certainly be very happy and honored to greet you in my office. You will be welcomed at any time.

May 21, 1989, to Mac

Thank you very much for your letter of April 7, 1989, and also for the letter of Mme. Maryse de Chantilly with a copy of manuscript of your outstanding work "Together We Build the World" sent to me earlier.

You are quite right that "only together can we build the world, and only upon universal partnership should it be done." But I cannot see clearly why it should start "from cross-examining the Holy Bible."

It is probable that no one can win your reward of $25,000.00 by defending the Holy Bible against your ten breaking points. But I don't think that the attack of the Holy Bible is the right way to "together we build the world" either. It is a way to win the battle, but lose the war. It is more difficult to want some people to be the partners after beating them badly.

It seems to me that there is no existing religion which can help the world unity very much, and at the same time, there is no existing religion which would stand strongly against the world unity either. For the sake of "universal partnership", it is better to keep peace with all of them, and not to make war against any one.

The most important thing is to have a sound philosophy for the world unity itself. It has had deep roots in history with a wide ground in science and technology. But it has to be different with religion fundamentally because it has to work for something material, not just spiritual; for something real, not just abstract; for life, not just for soul; and for some cash value, not just for eternal good after the death. We had better to perfect this kind of philosophy rather than to look for some new wine for some old bottle.

It is indeed, as you urged, "it's time for us to act together in a universal partnership spirit and devote our time and effort to the common cause. It's time for us to meet each other and design a common plan for our joint action. Action is what we need to bring our dreams to reality. Unity and cooperation are what we must reach to achieve our common goal."

I want to meet you just as anxious as you want to meet me. But I cannot get away until probably September. At the present time, I am writing a small book "The Strange World—a Report of the Mission from Moon". I want to have its manuscription with me when I come to New York this fall.

Enclosed is a copy of my letter of August 29, 1988 to Dr. Lucile Green for your review. Your comment and suggestion will be appreciated.

With Mr. Philip Isely, Secretary General, World Constitution and Parliament Association

Sept. 29, 1988, from Philip

Thanks for your letter of Sept. 6 with copy of your longer discussion sent to various persons.

We seem to be no closer to working together than when you AND your good wife came to Colorado and we had the nice visits and luncheon at Mt. Vemon Country Club, several years ago before your book was published.

I suppose a basic reason is that you do not accept the Constitution for the Federation of Earth as a valid starting point for the completion of a Constitution for World Government.

From reading your various papers, I get the idea that you have in mind a unitary type of World Government, and not a federation of existing nations, even a federation which includes direct representation of the people of Earth in one of the Houses of the World Parliament, as provided under the Constitution for the Federation of Earth? Is this correct?

I do believe that most of the people in the world government movement or world federation movement have in mind a federal type of world government (similar to USA) rather than a unitary type.

You mention that Emery Reeves admonished world federalists not to rush ahead with drafting a world constitution. That was in 1946, 42 years ago. We have hardly been rushing ahead, rather most of the world government movement as well as the peace movement has been wandering in the wilderness for 42 years because they were reluctant to come to grips with the necessity for drafting a world constitution to define what was actually required for world government and world peace.

Apart from the Committee to Frame A World Constitution (Chancellor Robert Hutchins and Associates) in 1946 to 1950, the WCPA is the only organization which has forged ahead in 42 years time.

Jan. 6, 1991, to Philip

I apologize for the long delay of reply to your letter of Sept. 29, 1988.

It is bad that we are no closer to working together than when I and my wife had a nice visit and delicious luncheon with you at Mt. Vernon Country Club seven years ago. Since then, I have checked again and again your draft of the Constitution for the Federation of Earth and other documents, made a special trip to observe your conference at the Fontainebleau Hilton Hotel, Miami Beach, Florida, June 18 to 28, 1987, and received a number of your letters, including special and long ones dated July 8, 1985 and Sept. 23, 1986, and also a letter from your president Mr. Ing Reinhard Ruge dated Feb. 26, 1988. Yet, we remain apart as far as before.

There is no need for me to explain my position. I like to take this opportunity just to tell you my opinion on the federal system which you emphasized in your letter.

It is true that most of the people in the world government movement have in mind a federal type of world government rather than a unitary one. I like federal system too, but I cannot take for granted that it can work well for world unity.

A generally accepted definition of classic federalism is "the principle according to which two levels of government, general and regional, exist side by side, each possessing certain assigned powers and functions. Each level of government is limited to its own sphere and within that sphere is autonomous and independent; neither may arrogate to itself powers assigned to the other; each operates directly upon the people and neither is dependent on the other for its legislation, taxes, or administration. Federal government is to be distinguished from a confederacy, in which the general government is dependent on the regional governments, and from a unitary system, in which the regional governments are dependent on the general government."

Accordingly all the regional components in a federal system are equal, somewhat independent, with certain sovereignty. These are the ideal features of classic federal system, and with these features in mind, John S. Mill stated in the middle of last century "there be not a very marked inequality of strength among the several contracting states" as a condition for federal system. If the nations are to be the components of a world federation, obviously there is no such condition in existence today. The strength of the nations as measured by population, area, and wealth, is too inequal. According to statistics of 1988, for example, the number of 100,000 population of Dominica looks like that of a small town in the United State, the area of 115 square miles of Maldives is much smaller than that of an average county in China, and the wealth of Antigua and Barbuda may be not as much as that of a quality bank in Japan.

To modify Mill's condition, a new theory allows the existence of even some marked inequality of strength among the components, but stresses that most of the components should belong to a middle-sized class, and that this class can form a dominant force to keep an equilibrium in the federation. This modified condition is not good for a world federation either, however. We have a few nations which are outstandingly large, and a great mass of nations which are small. What we are lacking is a class of nations in the middle, which can provide a dominant force. Among the approximately 170 nation, China, India, the Soviet Union and the United States have a population of about half of the world's total; the Soviet Union, China, Canada, Brazil, the United States, and Australia have a territory of about half of the world's total. This well-known fact alone illustrates why a dominant middle-sized class of nations is lacking today.

In contrast to classic federalism, there is a type of federation framed under the leadership of one of its components which is much larger in all important respects than all the others, such as Prussia in the German Empire and Russia in the Soviet Union. For Instance, the territory of Russia is about 72 percent, and its population is about 58 percent of the whole union. This type of federation furnishes no model for a world federation also, mainly because there is no nation at the present time which is large enough to provide such a leadership. The Soviet Union, which is the largest nation in area in the world, has only about one sixth of the world's land. China, which is the largest nation in population in the world, has less than one fourth of the world's population, and the United States, which for the time being is the largest nation in national income in the world, has only about one fourth of the world's income, according to recent statistics of the United Nations.

With the lack of equality in strength, a dominant middle-sized class, and an outstanding leadership among the nations, there are also difficulties for a world federation to arrange the relative position of the very inequal nations to be respresented in the world government, and to maintain their respective financial capacity. In arranging the relative position to be represented, there are some ways to make a compromise between the principle of equality and the numercial strength of the components. The common way is to set up a bicameral congress: one chamber representing relative numerical strength, composed of representatives elected according to the number of population, and the other chamber marking the principle of equality by being composed of an equal number of representatives sent from each component. The United States Congress is an outstanding example. This is possible only in a federation in which most of the components belong to a middle-sized class, and the weights at both extreme sides are not very heavy. Our world as of today furnishes no foundation for such a federation, as pointed above.

Other compromising ways include the division of the components into several classes such as the cases of India and the Soviet Union. The Soviet Union, for instance, classifies its components into: a. Union Repuplics; b. autonomous republics; c. autonomous regions; and d. national areas. Its congress, the Supreme Soviet, is divided into two houses, the Soviet of the Union representing the numerical strength, and the Soviet of nationalities characterizing the federal system. In the Soviet of Nationalities, the Union Republics are assigned 25 delegates each, the autonomous republics 11, the autonomous regions 5, and the national areas one. This kind of classification has been criticized as artificial and arbitary, and can hardly be considered as a sample for a world federation. It is possible only there is a special factor in the Soviet Union, which is the Communist Party, a unitary and monopolistic organization, and has completely controlled the whole Union until recently when Mikhail S. Gorbachev started to turn the Communist rule loose someway. Since then some of its components have tried to claim for sovereignty, independence, or more freedom to handle their own business, and have brought the Union to the edge of dissolution.

In respect to the financial capacity, the components have to support both the federal government and their own governments. If some components are too small or too poor, not only unable to support the federal government, but even their own governments, or can do so only at the price of financial dependence upon the federal fund drawn from the others, it will seriously affect the health of the federal system. The Union of South Africa, Australia, and some Latin American federal republics, have been confronted with this problem. In a world federation in which the component nations so greatly vary in financial capacity, this problem would be much more serious.

In order to reduce the marked inequality among the nations so as to provide a better condition for a world federation and to save some difficulties for it to arrange the relative position of the very inequal nations to be represented in the world government and to maintain their respective financial capacity, Leopold Kohr has proposed to break down the great powers into small states in his book *The Breakdown of Nations* originally published in 1957, with a new edition published in 1986. "Can it be done?" His answer was "Yes." But in the last chapter to the question "Will it be done?" His answer was "No."

Since its regional components are equal, somewhat independent, with certain sovereignty, the classic federal system is "inherently unstable" as remarked by a scholar. The United States avoided disruption only by the bloody lesson of Civil War, and since then, the three constitutional amendments—XIV, XVI and XVIII have notably increased the powers of the federal government, and judicial interpretation of the constitution has also led in this direction. As a result the United States has gone away from the classic federal system, and today its government is in federal form but in unitary substance.

Actually the trend to centralization of government powers in modern times is not confined in the United States. It is common to other federal nations. Switzerland has conferred new areas of jurisdiction upon the federal government to a considerable extent, and Australia and Canada have also made some important changes in this direction. It is mainly because they increasingly need a stronger federal government to handle their growing overall business. But the real driving force is the rapid advance of modern science and technology, which makes their people more and more interdependent economically, and keeps them closer and closer through convenient transportation and communication. It is the very force which is driving the whole world into one and is rendering it impossible for any people to live separately anymore. Clearly, therefore, the ideal features of classic federal system for a world government are diminishing, and the distinction between the federal and unitary forms of government is no longer important. What is important is the fundamentals: Humanity is equal, mankind is the only independent group, sovereignty belongs to all peoples vested in a world government to manage their general happiness, while the nations are respected as autonomous units with self-ruling government to take care of their local business. This can be done directly and why to bother with all the troubles involved in any federal system? Meanwhile, the traditional ideology about the independence of the nation, national sovereignty and nationalism, has become a serious hinderance to the great cause. It is necessary to wipe it out first anyway.

As you know, I have been friend with world federalists for a long time, and I have always respected for them and their groups. They are the good people who believe in common sense that the federal system is something good for peace, humanity, world unity and world government. My opinion on the federal system should not be misled to discount their such common sense which is a great source of our common cause. They are the good people who join in the federal course likely by intuition to do something for peace, humanity, world unity and world government. My opinion on the federal system should not be misunderstood to discourage their such intuition which is a great force of our common cause.

With Mr. Lyman Hinckley, *Fourfold Fellow Citizen*

July, 1990 from Lyman

This letter is an update of one sent to you in Oct/1988. I again express admiration for your effort to unite the world-government movement, and discontent that this effort has yet so little effect. Not that your scholarly work *One World* (1984) was anything but a good start; or that your *Two Years After* was other than a good sequel; or that your letter of Aug/14/

1986 to people in Spain, England, Australia, Italy, and others including me in the U.S., was anywhere but to the point.

You, 'could not agree' with my questioning that 'all natural resources belong to mankind, and all economic systems are entitled to operate'; or my conviction that there is no place in a real democracy of properly educated self-governing citizens for a *ruling class of experts; but you did not explain your disagreement.* You quote John Davenport that 'leaders as a character type are singularly intractable in teamwork that does not feed their egos'; *but you do not say how to overcome such a 'common weakness' in your own enterprise,* as in that of another admirable pioneer, Garry Davis.

Another letter in that chain of correspondence was from Philip Isely of Denver, the *likewise admirable moving spirit* of the World Constitution and Parliament Association (WCPA). He opines: 'There are separate world-government organizations because there are different strategies to achieve world government, and also because there are different concepts about the ultimate goal. This is not bad!! No one can prove in advance which strategy will win!! altho money talks loudest rather than perception of merit.' A double blindness: competition is the way to go, and victory is to strategy!

Then we have the Association to Unite the Democracies (AUD), a 50-year evolution from Streit's *Union Now,* strengthened by people such as U.S. Senators and a Supreme Court justice, proposing to collaborate with powers like the federal-economics Organization for Economic Cooperation and Development (OECD), getting as far one time as a Congressional bill for a World Constitution Commission to be co-chaired by then-living Truman and Eisenhower.

The great trouble in our thinking is *the deep-rooted concept of leadership as a person or group,* a *sectarian mouthpiece of God or a partisan champion of Our Kind of People.* And all along is *our authority of WHAT, in place of those warring ones of WHO: Self-evident Truths* and inalienable Rights in that 1776 Declaration, *'establish justice'* in that 1787 Constitution Preamble. Justice ('precisely defined' as Einstein would say), not God or any other sectarian or partisan entity, is the essence of secular faith in this secular nation.

The other great trouble is one which is entangling us ever more in its grip. From the old country came not only the *budding* principle of political democracy but the ancient tradition of *economic feudalism,* now *masquerading* as 'free private enterprise'. Yet even here we have a message of salvation uttered by two North Americans a century ago. It was Henry George who condemned the piratical usurpation of our legacy of public land; and it was his contemporary Edward Bellamy who exposed the abuse of money tied to goods.

Of all of the world-constitution drafts hopefully put together, not one has dared to break out of this deep political-economic prejudice. Of all of the leading *personalities* working for a lawfully governed world, not one has seen leadership as belonging to ideas, not to any of the people carrying them. This writer will refrain from signing his name to this letter, anxious to avoid any appearance of even aspiring to personal recognition. He is *not* the author of the work of which this letter is a part; only a compiler of many fine sources needing to come together.

Garry and associates are planning a 'world government constitutional convention' in Christchurch, N.Z., this September—as though there could be any respectable world government ('of world citizens' or not) without a 'trans-citizen' law of justice providing for it. AUD is urging me to 'Join the Cause of International Democracy!'—as if there were *any* real democracy, political *and* economic, anywhere yet.

Real citizenship in action means *right education;* and right education (as you would likely agree) means books. I cite once again the ones indispensable to seekers for justice with freedom.

1) *No Contest: the Case against Competition.* All competition everywhere! By Alfie Kohn. Houghton Mifflin Co., Boston, 1986. Available in paperback.
2) *Progress and Poverty.* By Henry George. Abridged edition. Schalkenbach Foundation, N.Y., 1980. Paperback.
3) *Looking Backward.* By Edward Bellamy. Many editions. Available in paperback.
4) *Equality* (sequel to the preceding). AMS Press, N.Y., 1970.

The principles of political and economic justice carried in these four books are *a life-or-death matter for our Earth and our race of creatures.* Who is disposed to help shape them into a prime instrument of citizen education? The principles of *agnostic* philosophy and reasoned secular faith are nowhere better *conveyed* than in the work at hand. Who would care to help make them into an inspiring community religion beyond all sects and parties?

As Einstein declared, *without the 'force and zeal of a religion' the effort for a peaceful world can hardly succeed.* Or as Rene Dubos put it more directly, *'Common action cannot be mustered because a common faith does not exist.' With enough strength in enough heads,* that is.

May 20, 1991 to Lyman

Indeed, as you expected, I have been "specifically interested" in your letter of July, 1990, which came with a bunch of your papers and "is planned as the beginning of Part C" of your philosophical world constitution. I want first to thank you for addressing to me specifically of this open letter. I want also to take this opportunity to say "Happy 97th Birthday" to your mother, which is 25th of this month.

Your letter is a general review on the movement for world government, peace, democrary, constitution, and so on. It is going so far that I am not in a position to say much except to explain briefly the three points in respect to my opinion, which are contained in the second passage of your letter.

The first is "all natural resources belong to mankind, and all economic systems are entitled to operate." I have discussed these two topics fairly in pp. 498–508 of my ONE WORLD. I like to make a few remarks, however, for some clarification; a. the proposition that all natural resourcesbelong to mankind is not to deprive the private ownership or the right to use by individual or corporation under law, but to allow no nation to claim any portion of natural resources as national resources. It is this kind of claim that causes international wars, blocks the adjustment of world environment and hampers the promotion of the happiness of mankind. b. By far most of the natural resources including the vast space, the immense oceans and the oil and non-fuel minerals under their beds, are the property of mankind ever since; the nations claim no more than thirty percent of all the natural resources as their national resources. It is not too big a problem to nullify their claims. c. This nullification is not unfair to anyone, but beneficial to everyone, if all the potential natural resources are taken into account, viewed in the long run, not in the short term, and weighed by social value, not by commercial standards. d. Furthermore, the real value of natural resources lies not in what they are, but in how they are processed by knowledge, and depends not on their static property, but on their dynamic function. Less than half a century ago the air was for breathing and burning only; now it is also a natural resource of the chemical industry, and the Vermont granite was only building and tombstone material; now it is a potential fuel, each ton of which has a useable energy content—uranium equal to 150 tons of coal. Clearly the mother of the value of natural resources is knowledge which is the common heritage of our civilization. e. The complete sentence on economic systems is "all existing economic systems are entitled to operate, compete, and to adjust by free will under the general management" of the world government. Necessarily this proposition will lead to a common system through compromise, or the best one beats all the rest. This is expected to take place under the world government, but is now under way already since the Soviet Union and the East European countries are changing their central-planning economic system drastically in favor of free enterprise. f. Finally I want to stress that economy is to make better living, better living cannot be achieved without high productivity, and high productivity can be obtained mainly through the progress made by science and technology. Thus the progress by science and technology is the key to the happiness of mankind.

The second, is "experts rather than politicians run the government." You disagree with this, because your conviction is that "there is no place in a real democracy of properly educated self-governing citizens for a ruling class of experts." Experts are those who are specialized in certain field of science or technology. Since the advance of modern science and technology has accelerated its way into the government, more and more experts are needed for public services, and less and less rooms is left for politicians to play politics. This is the primary reason for experts rather than politicians to run the world government. Another main reason is that the world government is established when all nations are merged into a single group. There would exist no other independent group with sovereignty with which the world government may have to wage war and enter foreign relations, and consequently, the traditional units of government for military and foreign affairs are no longer needed. These two units usually are where not only most of the money are spent, but also the dirtiest political tricks are played and feverish power struggles are engaged. Their omission from the world government means not only saving enormous expenses, but also stopping two evil sources of the government, and thus making it possible for the world government to emphasize services rather than politics, and for experts rather than politicians to run the world government. Their ommission would pave the way for the world government to concentrate in global management on important matters, such as population and food, environment and ecology, energy, space, water, forest, weather, natural calamities, and social welfare. All of these require experts to do the job, and citizens cannot do very much directly by themselves, no matter how they are properly educated for self-governing. The danger for the experts to become a ruling class seems not quite real, since they normally grow up with different backgrounds by different trainings, and are elected for the jobs in terms by the people directly or indirectly or through some other appropriate process. If they do eventually become a ruling class, it probably is a class for service rather than for power, and is not necessarily a bad development for a healthy democracy.

The last is "leaders as a character type are singularly intractable in teamwork that does not feed their egos," I quoted from John Davenport as our common weakness. "But you do not say how to overcome such a 'common weakness' in your own enterprise," you questioned. In this respect I like to remind you my announcement in an open letter to you and some other leading people two years ago: "I think our unity is more important than anything else in the pursurance of our common goal. I have set to work for the unity as the first job of my One World Movement. I will go along with any strong leadership all the way in this direction, and will submit the identity and fund of the One World Movement to a really united party without any hesitation." This announcement was later quoted in the *World Peace News* and somewhere else. I also like to tell you that in the conclusion of my new book *The Early One World Movement* which was just finished, I renewed my determination "to maintain my role as John the Baptist to look for a real leader."

V. Some Replies to Other Letters

To Dr. John Roberts

Oct. 23, 1987

Thank you very much for your letter of Oct. 13, 1987, which is full of good words with kind intention towards my book ONE WORLD. But I regret to say that your immediate impression on the book as revealed in your prompt notice was not quite right and may lead to big misunderstanding. It is indeed that my book contains annotations which are more extensive in scope and much richer in content than ordinary footnotes. But they are not just a "collection of facts, comment and analysis". They have been used only as references to support the text of the book with source, evidence, depth and weight. The text of the book explains my theories, principles, objectives and programs with a number of discoveries and innovations important to social evolution, world government, peace and happiness of mankind. It is the core of the book and is where the value of the book lies in. It is true that there are many annotations which have independent value. But as far as the book is concerned, the text is much more important and without the text the book is nothing.

Three years ago when a copy of galley proofs of the book was sent to Dr. Norman Cousins for preview, his immediate impression on it was somewhat similar to yours today. But he changed his opinion soon after in some way. I believe you will find the true story of the book and its real value if you spend

163

more time to check into it, both its text and annotations, thoroughly. This is important to our great common cause.

To Prof. Benjamin Ferencz

Sept. 18, 1989

I found your letter of Sept. 12 already in the post office box when I went to mail out my thank-you note. I admire your working efficiency very much. I want to thank you for your kind introduction to Mr. Stanley K. Platt. I have sent him two of my books relating to the great cause for his review. I want to thank you again for your nice work "A Common Sense Guide to World Peace" with your autograph. It is indeed a meaningful remembrance for our first meeting.

In respect to the Alliance for Our Common Future, I have checked over the condensed memorandum by Stanley K. Platt and the "Statement of Purpose" worked out by Rick Wicks. I have also read some other material about it since the conference that gave birth to it six months ago. It seems to me that it is not only just another agent of coordination, but even more pragmatic than some other similar organizations. It does not try to get out of the bandage of the nation-state and United Nations and is actually at least 40 years behind in knowledge and vision of the old-timers, such as Herbert G. Wells, Bertrand Russell, Emery Reves, and Albert Einstein. This is one of the reasons I could not be "optimistic" in answering the question you asked while we were discussing the current situation at the Harvard Club. What we need now is united actions under an united organization, not so much of academic coordination. For the very reason, you are urged to check over again my letter to Lucile Green and to reconsider my proposal to provide with a revolutionary leadership for the great cause of world unity in order to achieve a permanent peace on earth and the general happiness of mankind.

To Mr. Gary K. Shepherd

Oct. 27, 1989

I have had Vol. 2, No. 5 of the UNITED WORLD, and found The ''Sacred'' Flag by Guy W. Meyer and your ''Man the Killer?'' excellent. If convenient, please let me know Meyer's current address. I want to send him my books for his review.

Thanks for your sending me all previous issues of the UNITED WORLD, and for your comment on my ONE WORLD and TWO YEARS AFTER. I just want to tell you two things: First, I did not undercut my own arguments when I spoke of the ''law of group expansion'' as you mentioned. I believe that the law is of paramount importance and is the historical and philosophical foundation of the One World and consequently the world government. I spent many years to work it out. It would be helpful to the great cause if you will spend a few more weeks to find out the truth by checking over the whole thing and the related materials. Second, I agree with you that the ''monumental footnotes at times obscure the flow of the text,'' and it might be useful to issue an additional edition consisting just of the Popular Manifesto, without the Scholarly Annotation, as you and some other friends suggested. But a second thought has led me to write a new simple book THE STRANGE WORLD, a Report of the Mission from Moon, instead. The new book will probably be finished before the end of this year and published sometime next year. I will send you a copy for your review whenever it is available.

When I was in New York several weeks ago, I showed the UNITED WORLD to Tom Liggett, editor of the WORLD PEACE NEWS. He was very interesting to your publication. He is an outstanding fighter for the world government. I wonder if you would like to send him the UNITED WORLD, at least from Vol. 2, no. 4 on, to exchange for his WORLD PEACE NEWS, if you have not had contact with him. His address is: 777 U.N. Plaza, 11th Floor, New York, N.Y. 10017

To Mr. Henry C. Usborne

June 28, 1990

It is nice to hear from you again. Thanks for sending me the paper you presented at the Third Lothian Memorial Conference, including your experience in the movement for a world government, and your view on the current world situation, especially on Germany. Your experience in the movement for a world government is an invaluable lesson for us, and your advice for a disarmed German union is a far-reaching one. Such a German union may be a break-through for a disarmed European union to a disarmed world union. I have tried to note your advice to the public through some channels.

I like to take this opportunate to report to you that I have finished the manuscript of a new work THE STRANGE WORLD, a Report of the Mission from Moon. It is a small book and I will present a copy to you when published. Its theme is basically along with the line of your efforts for a world government in the last forty five years. After a careful study of the situation and problems of the world, it concludes that a world peace and happiness require a world unity which can be achieved only by getting rid of the independence and sovereignty of the nations as the Constitution of the United States did it in respect to the several states. Had the several states remained independent with sovereignty as under the Articles of Confederation, there would be no federal union at all.

The national independence and sovereignty are the original evils of modern civilization. They make the danger of nuclear war to threaten our survival and spend trillions of dollars every year to feed the killing machines for defense or aggression rather than to promote our livelihood and to save our environment. It would be impossible to have a real world peace and general happiness of mankind as long as they are existing. This is why THE STRANGE WORLD calls urgently for getting rid of the original evils to unite all nations into a world commonwealth.

166

To Prof. Benjamin B. Ferencz

Nov. 14, 1990

Thank you for your letter of Oct. 8, 1990 and the introduction. I appreciate very much your suggestions. I have
made some changes in the titles of "Long Life" and "No Way
to Escape." Others have been reconsidered, but no action has
been taken for various reasons. Among these most important
is the "Group Expansion." It is not just a term replaceable. It
is a great process of social evolution I discovered in history. It
has run for hundreds of thousands years everywhere with civilization. It is the root of world unity, the foundation of world
government, and the promise of a permant peace on earth and
a general happiness of mankind.

Since the group expansion is so important an evolutionary
process, I have tried hard to explain it, especially its development from the early single family, through the primitive
community, clan, tribe, to the nation; how it has promoted
peace and happiness, and the conditions for its operation. This
effort requires a broad and deep search into the origin of
the earth and mankind, the application of tools and energies, the progress of communication and transportation, the
development of weapons and war, the increase of knowledge,
and the change of economic life. It also requires a quick look
into the current affairs in both good and evil sides with all
sorts of problems. It is indeed a difficult job to explain a great
discovery on a scientific basis with so many topics of so many
fields involved.

Equally difficult to explain is the situation in which the
rapid advance of modern science and technoloty has made
possible for a world unity, and the serious threat of nuclear
war has made necessary for a world unity, but the evils of the
independence of the nation, national sovereignty, and nationalism, are blocking the way very badly for the group expansion to achieve a world unity. It is urgent, therefore, to sweep
out these evils as the primary task of a world revolution without violence.

167

The group expansion is an uniting process much wider and more practical than federation. I happen to know the latter very well too, since I studied the "Conditions for Federation" for almost two years as my Ph. D. thesis at the University of Nebraska. I also discussed the "Problem of Federation" as a section of my ONE WORLD.

To MD. Nurul Alam, Director-General, Dayemi Complex Bangladesh

July 4, 1991

Thank you for your prompt and enthusiastic response to my book ONE WORLD, willing to join in the membership of the One World Movement, to develop its organization, and to support its fund. Thanks also for the information about your Dayemi Complex Bangladesh, and your International Organization for Peace, Disarmament, Development and Human Rights.

Six years ago, soon after starting to organize the One World Movement, we found that there had been over the world several hundred groups professing to strive for world unity, world government, world federation, world citizenship, world peace, humanity and the like. It is apparent that there is no need for the world to have one more this kind of group, but there is an urgent need to unite this kind of group into a solid force to work as a team for a common goal. Promptly we started to try to get these groups into a world unity party, and stopped the building up of the One World Movement and vowed to submit its identity and fund to the world unity party. After six years try, however, we have realized that it is not only almost impossible to unite these groups into one party, but even very difficult to reach a workable cooperation among them.

We are in a dilemma now. Back to develop the One World Movement alone, or to start a world unity party with a few leading people to struggle for world unity with a world government, through a world revolution in political ideology to eliminate the independence of the nation, national sovereignty, and nationalism as the primary task? Before a decision in this respect is made and before our position in this respect is clearer to you as well as to other concerning people, we are unable to accept your kind support, nor to support your organization materially. Nevertheless we appreciate very much the chance you have offered to us. Thank you again.

VI. Early Correspondence With Dr. Norman Cousins

The release of these letters is in memory of Dr. Norman Cousins, Chairman of the World Federalists Association, who passed away on Nov. 30, 1990. It is a great loss to the great cause of world government. These letters are supposed not to reveal until the day when I have a chance to redeem myself for not mentioning his name and contributions to the great cause in my book ONE WORLD, to discuss personaly with him over my proposal to him for the One World Movement, and to examine thoroughly the difference between him and me about the problem of how to achieve a world government. The difference is, as it is well known, that he preferred to carry the great cause in a federal way through the United Nations, while I have projected a world revolution in political ideology to eliminate the independence of the nation, the national sovereignty, and nationalism, as the first step to achieve a world government. In my opinion, the United nations cannot be utilized to carry the great cause through unless there is a drastic reform for it to change its nature from an association of the nations to a true world government, and this change also requires primarily the elimination of the independence of the nations, the national sovereignty, and nationalism.

From Norman

Many thanks for your letter and the privilege of reading the galley proofs of your new book. I am profoundly impressed with the extent of your research but I confess that this book seems to me to be more an assemblage of footnotes than a cohesive account. I confess I am troubled, too, by the fact that one of the most important books in the field, *World Peace Through World Law,* by Clark and Sohn, receives just a single footnote. Grenville Clark was a key figure on the "One World" constellation and is otherwise ignored. The World Committee of World Federalists is important but I see nothing about the major U.S. group, the United World Federalists (now the World Federalists Association). I find nothing about Robert M. Hutchins or Mortimer Adler. Wendell Wilkie, who wrote a book of the same title as your own, receives no more than a footnote.

To Norman

May 30, 1984

I am very much surprised by your quick reply to my letter asking your review on my book ONE WORLD, and am equally surprised by your quick judgement that the book seems to be more an assemblage of footnotes than a cohesive account. I thank you for the reply but regret to say that the judgement is a great misunderstanding. My book is a cohesive expounding of new ideas in theory as well as in practice relating to humanity, world peace and government, and the happiness of mankind. It is not an assemblage of old views in these respects, and is not their account whatsoever. This is why you have been "troubled" with the missing of so many familiar events and names. Believe me, I am not quite unfamiliar with them. For instance, I have had a high respect to Robert M. Hutchins since his brother Francis told me about him forty years ago in China. I have admired the simple-mind leader, Wendell Wilkie, long before I moved into the Hoosier State. But I mentioned in my book only the draft of a world constitution sponsored by Hutchins and only a short note about Wilkie, because I found in their views nothing much more necessary to be referred today. As regards the world federalist organization, I did note it with various titles in page 543.

It is not my interest to argue about what I wrote, especially about my new ideas. They stand firmly on sound and scientific grounds and can be tested to the truth. I can ignore any misunderstanding by any body but you, because you are the foremost leader for a world government. As such a leader, you have the right as well as responsibility to make a fair and just review. I am sure you will find out that my book is a cohesive expounding of new ideas if only by checking through the terse text, which is the skeleton of the work. All the references are supporting material. I am humbly writing you again not just for the book but mainly for the great cause for which you have been struggling for many years.

From Norman

July 2, 1984

My comment on your book was not intended as criticism. I stand in awe of your ability to mobilize as much research material as you did. And I concur with your judgment that this is nothing that ought to be argued about. Let me rest the matter with the observance that your scholarship is titanic, but that it is carried to the point where it gets in the way of the reader's connection to your central presentation. Having been involved in book reviewing for about a half a century, I have developed a very substantial respect for the position of the authors, especially under circumstances of total commitment. At the same time, I have come to recognize that the critic is obligated to be not only constructive in his assignment but as candid as possible.

Please accept my continuing congratulations on your literary efforts as well as your continuing service to the cause of world peace and world law.

To Norman

July 25, 1984

Thank you very kindly for your letter of July 2, 1984, and the observance on my book ONE WORLD. As a matter of fact, I was not quite unaware that too much academic would cause some trouble to the general reader. This is why I tried to separate all supporting materials from the text, and also to start the last chapter with a summary of all the previous ones. I will keep your observance in mind for further efforts.

Now the book is published. I am humbly presenting you a copy with compliments. Meanwhile I like to take this opportunity to seek for your counsel for the One World Movement.

As you know, the Movement is initiated by the book with the evolutionary law of group expansion as guiding theory, the nation as primary target, permanent peace and general happiness as ultimate objectives, together with a blueprint for world government, and a practical program for actions.

Actions include: 1. to build up the Movement to be a world revolutionary force and to unite all groups who strive for world government, peace, humanity and the like, into the Movement; 2. to establish a world university as a training and working center; 3. to set up a worldwide information system; 4. to launch a world revolution with campaigns for liberating all peoples from the national independence, national sovereignty, and nationalism; for promoting humanity and world patriotism; and for survival, such as anti-war activities and demand for total disarmament; 5. to get financial and other supports from public and private sources; and 6. to develop a provisional world government and to work out a constitution for a permanent world government.

The Movement is just an infant at the moment. Your wisdom and experiences are needed for its growth. Any your guidance will be highly appreciated. Leadership for the Movement is an historical challenge to you.

To Norman

Nov. 16, 1984

I like to enclose a letter written early (July 25, 1984) to you but not mailed out, as the first part of this letter. It was held, because I thought I had to say something more about the last sentence.

Actually I want to say is that the One World Movement needs you to be its leader as chairman, president, or with some other suitable title. This kind of title is nothing new to you, but it is an endeavor rather new with a guiding theory, a primary target, two clear objectives, a blueprint and a practical program. It is an endeavor of world revolution with non-violence campaigns.

The initial works of the One World Movement include: 1. to announce formally its launch, 2. to invite leaders of important groups in common interest for a One World Conference, 3. to initiate a worldwide anti-war demonstration, 4. to start the organization of the One World University, and 5. fundraising.

To lead the One World Movement with such a scope of initial works is indeed a big job. It is actually a primary job of salvation for mankind and civilization. It is now an historical challenge to you.

As the writer of the book ONE WORLD and a sponsor of the One World Movement, I am sincerely and eagerly making myself available for your consultation and assistance anytime and anywhere.

VII. Try For Unity

1. Proposal in WGOC Philadelphia Meeting, Aug, 11, 1987

Last year in our Milwaukee meeting I expressed my idea to unite all of us into a political party in a multiple letter. Now I am following up to make a formal proposal:

Let's urge the World Federalists Association and the World Association of World Federalists to start the unity of all world federalists and other groups that strive for world unity, world government, world citizenship, world peace, humanity, and the like, into a single political party, and to set a preparatory committee immediately to do the initial works including:

a. To select a name for it (such as World Federal Party, World Unity Party, World Government Campaign, World Citizens Assembly, One World Movement, and so on);
b. To lay down a fundamental philosophy or guiding theory for it;
c. To establish clear objectives for it;
d. To work out practical programs for its action;
e. To make a project for its organization;
f. To search for a world flag and a world anthem for it to start use;
g. To draft a statute or bylaw for it;
h. To draft a declaration explaining its philosophy, objectives, programs for action, etc.;
i. To fix up a date, place and procedure for its inauguration.

2. Proposal in WGOC New York Meeting, June 10, 1988

To follow up the effort of uniting into a political party all groups that strive for world unity, world government, world federation, world citizenship, world peace, humanity, and the like, as urged in my letter of April 26, 1985, expressed in the WGOC Milwaukee meeting of Sept. 12, 1986 with a multiple letter, and suggested in the WGOC Philadelphia meeting of August 11, 1987, I propose:

a. To organize a World Unity Party or to develop the One World Movement to achieve a world unity, based on the theory of group expansion as a social evolutionary, historical and universal law.
b. To establish a world government through the elimination of the independence of the nation, national sovereignty and nationalism.
c. To achieve a permanent peace on the earth by abolishing war through the merger of all nations into one world.
d. To promote the general happiness of mankind with the balance of humanity, technology and ecology.

3. Letter of Aug. 29, 1988 to Dr. Lucile Green, as An Extending Appeal

Thank you for sending me the Minutes of the WGOC meeting, June 10, 1988, with your special note to me. I have not received your report of June 12, as you mentioned in the note. Would you please send me a copy again? Thanks also for you and Dr. Harry H. Lerner's letter of July 10, 1988, explaining the idea of Peoples Assembly for the U. N. and urging to join in the International Network for a U. N. Second Assembly. Meanwhile I have received a letter from Dr. Hannah Newcombe of Canada, telling her vision about the World Citizens Assembly as a U. N. second chamber or an auxiliary organ of the U. N. General Assembly; a letter from Mrs. George W. Dana, stressing the importance of Citizens Global

176

Action, and a good number of letters from other the like organizations asking for cooperation or support.

Lately I have received Mr. Lyman Hinckley's article "Coordination for Survival", and more information about the new World Citizens Assembly, including Dr. Genevieve Marcus' some thoughts for it, and the Minutes of its Planning Committee meeting, June 24, 1988, reported by Richard Jordan. In the meeting "Tom Liggett mentioned that the goal of the June 12 meeting was still 'foggy' to him . . . and stated that one thing was made clear, and that was that the U. N. Charter affirms the 'sovereignty of states' and not a 'federation'. Thus, the U. N. would seem to be a large block, in his view, to our thoughts of achieving some type of federation." Then Dr. Harry Lerner came "to clarify the June 12th meeting decisions that we were all sufficiently like-minded in our many years of working to achieve world unity, but merely differed in our approaches." Also received are a kind invitation from the World Constitution and Parliament Association, urging to participate in the conference of the Preparatory Committee for the World Constituent Assembly, to be held on Nov. 19 and 20, 1988 in New York; and the letter dated Aug. 4, 1988 from Dr. Lisinka Ulatowska, with a draft of pamphlet for the new World Citizens Assembly and other papers. I am impressed in the enthusiasm Dr. Ulatowska has had in handling the new job. The draft of pamphlet begins with a quotation "As life's inherent unity is permitted to emerge, durable solutions follow naturally." It describes the new World Citizens Assembly as a network of groups and organizations with the possibility to develop into a world peoples' parliament.

For a multiple reply to the above letters and documents, I like to take this opportunity to explain briefly the stand of the One World Movement I represented under the present situation.

As you know, I have tried for years to unite into a political party all groups that strive for world unity, world government, world federation, world citizenship, world peace, Humanity, and the like, as urged in my letter of April 26, 1985, expressed in the WGOC Milwaukee meeting of Sept. 12, 1986 with a multiple letter, suggested in the WGOC Philadelphia meeting

177

of August 11, 1987, and proposed in the WGOC New York meeting of June 10, 1988. My last proposal may be reiterated as follows:

a. To organize a world unity party to strive for world unity;
b. For the establishment of a world government through the merger of all nations into one world;
c. To achieve a permanent peace on the earth by abolishing war through the elimination of the independence of the nation, national sovereignty and nationalism, and
d. To promote the general happiness of mankind with the balance of humanity, technology and ecology in relation to world population and resources.

"We now have in the world some hundred groups with probably millions of members striving for the same ultimate goal." I noted in an early letter, "if we remain separate to stress certain minor differences, no one can accomplish much; but if we stand together as one revolutionary force, nobody can stop us. The time requires us to unite into one party more urgently than ever before. Let us put our unity ahead of anything else. Let us unite now. To unite ourselves is the initial step toward uniting the world."

So simple is the proposal and so obvious is the reason. But it is for real and should not be regarded as "a strategy" in spite of "skepticism among many who have tried this idea and failed." I wonder if there is anyone who has ever actually so tried and failed. Nor I think that the new World Citizens Assembly can be a vehicle for it. The best one can hope from the newly formed organ is that its development may have some impact to reduce some weakness of the U. N. structure. However, the weakness of the U. N. structure is only the symptom easily noticed, and is not the disease itself. The disease is: the U. N.'s nature is looser than a confederation. Actually it is an association of its member nations, and its member nations are its real masters with a dominant position fortified by its Charter such as "sovereign equality" in Part 1 of Article 2, "equal right and self-determination" in Part 2 of Article I and Article 55, "territorial integrity and political independence" in

178

Part 4 of Article 2, "domestic jurisdiction in Part 7 of Article 2, "self-defense" in Article 51, "regional arrangements" in Part 1 of Article 52, and the veto rule in Parts 2 and 3 of Article 27. It is the dominant position of its member nations that makes its structure so weak. It would be very difficult to strengthen the U. N. structure unless this dominant position has been changed and its fortification has been removed. But this position and its fortification are not something built just in the air. They have a wide ground in the independence of the nation, national sovereignty and nationalism. As long as their wide ground exists, they will remain strongly. In other words, the real work to strengthen the U. N. structure should begin with the elimination of the independence of the nation, national sovereignty and nationalism.

The elimination of the independence of the nation, national sovereignty and nationalism also is a prerequisite for a permanent peace on the earth.

As it is well known, in 1982 the world had 50,000 nuclear warheads, equal to 20 billion tons of TNT, or 1,600,000 times the yield of the Hiroshima bomb. This amounts to over 3 tons of TNT per person of the world population, and we all know that a pound will suffice. Meanwhile, five more nuclear weapons have been produced every day as if there were a shortage. Under these circumstances, if a nuclear war should erupt, it "would with little doubt mean the end of our civilization, and probably the end of the human race," as Linus Pauling warned. This threat could not be eased by Detente, Deterrence, Non-proliferation, SALT, Star War, or other means such as freeze nuclear weapons, promise not to use them first and the scraping of intermediate-range nuclear missiles, as long as there are chances for war. Even if all the existing nuclear weapons were destroyed all at once by some arrangements of miracle, they can be reproduced easily and quickly with advanced techniques when demanded by great and bitter wars for desperate use by war-mongers or fanatic zealots. There is no way to free mankind from a nuclear catastrophe completely except to abolish war itself. Is it possible?

Yes, it is possible by cutting off the root of war, not by checking its causes that are too many and too elusive. The root of war is the independence of human groups, since war is generally waged by groups of independence or for independence. There has been seldom a war of large size engaged by groups that have no independence. The groups that have independence include in ancient ages clan and tribe and in modern times, the nation. The interclannish wars were abolished when the independence of clans was eliminated, and the intertribal wars were abolished when the independence of tribes was eliminated. Consequently modern international wars would be abolished when the independence of the nation together with its symbol—national sovereignty and its agitator—nationalism is eliminated. How to eliminate the independence of the nation together with its symbol and agitator? There is a particular and effective way: To merge all nations into one world.

Actually the independence of the nation, national sovereignty and nationalism are the remaining blocks to the merger of all nations into one world. This merger is the consummation of the group expansion which has been at work for several million years everywhere by merging smaller groups into larger ones, from the early single family, through the primitive community, clan, tribe to the nation. To merge all nations into one world is only one step further, but it is the last step of the expansion process.

When all nations are merged into one world, there will be no other group that has independence, therefore, no root of war exists any more. There will be only one sovereignty that belongs to all peoples as a whole and is vested in the world government, and will be no any room left for nationalism while humanity is alone prevailing. Under these circumstances, necessarily, war is abolished and a permanent peace on the earth is assured.

The merger of all nations into one world is a consequence of the long process of group expansion over the whole world as a social evolutionary law. It is an historical necessity, not only desirable but also logical, and not just anticipated but even inevitable. It is the foundation of world unity and the guaranty for the success of world government. For these reasons it should be firmly adopted as the guiding theory of the great cause.

The group expansion, although at work all the time everywhere, is subject to physical conditions developed primarily by science and technology with tools and energies to make changes and improvements in economic life, transportation and communications, and weapons. The rapid advance of modern science and technology has now made all physical conditions ready for the merging of all nations into one world: the economic life of locally independent agriculture has been replaced by one of world-wide interdependent industry; the fast transportation and communications have swept away all national border lines, leaving no room for national territorial integrity, and have shrunk the vast world into a small kingdom for a world government to take care of it easily, and finally there has been on the earth no place where deadly weapons cannot reach within minutes to destroy everything, reducing the entire world to merely a small standing tactical theater, and everybody a permanent hostage. Hence, clearly the time is ripe for the merging of all nations into one world. The only job we have to do now is to sweep away the remaining blocks to the merger: the independence of the nation, national sovereignty and nationalism.

All nations after the merger will remain as autonomous political units, a status similar to that of the several states in the United States of America after the Civil War. Human rights will be protected by world law which is superior to any local law and governs the individual directly. The world government will have a supreme authority not only to maintain law and order over the whole world, but also to manager the general happiness of all peoples with the balance of humanity, technology and ecology in relation to world population and resources. Only a world government with a supreme authority can keep such a balance to manager such a great business.

So far, so much, is an explanation of the stand of the One World Movement I represented under the present situation. It also is an interpretation of the proposal I made to organize a world unity party to strive for world unity in order to establish a world government. In addition, I like to reiterate some points I made before the proposal, beginning with an initial conference to decide a statute or bylaw which includes:

181

a. Official name of the party;
b. Temporary organ (My proposal is: A council, a president, several vice-presidents—one for organization, one for information, one for world peace, one for mankind happiness, one for finance, and one at large, with a secretary-general.)
c. Program for actions (My proposal includes: I. to build the party to be a world revolutionary force; II. to set up a world-wide information system; III. to establish a world university as a training and working center; IV. to campaign for liberating all peoples from the national independence, national sovereignty and nationalism, and for promoting humanity and world patriotism; V. to strive for the abolition of war; VI. to plan for happiness of all peoples in respect to population, resources and environment; VII. to get financial and other supports from public and private sources, and VIII. to develop a provisional world government and to work out a world constitution for a permanent world government.)
d. Designs of a world flag and a world anthem, and
e. Declaration of the party including its guiding theory, primary mission, objectives, blueprint of world government, and programs for actions.

My proposal for a world flag, a world anthem, and a draft of the declaration may be found in my book *Two Years After,* pages 63, 64 and 73–93. Copies of the book are available. After all, I have looked for leadership for a world unity party in various ways. From the very beginning I have hoped world federalists to lead us in the struggle for world unity. Unfortunately they have not united themselves yet and have not had a clear criterion for world federation with appropriate policies. If the federation they have pursued for the world is much different with the U. N. which is looser than a confederation, why don't they stand up to be an opposite speaker or a strong reformer, rather than just play as a cheerleader?

To those who have ventured ahead with a world government, world parliament, world cabinet, or world constitution, I have my highest respects for their great courage and devotion. But practically I could not see much use to have a saddle before raising a horse. Indeed, Emery Reves once said in his

Anatomy of Peace: "There is no first step to world government. World government is the first step." Obviously he was urging to go directly for world government, because there has been no short stop or halfway station left for us anymore. I don't think it can be a basis for "world government, ready or not." In the same book Reves expressed no interest to any too early detailed draft of world constitution and indicated that principles and standards should come first. Anyway, I salute the great adventurers for the great cause, and sincerely hope that they would supply us with a more realistic leadership.

Now I want to appeal to all other groups to single out world government as a common goal and to join in a world unity party for its achievement. This is the only way for everyone to know clearly and exactly that what we are striving for and how to join forces for the success. In this respect, I like to quote two great lessons from Albert Einstein for further consideration. One is "A new type of thinking is essential if mankind is to survive and move to higher levels;" and the other: "There is no salvation for civilization, or even the human race, other than the creation of a world government."

Early this year, in urging the like-organizations to unite into a single political party, I wrote to Dr. Everett Millard, "I think our unity is more important than anything else in the pursuance of our common goal. I have set to work for the unity as the first job of my One World Movement. I will go along with any strong leadership all the way in this direction, and will submit the identity and fund of the One World Movement to a really united party without any hesitation." This part of the letter was later quoted in the *World Peace News.* This is my determination and commitment to a world unity party for the achievement of world government. My determination is serious and my commitment is firm. Meanwhile my principles as simply explained in this letter are serious and firm too. I will not trade my principles for anything else.

With my determination and commitment, I am humbly submitting my viewpoints to you for your preview. I will appreciate it very much if you and Tom Hudgens would help to introduce my proposal for a world unity party with the necessary interpretations formally to the November meeting.

Copies of this letter will be sent to about a dozen of other leading persons for their comments. I will know better what is going to do next after hearing from you and other friends.

4. Responses

Soon after the publication of my book ONE WORLD in 1984, I started the One World Movement with a try to unite all groups that strive for world unity, world government, world federation, world citizenship, world peace, humanity and the like. I started this try with an open letter of April 26, 1985 to the leaders of these groups and followed up with a suggestion in WGOC Milwaukee Meeting, Sept. 12, 1986, a proposal in WGOC Philadelphia Meeting, Aug. 11, 1987; another proposal in WGOC New York Meeting, June 10, 1988, and finally with a letter of Aug. 29, 1988 to Dr. Lucile Green, as the Chair of WGOC. About 20 copies of this letter were sent out as an extending appeal to seek for sponsorship and leadership for a world unity party. I have received so far 16 formal responses listed in order of date as follows:

Sept. 14, 1988, Mr. Tom Liggett, Editor of the World Peace News

Sept. 19, 1988, Dr. Norman Cousins, Chairman of the World Federalists Association

Sept. 20, 1988, Dr. Doug Everingham, World Federalist, Former Vice President of WHO Assembly and UN Delegate

Sept. 22, 1988, Mrs. Elizabeth R. Dana, Secretary of the Federalist Caucus

Sept. 27, 1988, Mr. John H. Davenport, Secretary of the Popular Initiative and Referandum Committee

Sept. 28, 1988, Mr. Bruno Micheli, Editor of the Evolution

Sept. 29, 1988, Mr. Philip Isely, Secretary General of the World Constitution and Parliament Association

Sept. 30, 1988, Dr. Lucile W. Green, Chair of the World Government Organization Coalition

Oct. 3, 1988, Mr. Henry Usborne, Joint President of the Parliamentary Group for World Government

Oct. 3, 1988, Dr. Bennet Skewes-Cox, President of the Academy of World Studies

Oct. 3, 1988, Mr. Walter Hoffmann, Executive Director of the World Federalist Association

Oct. 7, 1988, Mrs. Stella Dunn, Hon Organizer of the Project for Peace

Oct. — 1988, Mr. Lyman Hinckley, Fourfold Fellow Citizen and Leader of Our Right Start Associates

Nov. 7, 1988, Messrs Tom Ehrenzeller and Rick Wicks, Officers of the World Democracy News

Sept. 23, 1989, Prof. Benjamin B. Ferencz, Pace Law School

Oct. 11, 1989, Mr. R. Ward Harrington, President of the American Movement for World Government

In addition, there are a good number of letters expressing some opinions on the subject from friends who happened to have learned my extending appeal from some other sources. My deep thanks to them are just as much as to all friends in the above list. But I will not discuss separately with their opinions which can be generally represented by the formal responses.

I had planned to review the responses for an assessment soon after finishing my new book THE STRANGE WORLD, A Report of the Mission from Moon, sometime in the early 1990. But a coughing trouble after my trip to the Far East had prevented me from doing anything regularly for almost eight months in this year. I have gotten my new book ready for publication since having recovered from the illness, and now proceed the review as the last part of my another new book THE EARLY ONE WORLD MOVEMENT.

The formal responses thus far received are 16 in number, but they have made a file of half-a-foot high, not only because some of them run into many pages, more because some attach references like a book. It is impossible for me to check into all the details. I have to pick up only the important points with a few of them appended as samples.

The quickest, the shortest, and also the strongest response is the one from Tom Liggett. "Please consider me a sponsor," it says, "Your insights, etc., of Aug. 29 have been ours since long before we started publishing WPN in 1970."

I was surprised too by Norman Cousins' quick response which is quoted here in full:

"I am in your debt for your letter and for sharing with me a copy of your letter to Lucile Green. You are to be commended on your desire to unite world government groups into a single organization. I am not certain, however, that the effect of such a merger would lead to greater strength. Previous such efforts over the years have had the unhappy result of a boiling down rather than expansion. People who were in leadership positions were no longer in posts where their creative initiation was being put to best use.
The real problem of the world government movement, it seems to me, is not so much the absence of a single thrust as the failure to attract young people. I realize that it will be said that amalgamation will add to the attractiveness of the movement for young people. But their lack of interest, it seems to me, is not organizational but philosophical. Perhaps we can all work on this problem."

I was not so surprised though by Doug Everingham's response of almost 5,000 words, because he had kindly written me long letters before. He always has some extra energy to do some extra works. He started with that "I agree with your general theme but am not clear how you think that Lucille's WGOC falls short of what you want." He then went on to discuss with almost every aspect in and sometimes beyond my appeal. He adopted the Safe Earth Network as the title of the proposed world unity party, and nominated Philip Isely to be its Secretary-General, and also nominated Tom Liggett to be the Editor of its information system. He oked the temporary organ of the proposed party in general, modified the United

186

Nations' flag as a world flag, and reminded that a world anthem has already composed by Everett Millard with minor changes proposed by himself. He also reminded that world university has already existed in several forms and there have been already good declarations to which he subscribed. He figured out that the provisional world government has already existed but in embryo and the blueprint of world government has been under development, and that such a saddle is not without a horse and "something that may be more horse than saddle." He extended his concern as far as suggesting the World Citizens Assembly to join in the World Constitution and Parliament Association "or tell us why not." And he even mistook the party I proposed as the new World Citizens Assembly from which the best one can hope is to reduce some weakness in the structure of the United Nations.

Most part of his thesis, however, is devoted to the argument for the United Nations together with the independence of the nation, national sovereignty, and nationalism. After enumerating the value and merits of the United Nations and discussing the terminology of confederation, federation, sovereignty, etc. at length, he declared:

"The coming world government will not throw out the baby along with the bathwater, or the embryo world parliament and civil service along with the nationalist-cum-international-anarchist trends in all national sovereignties."

Meanwhile he told me that "I find your recipe for removing independence by a 'merger' of all nations is too big a bite for most digestions," and that

"So I feel you are too dogmatic in saying we must abolish nationalism, national sovereignty and independence. Better to say we must build a wider patriotism in common cause with all world citizens, tolerating and prizing divided sovereignties in national matters but global sovereignties with rational regulation in matters of vital global survival where divisive sovereignties are disastrous. We must eliminate only those aspects of nationalism, independence and sovereignty, not those which concern national pride in sport, culture, research, industry etc.''

Since Dr. Lucile Green, as the Chairman of the World Government Organization Coalition, has found that ''Doug's views as an experienced politician very sobering,'' his long letter is excerpted as an appendix for reference.

Elizabeth Dana also always has some extra energy to do some extra works, in action as well as in talking. She has been not only very active in the Federalist Caucus, but also advocating the Citizens Global Action, and even interesting in the Parliamentarians Global Action. She told me first that ''As you know, I strongly support your idea that what we must move toward is the establishment of a transnational political party that embraces our views on the need for global institutions capable of keeping the peace.'' Then she said that she was not clear what the responsibilities would be of a sponsor for a world unity party and that ''if it involves persuading people to give up their present party affiliation in order to join this one, I could not do that, as I am presently not prepared to make such a switch myself.'' Obviously she has been serious about the sponsorship for a world unity party and the affiliation of other parties. She also mindfully noted that ''I share your view that what is needed, ultimately, is a party type of structure, that enables individuals to relate across organizational and national lines, toward a common purpose. But most group leaderships seem unable to think beyond the narrower scope of what groups would agree to do together.''

The first sentence of John Davenport's response is unusually serious: ''In answer to your 6 September 1988 letter, of course I will be glad to be a sponsor of a world unity party for achieving world government.'' Then he gave me some hints based on his own experience, about how to approach people for leadership: ''Get hold of an authentic Chinese Mandarin

188

costume - lots of gold braid and lace and whatnot. Wear it in every public appearance;" "To paraphrase Confucius, every journey begins with you;" "Give everybody whom you approach a smile and a Chinese fortune cookie;" "Don't say anything about world government;" "You are going for mayor, not dog-catcher;" and so on. Unfortunately I cannot go along with his wisdom, because I am not running for leadership, but looking for leadership. In this regard he remarked: "Go along with strong leadership is what everybody else is doing. Lots of horses, lots of saddles, but no riders." As regards the title of the proposal party, he called it on the envelop to me from Spain "The World YOUnity Party."

Bruno Micheli's interesting in a world political movement was clearly expressed in his letter to Lucile Green dated Nov. 29, 1986, of which I was honored with a copy. He started with the question: "Let's Abolish War" is an impressive and comprehensive slogan, but will it be enough jointly using it to reach the goal? "Tom Hudgens' and John Kiang's suggestions for a Union of COGCC organizations would represent significant steps forward, provided they are based on a commonly agreed upon program of action;" he followed, "John Kiang's proposal for One World Movement seems to me nearest to what we all actually need;" and "As you probably remember, way back in July 1980, during the III World Citizens Assembly held in Japan, I proposed the establishment of a World Political Movement."

In response to my extending appeal, he remarked, however, that "My long personal experience has shown that it is practically impossible uniting various Groups, while it is possible to unite Individuals, when there is a clear, serious, reasonable, realistic, sufficiently detailed, well balanced and acceptable program of action;" and that "You are for a revolutionary force, while, as you know, I am for an evolutionary one."

Philip Isely said almost nothing except acknowledging receipt of my extending appeal, perhaps because he has made his opinion in this respect clear enough in a letter to me early. This letter dated July 8, 1985 is appended practically in full, and abstracted here:

Concerning the proposal to unite the world government and peace groups, the history from 1945 onwards is strewn with all sorts of attempts, such as made by the World Association of World Federalists and the World Government Organization Coordinating Committee. "Those unifying efforts which did not support a particular line of action in comparison to others were weak and did not attract much support. Those which supported a particular line of action, even tho nominally endorsing a variety of approaches, ceased to be unifying movements and became organizations to carry out a particular program, which meant that those favoring other lines of action continued separately."

"The point is that only an organization which endeavors to carry out a particular line of action is meaningful and attracts support; and only a specific line of action makes any sense and will get anything accomplished. It is impossible for all the world government and peace organizations to agree on a specific line of action. Their alliances or coalitions cannot make any headway."

Lucile Green's "think out loud" letter is appended in full and essentially quoted here:

"First of all, I think your analysis about nationalism and national sovereignty as the root cause of the arms race is accepted by most of us in the WG movement, as are the weaknesses of the UN which you identify specifically in its Charter. Most of us agree that the goal must be elimination of war itself rather than amelioration of its horrors by arms control, nuclear or other kinds of "disarmament." The differences arise over the most effective and practical strategies to achieve this."

"Right now I don't know what path is going to make a breakthrough to the elimination of the independence of the nation, national sovereignty and nationalism."

190

"As to a political 'party' for the realization of world government, it has been discussed several times in WGOC meetings and put on the WCA agenda. It has not received much support for several reasons: 1) a 'party' is perceived as a divisive rather than a unifying strategy at this time, for membership would preclude participation in other political parties. 2) parties—at least in the US—are extremely expensive to launch and maintain and have not been effective in promoting their goals. 3) the left-of-center parties in this country have been disasters, such as the Peace and Freedom Party, the Citizens Party and the Unity Party of John Anderson. They may even have contributed to the frightening Reagan 'landslides'!"

"On the other hand, the new WCA could create a constituency of globally-minded voters for global issues, global statesmen and—eventually—a global government without being a 'party' as such. Instead, it would be more like an annual convention, putting its collective support behind a few selected vital issues. This is the approach of the Federalist Caucus and Citizens Global Action, which makes sense to me."

"Finally, to be politically effective requires numbers, and I have found in my fifty-plus years in the peace movement that world government per se just doesn't have much appeal—too complicated, perhaps. 'World citizenship' on the other hand communicates well and, in fact, is 'in.' "

All of us remember that Henry Usborne was the leader of the Crusade for World government launched forty years ago. Today he still remains as ardent and pious as his early years for the great cause. His response in which almost every point he made is meaningful is quoted here in full for appreciation:

"I agree with you that it would be most useful to persuade all the genuine peace-makers to merge their forces into one world movement. But I think it is important that you should be selective and incorporate in your movement only those who recognise, as you do, that structured peace can be secured only when the nation-states will agree to surrender sovereignty to some sort of supranational federal government.

I have described the essential element which has to be surrendered as its 'elemental sovereignty.' You evidently call it "the independence of the nation: its national sovereignty and nationalism". What I think we both mean—and indeed all federalists must mean—is that the nation-states must join a federal union which has the legal power to forbid them to. have their own *Armies-in-national-uniform-using-war-making-weaponry*. This is the right that all sovereign nations now possess which they will have to surrender to a federal government if structured peace is ever to be created.

In the NOTES FOR PEACEMAKERS, which I now enclose, I have argued that these 'federalists' must be distinguished from those other good people, like the Greens, the Quakers and the campaigners for nuclear disarmament, who seem to think that the world can become a better and safer place without any kind of supra-national federal government being created. We federalists don't agree with them.

I therefore suggest that your world unity party should be composed only of those of us who are working for a global federal government of one sort or another. I conclude that a World Government Party might be a better name for it. After all everyone is in favor of world unity—who can possibly be against it? But very few people have your courage to state categorically that it is global government that you are seeking,

If your world unity party would care to call itself The Crusade for World Government, which is exactly what it has to be, I would be happy to join it.

But if you do succeed in creating such a world federalists' party I hope you will accept that there are currently many different opinions as to the kind of federation it is wisest to be advocating."

192

Bennet Skewes-Cox took very serious steps in response to my extending appeal. He told me that:

"Your proposals will be referred to our Academy's Board of Directors at our next meeting, and they in turn will transmit their considerations to whoever represents us at the November meeting of the W.G.O.C. which I unfortunately will be unable to attend."

Unfortunately too I was not able to attend that meeting and has had no further information in this regard.

Walter Hoffmann's response is a kind rejection:

"Thank you for sending me a copy of your letter to Lucile Green of August 29, 1988. While I applaud your efforts and those of others, my own view is that sponsorship of a world unity party at this stage is too premature. More work must be done, in my view, to change peoples attitudes before we can push that.

I, however, encourage you to continue doing what you think is best."

In the heavy documents I have found that as early as in Sept., 1982, during the WGOC Meeting at the Grand Hotel in Brighton, England, Stella Dunn with Lucile Green raised the need for a World Federalist Party. In a letter to me dated June 5, 1985, she wrote: "I certainly agree that political and global-minded World Citizens need a political framework through which to unite and develop their activities;" and she proposed the establishment of a Small World Federalist Political Committee. On Aug. 30, 1986, she wrote to Lucile Green, however, "I now realize that the name World Federalist Party as previously proposed would probably not be fully understood by the majority of political activists at the ordinary

193

grass roots level. It is proposed that the name World Unionist Party might be a better alternative, for it would be more directly explicit.''

In response to my extending appeal, Stella Dunn further noted that ''it was already agreed at last year's World Federalist AGM in London, that the word Federalist is not likely to have much appeal to members of the general public, to whom the name World Citizens Party would be more meaningful.'' She also noted that ''I learn from the annual mailing to subscribers, of the Federalist Caucus, of Portland, Oregon, that Garry Davis, of the World Service Authority in Washington, is standing for election as a World Citizen Party candidate— which is presumably much the same kind of party that you are trying to establish. And there would obviously not be much point in having two similar world parties geared to promoting similar policies; but bearing a somewhat different name and functioning under a different leadership;'' ''So perhaps you would find it helpful to contact Garry Davis about the matter.''

As a matter of fact, I have had contact with Garry Davis for years. Besides regular correspondence, I visited his headquarters in Washington once and he made a trip to my home once for long discussions. There are differences between us, indeed. Simply, to me, he has gone too far, and to him, I have not gone far enough. I have admired him very much nevertheless. He is a good orator and has worked for the great cause all the time under all kinds of pressure. Thus he is an outstanding leader. Unfortunately, there is not much support for his action, especially for his World Service Authority to issue passports and some other papers. His Middlebury Address launching the campaign for the election of the U. S. presidency ''is a prose poetry, interesting and beautiful,'' I remarked in a letter of him dated May 20, 1987. It is excellent for running for world president, but not very practical for running for a national president.

Let's back to Stella Dunn. In the cloud of various party names, there is one thing which is clear to me: She is standing for a world political party.

Lyman Hinckley responded to my appeal with a very long letter and a follow-up like a book later. His first remark may be quoted here as a summary:

"I have great admiration for your endeavor to unite the world-government movement. The leaders of the various groups have given little or no thought to this vital matter, with the exception of Lucile herself, who has at least attempted a sort of United Nations unification with the WGOC project.

Her type of project and yours represent the two visible alternatives at present: either the various groups, like UN sovereign nations, establish some sort of clearing-house for what little common action may be possible, or one of them undertakes to absorb the others by convincing them of its superiority in merit or elsewise.

I conclude regretfully that neither effort will achieve any real unification."

"Real unity is articulate agreement on beliefs and purposes," he said this before again and again. Now he stressed the importance of "moral health," "secular faith" and later, "common faith, just law, and moral public management." At one point he made another remark which is directly important to the subject:

"As I see it, there are two main themes in your proposal:
(1) That group expansion is a phenomenon going on throughout history, and needs only understanding and facilitation for its inevitable completion in our critical age.
(2) That further group expansion is obstructed by national independence, national sovereignty, and nationalism; hence these must be abolished.

Throughout the ages until 1945, group expansion was accomplished by conquest, or conversion, or both. The atomic age has put an abrupt end to that. There is now no prospect that any group, political or religious, can expand in the historic sense. But a quite different 'group' has come to be, namely a single interdependent worldwide community. The whole matter of nationalism and national sovereignty can be bypassed with this reality, together with one more citizenship added to our present three, namely world citizenship, inherent from having been born into that now existing community. (Projection of U.S. Const. Amdt. XIV. Sec. 1) An attempt to abolish nationalism would appear to be not only impossible but unneeded.''

Tom Ehrenzeller and Rick Wick's response to my extending appeal is very cautious with responsible considerations:

''We support the idea of a world unity party as a vehicle for public education, although we have some reservations about the degree of our potential involvement. We would consider being a co-sponsor of such a party at this time, but primary sponsorship could affect our objectivity with regard to other organizations and points of view and might jeopardize our non-profit status with the IRS. We can imagine a time in the future when the world unity party becomes successful as an active political force: then we would need to withdraw our sponsorship. We assume that when that becomes necessary our name will be dropped from any organizational literature. Meanwhile, we are happy to help in any way we can.''

Benjamin Ferencz's response is quick and intimate and is worth to be appended in full. He remarked warmly first:

''I certainly agree with your argument that the idea of unrestrained national sovereignty must be eliminated if we are to have ''One World'' of peace and happiness. Your proposal for a world unity party and your outline of its programs are certainly sensible and present a rational focus for consideration by individuals or groups desirous of eliminating the present war system. It reminded me of similar plans put forth by Kant, Rousseau, Bentham and other thinkers before them. The problem still remains: How do we get from here to there?

Then he called for caution: "Are you not being impatient, or expecting too much too soon?" "Your should recognize that we are making significant progress . . . If all of us continue to do our best—as you are doing—I believe we will win the race between civilization and disaster." He has been going along with the United Nations since his very early years when he was a chief prosecutor in the famous Nuremburg war crime trials. He recorded highlights of the United Nations year by year in his famous book PLANETHOOD. It is no wonder that he prefers progress along with the United Nations rather than changes through some radical actions.

The last response so far is reached for review now. It is from Ward Harrington. "It is very gratifying to see the clarity of your conviction of the need for an authentic world order under an effective governmental institution." After the encouraging words, he warned:

"You urge the establishment of "one party", to bring into unity all of the organizations and people who are striving for some solution to the problem of anarchy, injustice, and the threat of nuclear extinction. Serious doubts arise in my mind as to the efficacy of such an approach. The crux of the problem, I feel, would be that the influence of major elements in many of these organizations would hold back any action of an effective nature. . . . The clarity of the focus and commitment which you bring to the matter, would be blocked by those who rather than revolutionists are bootlickers of the prevailing establishment figures."

He further pointed out that "You very properly identify a key part of the problem as the independence of the nation with its absolute assertion of sovereignty," and reminded

"There is a need for you to accept the full implications of your recognition that the task before us involves revolutionary change. How can we overthrow the existing independent and sovereign nation-state institutions in a non-violent manner.

197

Revolution by non-violent means lays a very demanding burden on us, but that is what has to be achieved. A mass movement with all the other organizations that have some interest in this, is the least likely way to accomplish the needed revolution."

Finally I believe that, after he had chance to check over my books, he would find that we are in full accord with the revolutionary approach for the great cause. We know quite well that we cannot "wishing away" of the problem, and there is no way to eliminate the independence of the nation, national sovereignty and nationalism, except through a revolutionary change. "We have a big job achieving that goal and we will not achieve it by nice words or gentle persuasion." I am very happy to know that there has been a revolutionist as the leader of the American Movement for World Government, and I like to append his response to my appeal in full with compliments.

5. Assessment

Among the 16 formal responses to my extending appeal for a world unity party, as far as I can detect out, there are only 4 which are positive, equally 4 are negative; 2 are not decided yet, 3 tend to be positive, and also 3 tend to be negative. It is virtually a tie, in addition to various important opinions which may be remarked as lessons or prompt for more explanation.

a. First of all, I am greatly encouraged by the wide acceptance of my analysis about nationalism, national sovereignty as the root cause of the arms race, and the weaknesses of the United Nations caused by its Charter, as noted by Lucile Green. She also noted that most of us agree that the goal must be elimination of war itself rather than amelioration of its horrors by arms control, nuclear or other kinds of disarmament.

b. As regards the United Nations particularly, I am not the one who wants to throw out the baby along with the bathwater, but I cannot agree with those who like to keep the bathwater for the baby. What I have tried to do is to change the nature of the United Nations from a looser than confederation into a world government through the elimination of the independence of the nation, national sovereignty and nationalism. This is in the line of the opinion of Alexander Hamilton when he said in the FEDERALIST, no. 6 that "To look for a continuation of harmony between a number of independent, unconnected sovereignties, situated in the same neighborhood, would be to disregard the uniform course of human events, and to set at defiance the accumulated experience of ages." Hamilton's opinion was expressed two hundred years ago for the formation of the United States and is clear a guide for us to struggle for a world government.

c. The term "sovereignty" has been a very hot topic for discussion in modern times. But the more is the discussion, the more is the confusion. Lately it has been applied for common organization and even individual, and has been mixed with some words such as pride, integrity, dignity, privilege and prestige. But in political ideology, it has a proper meaning. It is the symbol of an independent group. Thus, sovereignty and independence cannot be separated from each other. Professor Lassa F. L. Oppenheim pointed out that "Sovereignty as supreme authority, which is independent of any other earthly authority, may be said to have different aspects. As excluding dependence upon any other authority, and in particular from the authority of another State, sovereignty is independence. It is external independence with regard to the liberty of action outside its borders in the intercourse with other State which a State enjoys. It is internal independence with regard to the liberty of action of a State inside its borders." The sovereignty as symbol has developed from primitive times as totemism. Its early modern exponent was Jean Bodin who wanted to use it to unite France into a nation through a strong central government. Unfortunately it merely served as a pretext for the rise of despotism. After having been applied from internal affairs to external relations, it became a new doctrine of international separation and anarchy.

d. Nationalism has also developed from a force of internal unity to a factor of international disorder in modern times. It originated from barbarism and tribalism. It commands a paramount loyalty and duty to one's own nation, leading to rivalry and hostility with other nations. It wants one's own nation to be militarily stronger, leading to strategical struggles against other nations, and it asserts one's own national interests emphatically, leading to economic egoism in dealing with other nations. It always exploits public sentiment, manipulates history and distort facts for its own interests. It is the aggressive force for imperialism and also the conservative elements for isolationism. And necessarily it is the strongest agitator of the independence of the nation and national sovereignty.

e. The problem of world federation is also tied up with the independence of the nation, national sovereignty and nationalism. According to classic federalism, in a federation all the regional components in name of province, state or nation, are equal and somewhat independent with certain sovereignty, and also with certain pride and integrity. These ideal features, however, are subject to a condition that there be not a very marked inequality of strength among the components, as emphasized by John S. Mill a hundred years ago. Unfortunately there is no such condition in existence among the nations today. Their strength as measured by population, area and wealth is too inequal. According to statistics of 1988, for example, the 100,000 population of Dominica looks like that of a small town in the United States, the area of 115 square miles of Maldives is much smaller than that of an average county in China, and the wealth of Antigua and Barbuda may be not as much as that of a quality bank in Japan. On the other hand, China alone has almost one fourth of the world's population, the Soviet Union has about one sixth of the world's land, and the United States has approximately one fourth of the world's income. This marked inequality of strength among the nations would make it very difficult to bring them into a world union with ideal features of classic federalism.

f. The elimination of the independence of the nation, national sovereignty and nationalism is a job unprecedentedly big and important. It can be done only by a world revolution which should be carried out as soon as possible by all means except violence. The principle of non-violence distinguishes it from all conventional revolutions. Because of this, it may be not so sensational and so exciting. But reason will prevail, since it is virtually a revolution in political ideology to wipe out the traditional prejudice and superstitions everywhere and to free all peoples from the prison of the nation forever.

g. The world revolution cannot go by itself. It is necessary to have a political party to carry on. Thus a political party is its soul and it is this soul we are searching for. The name of the world unity party is just a suggestion. It is open to discussion and adoption. Various names have been proposed, such as world government party, world citizens party and world federal party. Some people dislike the word "party" and suggest to use such word as assembly, caucus and network. They argue that "party" is too great and too political. Actually we want not only that the name of the party great enough and clearly political, but also to make it known that it is a revolutionary party. Its main objective is to change the existing political structure through the elimination of the independence of the nation, national sovereignty and nationalism in order to establish a world government. It differs with ordinary political parties of which the normal purpose is to seek votes for offices with some platforms under the established governmental systems. It is a world party, not a national party. It is not overlapped with any party of any nation, and certainly not a third party of the United States like some people have worried about. But members of any national party can be members of the world party. Membership of the world party is projected to require a pledge of loyalty to humanity, of allegiance to mankind, and of devotion to world unity; together with a promise to fellow the principles and to work for the policies, decisions and orders of the party.

h. While the world party is the soul of a world revolution, a world university is designed to be the center of the soul in the early stage. It differs with the ordinary universities and even with the existing world universities mentioned by Doug Everingham. It will not offer regular academic courses, which other universities can do well. It will concentrate on developing a solid nucleus of disciplined personnel to work for the world party. Students will be recruited from all countries, and they will be sent to staff the local units of the world party after

201

graduation. Most of the faculty members are the leading staff members of the world party. They will study and discuss over theories, policies, problems and strategies for the world revolution with students thus making the world university a workshop of the world party. The faculty members will also work together as the general staff of the world party to provide guidance and coordination of all its activities, and to run an information network. They stand ready to help the establishment of a provisional world government and the draft of a world constitution.

i. The primary task of the world revolution is to eliminate the independence of the nation, national sovereignty and nationalism. They are the main stumbling blocks on the way to the merger of all nations into one group. The word "merger" looks not so good to some people including myself. But the process of merging small groups into larger ones has operated for hundreds of thousands years everywhere. It is a process of group expansion from the early single family, through the primitive community, clan, and tribe to the nation. It is a fact, no matter you like it or not. To merge all nations into a world group is nothing new. It is just one step further of the group expansion, but is its last step. The merger of all nations is not "too big a bite for most digestions," since the world has been shrunk by modern transportation and communications into a "village" as some writers called it. The world is no longer too big to be a group. It is too big only in the idea of those who ignore the rapid advance of modern science and technology.

j. When the process of group expansion merges all nations into one group for the whole world, a world commonwealth will be spontaneously brought forth with a world government. Vested in the world government is a supreme authority derived from all peoples as a whole, and subordinated to it are the nations as autonomous local units. Surely they cannot have independence, sovereignty and something like nationalism anymore, nor to claim secession. Also they cannot engage in diplomatic business, enter into military alliance, produce and store arms, wage war, and impose tariffs between them. Nevertheless they are regarded as self-ruled people. Their culture, economy and government are respected as much as possible. They are encouraged to promote local business and social welfare. But they are not allowed to do anything against law, policy or measure of the world government. Instead they are obliged to carry them on by all means. Generally speaking, their status is similar to that of the state in the United States of America today. In the world commonwealth human rights and obligation will be well respected without any distinction as to race, sex, language or religion. All peoples will be protected by world law which is superior to any local law, governs the individual directly and leaves no room for the existence of international law.

k. The world government is projected to consist of a world judiciary, a world administration and a world council. Judiciary will be independent. Administration will consist of various service units, but no military unit, nor any unit for foreign affairs. The world council will be the central organ of the world government, and will be composed of a house of commons and a house of experts. Its president, elected by itself, will serve as the world president in formality and ceremony, and to coordinate the functions of the judiciary, administration, the commons and experts. Traditionally the units for military and foreign affairs in the government are where not only most of the money are spent, but also the dirtiest political tricks are played and feverish power struggles are engaged. Their omission from the world government means not only saving enormous expenses, but also stopping two evil sources of the government, and thus making it possible for the world government to emphasize services rather than politics, and for experts rather than politicians to run the world government. Experts are those who are specialized in certain field of science or technology. Since the advance of modern science and technology has accelerated its way into the government, more and more experts are needed for public services, and less and less room is left for politicians to play politics. This is another reason for experts rather than politicians to run the world government. For experts to run the world government means not only that they provide leadership for all service units of the administration, but also that they participate in lawmaking and policy decision. This is why a house of experts is projected as a brand new branch as well as a brain bank of the government. When politicians run the government, a system of check and balance of power can help to keep the government from going too wild, while experts run the government, more services are expected, and big government may be not necessarily so bad as to be subject to "violent objections."

l. The reason for the omission of the units for military and foreign affairs from the world government is simple. The world government is established when all nations are merged into a single group. There would exist no other independent group with sovereignty with which the world government may have to wage war and enter foreign relations. Therefore, the traditional units for military and foreign affairs are no longer in need. War between nations would pass into history, and a permanent peace on earth would take place. This peace is the goal of the merging process of group expansion, and also the objective of our effort for world unity. It is real, and is not too good to be true. It is not too remote to reach, and can be achieved by the last step of the group expansion. Although we stand firm against any war, it is the permanent peace for which we are concentrated to struggle through the merging process. We cannot afford to do much for any other kind of peace, such as temporary peace, regional peace, and grass-root peace, in any other way. There have existed in the world hundreds of peace groups, and some of them have contacted us for cooperation or assistance for their various peaces or in their particular ways. We are sorry that our negative response or no response may have disappointed and puzzled them somehow.

m. We may in the same way also have disappointed and puzzled some humanitarian groups who contacted us for cooperation or assistance, even from foreign countries. We are sorry that we are not able to make any philanthropic contribution. To be sure we are working for humanity, but for humanity as a whole in the long run, not for any individual or any special case. Along with the permanent peace on earth, the general happiness of mankind is another objective of our effort for world unity. When the permanent peace is achieved, all the current military expenditures can be transferred to finance the general happiness. With the enormous financial re source and manpower, the world government would be able to do the big job with big measures, not to patch up little by little. Big measures may include: raising of the living standards in the poorer regions; control of the population; saving and developing energies, non-fuel minerals, forest products, and water; improving and increasing food production; preventing and reducing natural calamities; protecting the environment with conservation by minimizing the destruction of natural resources, holding down pollutions, and relieving urban overcrowding; maintaining equilibrium of humanity and ecosystem; Unifying and equalizing economic systems, and keeping growth with balance.

n. There are some notes in the responses to my extending appeal for a world unity party, which may be considered as important as hints or suggestions for adjusting our strategy in the future: Young people's lack of interest to the world government movement, according to Norman Cousins, "is not organizational but philosophical." We should unite with, remarked Henry Usborne, only those who recognize "that structured peace can be secured only when the nation-states will agree to surrender sovereignty to some sort of supranational federal government." Bruno Micheli reminded that "it is practically impossible uniting various groups, while it is possible to unite individuals." Ward Harrington stressed that we should develop an agile and speed "attack force." And Guy W. Meyer emphasized as noted by Gary K. Shepherd in the UNITED WORLD, Vol. 3, no. 6, p. 7 and 8, on what he calls "circle" as the structural basis of the movement. It is often termed organic, for it works very much like the living cells within a body. It resemble the Quaker weekly meeting a great deal. Meyer also emphasized that "the world unity movement will never get anywhere with conservative proposals. We must make broad, emotionally stirring, radical proposals, that will frighten as well as fascinate, ideas that will stir the emotions as well as the mind, if we wish to motivate people to act."

o. Finally I like to report that in the difficult struggle for world unity I have been encouraged by the shinning of four stars in the dark media sky, shedding clearer views on the problems of the United Nations, peace and war, the independence of the nation, national sovereignty and nationalism. They are: the WORLD PEACE NEWS, the ACADEMY FORUM, the WORLD FEDERALIST, and the UNITED WORLD.

The WORLD PEACE NEWS is better known to us. It has been published for twenty years under the outstanding leadership of Tom Liggett. Doug Everingham commended Tom as "a redoubtable campaigner for scrapping national sovereignty in favor of world government, but he realistic enough to know that one of the forums where this must be fought for is the UN, even when he calls it a block to world government." Tom has been working under a very difficult and complicated circumstance all the time. I wonder if he ever feel something like what Norman Cousins once confessed: "People who were in leadership positions were no longer in posts where their creative initiation was being put to best use."

The ACADEMY FORUM is a new publication of the Academy of World Studies whose president, Dr. Bennet Skewes-Cox is the author of The UNITED NATIONS from LEAGUE to GOVERNMENT based on his original study of 1947, the first analysis of the UN Charter article by article. He concluded that a league and a government are so different that any future world government would probably be the result not of amending the UN, but starting at scratch. . . . the same conclusion reached by the drafters of the U. S. federal constitution. They simply scrapped the old Articles of Confederation and drafted an entirely new instrument at Philadelphia. Under the guidance of Dr. Skewes-Cox the ACADEMY FORUM started to publish in November, 1989 when the 102 non-aligned countries issued a call for a UN decade of international law. This call was hailed widely, but the Forum remarked that it is "a major contribution but unfortunately is at odds with itself." It moved "both toward law and the abolition of war on the one hand and toward a strengthening of national sovereignty on the other. These are positions at odds with each other. These positions were often placed together in the same paragraph and even in the same sentence." The title of another major article in the first issue is that "Vernon Nash Was Right: the World Must Be Governed."

The WORLD FEDERALIST is published by the Institute of Mudialist Studies in England and edited by Dr. John Roberts. As a bulletin of federalists, it is bound to include various information and opinions. But Dr. Roberts is steering an editorial policy toward the right direction. After reading its no. four, 1987, I wrote to Dr. Roberts: "I am encouraged by finding in it your position in respect to the nation-state, sovereignty, nationalism, peace, war, etc. is more clear and firm than that of many other federalists, and is, therefore, more close for us to struggle for our common cause. In this regard, I am enclosing a copy of my letter to Mrs. Stella Dunn for your review, as my observation on the August events of Philadelphia where you and I met for the first time.

The UNITED WORLD is edited by Gary K. Shepherd and published in a college town Carbondale, Ill. Although I have admired Gary very much ever since I had chance to read his writings three years ago, nothing I know about him personally. What I know is that the UNITED WORLD is a publication devoting exclusively to the cause of uniting the world. Gary is able to write with clear thinking, strong wording and firm standing. His Editor's Corner on the campaign against the recent Gulf War, for instance, "To all appearances, this campaign is slated to be just as short-sighted, just as limited, just as narrowly focused as have been such campaigns in the past. The scenario for this one seems to be something to the effect that the U. S. soldiers should not be sent off into the desert to fight for oil, or cheap gas, or some such catchy slogan. . . . The implication is that in another time and for another reason, it would be perfectly acceptable for soldiers to kill and die. This reduces the entire question of war to one of whether the ends to be attained are worth the means used." The UNITED WORLD is a growing star, but it may fall down from the sky all at once. "Things are getting down to the wire here at UNITED WORLD, money wise. At the present time, it looks like, unless we get a sudden influx of subscribers, then the next issue will probably the last that we will be able to publish. . . . We desperately need your help. Remember the old saying, if it is to be, it is up to me. Send $12.00 for a year's subscription to: UNITED WORLD, 203 W. Walnut, Carbondale, IL 62901.''

6. Outlook

According to my assessments, the positive and negative responses to my extending appeal for a world unity party are virtually a tie. It is a point good for optimism, and also bad for pessimism. No matter how bad it is, however, it is not the end of the world, nor the end of my try for world unity. With the lessons I learned, the opinions I heard, and the explanations I made, I am more than ever before convinced that our proposed principles for world unity are sound. They are summarized as follows:

a. The group expansion through merging process is the historical and philosophical foundation of world unity.

b. The merging of all nations into a world commonwealth with a world government is the consummation of the group expansion.

c. The world government would be able to achieve a permanent peace on earth and the general happiness of mankind.

d. While the current threat of nuclear holocaust to the existence of mankind together with the serious deterioration of the world environment has demanded urgently the rescue of a world government,

e. The reactionary force of the independence of the nation, national sovereignty, and nationalism is blocking the merging process very badly.

f. Clearly, therefore, the reactionary force must be eliminated before it is too late. But there is no way to do it except by a world revolution in political ideology.

g. The world revolution needs a dedicated world revolutionary party to carry on by all means except violence. The world unity party is designated for the job.

h. The world unity party is the soul of the world revolution. Its primary mission is to eliminate the independence of the nation, national sovereignty, and nationalism. Its goal is to unite the world and establish a world government for peace forever and happiness everywhere, and

i. Membership of the world unity party, as a salvation, requires a pledge of loyalty to humanity, of allegiance to mankind, and of devotion to world unity; together with a promise to fellow the principles and to work for the policies, decisions and orders, of the party.

We have tried to explain our principles for world unity for years. We hold them firmly and will not trade them for anything else. However, we have to adjust the programs for them for the short run as simple as follows:

a. To consolidate the historical and philosophical foundation of the world unity.

b. To start the world unity party with even a few leading people.

c. To concern and work only for world revolution against reactionary force in political ideology.

d. To cooperate with a dedicated educational institute to train spostles, and

e. To cooperate with a dedicated news media to spread information to the public.

Finally I like to take this opportunity to renew my personal determination here:

a. To continue effort for world unity as my life-time mission.

b. To maintain my role as John the Baptist to look for a real leader, and

c. To publish my new book THE EARLY ONE WORLD MOVEMENT, to revise and enlarge my earlier work ONE WORLD, to have them translated into Chinese, French, Spanish, Russian and some other languages, and to distribute them to great libraries over the world, as far as my own fund can go.

I agree with your general theme but am not clear how you think that Lucille's WGOC falls short of what you want.

The emergence of the world's first ever set of moral principles acceptable to all nationally sponsored religious and philosophies in Declarations of Human Rights, surely an essential basis for the very principles you and Emery Reeves want set down as a start.

The coming world government will not throw out the baby along with the bathwater, or the embryo world parliament and civil service along with the nationalist-cum-international-anarchist trends in all national sovereignties.

Unfortunately I feel much of the disunity among federalist movements is based on the destructive aim of first destroying the UN because it is based on national sovereignty. It is also based on a striving to come to grips with the failures of national sovereignty.

Tom Liggett is a redoubtable campaigner for scrapping national sovereignty in favor of world government, but he realistic enough to know that one of the forums where this must be fought for is the UN, even when he calls it a block to world government. I would nominate him as Editor of the proposed coalition/party/network if he will take on the job.

With due respect for the World Citizens Assembly (WCA) idea of evolving into a parliament, I think this idea to the extent you have explained it is just a later, smaller, weaker, slower version of Philip Isely's World Constitution and

Parliament Association (WCPA) with its Provisional World Parliament (PWP). Therefore I would suggest they join WCPA or tell us why not. I want to see a few amendments to WCPA at its next conference and have sent these to Philip. Has WCA done so? If not, they should hurry to get on the agenda. It will be self-defeating if they turn their back on this large movement and so alienate some if not most of its members. I would nominate Philip as Secretary-General of the coalition/party/ network if he agrees and does not feel it would be too much diluting his energies into peripheral organizations.

You refer (page 2 lower part) to the best hope of your 'party' being to reduce some weaknesses of the UN structure.

So I feel you are too dogmatic in saying we must abolish nationalism, national sovereignty and independence. Better to say we must build a wider patriotism in common cause with all world citizens, tolerating and prizing divided sovereignties in national matters but global sovereignties with rational regulation in matters of vital global survival where divisive sovereignties are disastrous. We must eliminate only those aspects of nationalism, independence and sovereignty, not those which concern national pride in sport, culture, research, industry, etc.

The most violent objections to world government come from those who fear big and bigger and especially biggest government because governments like other groupings as they get bigger get less human in their dealings. We have to get across some reasons for this:

- the lack of grassroots input, which will develop with reverse (viewer input) TV etc. technologies;
- lack of responsibility of the media to a supranational constituency—the fourth estate is still elected mainly by circulation figures and viewer ratings;
- lack of fast translation services in news, travel, cultural activities etc.;
- and lack of education in the rights of foreigners, aliens, strangers, neighbors, others.

Similarly I find your recipe for removing independence by a 'merger' of all nations is too big a bite for most digestions.

211

Merger is not a good word to use in teaching such people. They fell enveloped, threatened by it, seeing it as a merger of bigger and bigger government. They must learn to trust other peoples and be the mergers with them. Federation is a better word but needs precision in definition and use to show
• it extends democracy and that means your voice and mine,
• it does not hand democracy over to a bigger menace but takes it from the main menace and gives it to the umpires, referees, judges, police forces, lawmakers we choose to tidy up the lawless state of the world in international concerns.

So for the official name of the 'party' I would not use 'party'. That implies a 'partial' sectional interest. 'Coalition' appeals more because it exists to reconcile parties. *'Network'* appeals more because it implies interconnection and hopefully intercommunication, without which the structure collapses. We need to build a world culture. Perhaps the first step is a system of certificates, diplomas and degrees in understanding the very issues put herein, with media, transnational companies, governments etc. eventually invited to donate prizes for the best media, educational compilations. I've already suggested to Suter he try to get a world mailing list for a 'Safe Earth Network'. That is my choice of a title.

The temporary organ you propose is OK but each official needs to have a better defined function. Is the finance vice-president to engage in fund-raising or is he merely to be the main supervisor of a paid fundraising setup? I prefer the way Isely is going with sub-committees working on specific problems. He has enough vice-presidents on his letterhead already with no very specific tasks ex officio.

The world university already exists in several forms, e.g. In Costa Rica, Japan and I think Scandinavia. Contact needs to be made with these and other peace education groups at national and international level. Kindergarten is more important than university, primary more important than high school.

The campaign for liberating peoples from national independance, sovereignty, nationalism and war I would rename as a campaign for liberating peoples from nationalist isolationism and military lawlessness to gain an international democratic voice and system of justice in matters of world

212

survival. Overriding national authorities which threaten survival but which will remain answerable only for things affecting their own territories separately.

The provisional world government already exists but in embryo. Unless you have a quicker, more sweeping, better way to propose, the Safe Earth Network should take this as the base for this part of its program (or plank of its platform).

Designs for flags and national anthems are often decided by public competition. There would be nothing to stop the Provisional World Parliament conducting such competitions. Everett Millard has already composed a world anthem to which I've proposed minor changes. The world flag ought to be like the UN flag but perhaps with the dividing lines omitted to remind us of the abolition of national borders for some vital purposes. The laurel wreath or olive branches could also be omitted since all governments claim to aspire to such ideals but only one undivided world can achieve them.

There are already good declarations to which I've subscribed and it may be that Keith Suter has a collection of them from which to devise a shorter, clearer, more generally acceptable version.

The blueprint of world government is under development by WCPA and PWP. You say you see little use for such a saddle without a horse. The horse must be public opinion. It can be approached by many roads: WCPA, Liggett's UN reporting, peace curriculum design, media-attracting events, surveys, competitions, talks to organizations, and the injunction granted against atomic weapon nations in the Provisional District World Court in California for PWP, something that may be more horse than saddle.

Appendix II
Mr. Philip Isely's Letter of
July 8, 1985

Concerning your proposal for a conference to unite the world government and peace groups which can identify common aim, the history of the peace and world government movements from 1945 onwards is strewn with all sorts of proposals and attempts to unite the world government and peace movements under common banner. Certainly, you must know of many of these attempts.

In the world government area, the World Movement for World Federal Government, formed in 1945 at Montreaux was the first after 2nd world war. This later became World Association of World Federalists. Altho nominally including support for various ways to achieve world government, in practice the only approach which was given encouragement by this organization was the amendment of the U.N. Charter under the charter review and amendment procedures of the U.N. For example, other methods were discouraged, including the ideas of "Peoples World Convention" and "World Constitutional Convention." although nominally endorsed in their statement of purpose.

Again, more recently, about a dozen years ago the World Government Organization Coordinating Committee was formed. Because the preponderance of membership favored either amendment of the U.N. Charter approach or the World Citizen registry approach, the Constitutional Convention and Provisional World Parliament approaches did not receive attention.

214

There are many other examples, both in the World Government movement and in the general peace movement. Those "unifying" efforts which did not support a particular line of action in comparison to others were weak and did not attract much support. Those which supported a particular line of action, even tho nominally endorsing a variety of approaches, ceased to be "unifying" movements and became organizations to carry out a particular program, which meant that those favoring other lines of action continued separately.

The point is that only an organization which endeavors to carry out a particular line of action is meaningful and attracts support of those who believe in the merits of the particular line of action. Alliances or coalitions which do not promote a particular line of action, but endeavor to be a common meeting ground or "umbrella" for a variety of ideas about what to do, either do not make any headway, or unite for some short-term single issue goal, or leave out everybody who does not agree with what the majority votes for when the "umbrella" becomes committed to a particular line of action and ceases to be an organization which endeavors to represent all.

The other point is, that only a specific line of action makes any sense, and only a specific line of action will get anything accomplished.

The third point is that it is impossible for all the world government organizations and for all of the peace organizations to agree on a specific line of action, unless it is so general and unspecific as to be meaningless—as the present line of the world citizens organizations: "campaign to abolish war."

If you are interested in actual accomplishment, rather than a theoretical unification of the world government and peace movements, then it would be necessary for you to carefully analyze the contents and merits of the specific line of action.

The W.C.P.A. already has a well defined program of action, with many specific items already well developed. It welcomes all who really want to accomplish definite and specific results to achieve world government; rather than mess around in the generalities of another coalition which either will be too general to be meaningful, or will reflect the dominance and prejudices of those who guide it so as to leave out others.

Actually, the program with the most merit may not have the largest membership—at least at present.

The WCPA, while being organized worldwide, cannot brag about having the largest membership at present, but can offer the program with the most merit to achieve the goals, and in that respect offers an "umbrella" to all individuals and organizations which want to join in effective action to reach the goals, while not requiring membership in the W.C.P.A, itself, through the action plan of the Provisional World Parliament.

Thank you for your letter of August 29, which I have before me along with one from Douglas Everingham dated September 20—both very important and thoughtful contributions relating to the direction of our activities, especially as we are in the process of forming the new World Citizens Assembly in New York. Let me try to "think out loud" about your propositions and what may be possible to do about them as we try to shape a more unified movement.

First of all, I think your analysis about nationalism and national sovereignty as the root cause of the arms race is accepted by most of us in the WG movement, as are the weaknesses of the UN which you identify specifically in its Charter. Most of us agree that the goal must be elimination of war itself rather than amelioration of its horrors by arms control, nuclear or other kinds of "disarmament." The differences arise over the most effective and practical strategies to achieve this. Here I find Doug's views as an experienced politician very sobering. For example, he says about the UN, "Don't throw out the baby (whole structure) with the dirty bathwater," and lists numerous accomplishments that could go into the foundation of a real world government. Couldn't the new WCAssembly embrace these items somehow in its structure, for example, by establishing commissions on human rights, environment, world law/world court, etc rather than setting out to overthrow it?

Right now I don't know what path is going to make a breakthrough to the "elimination of the independence of the nation, national sovereignty and nationalism", and until I do I will support both WCPA and UN reformers. I suspect the WC Assembly will do likewise, given its broad constituency. Even the much narrower WGO Coalition contains both groups.

As to a political "party" for the realization of world government, it has been discussed several times in WGOC meetings and put on the WCA agenda. It has not received much support for several reasons: 1) a "party" is perceived as a divisive rather than a unifying strategy at this time, for membership would preclude participation in other political parties. 2) parties—at least in the US—are extremely expensive to launch and maintain and have not been effective in promoting their goals. 3) the left-of-center parties in this country have been disasters, such as the Peace and Freedom Party, the Citizens Party and the Unity Party of John Anderson. They may even have contributed to the frightening Reagan "landslides"!

On the other hand, the new WCA could create a constituency of globally-minded voters for global issues, global statesmen and—eventually—a global government without being a "party" as such. Instead, it would be more like an annual convention, putting its collective support behind a few selected vital issues. This is the approach of the Federalist Caucus and Citizens Global Action, which makes sense to me *at this time*. Who knows what *more* will make sense in 5 years?

Finally, to be politically effective requires *numbers,* and I have found in my fifty-plus years in the peace movement that world government per se just doesn't have much appeal—too complicated, perhaps. "World citizenship" on the other hand communicates well and, in fact, is "in." Therefore, in my thinking-out-loud I come to the idea that you could do well to do what you ask nations to do—merge some of your structures (outlined on p. 4) with the emerging WCA structure to be discussed Nov. 9 & 10. If you agree, I'd be glad to help.

Thank you for your letter of Sept. 18. Let me confess the secret of my speedy responses; I just don't have time to be less efficient. To avoid having to re-read a letter or pick it up twice, I try to reply immediately. Since you asked me to re-read your letter to Lucille Green of Aug. 29, 1988, I have done so and am pleased to send you my additional comments.

I certainly agree with your argument that the idea of unrestrained national sovereignty must be eliminated if we are to have "One World" of peace and happiness. Your proposal for a world unity party and your outline of its programs are certainly sensible and present a rational focus for consideration by individuals or groups desirous of eliminating the present war system. It reminded me of similar plans put forth by Kant, Rousseau, Bentham and other thinkers before them. The problem still remains: How do we get from here to there?

Are you not being too impatient, or expecting too much too soon? How are we to reverse traditions of nationalism that have been ingrained for centuries? Do we have the funds available to launch a massive media campaign which will soon be able to overcome the complacency and power of "the military-industrial complex? Of course, drastic change is necessary if we are to save our planet from destruction, yet the mention of "revolution" or "a world revolutionary force" turns away those who associate such terminology with bloodshed and oppression. I fear that the changes we both seek— despite the urgency of the need—can only come about slowly.

Oliver Wendell Holmes said: "The mode by which the inevitable comes to pass is effort." I believe that all we can do is to put forth our best effort and hope that "One World" can become a reality some day. I am not clear about what more you would want me to undertake than I am already doing as best I can.

You should recognize that we ARE making significant progress. The nation-state can no longer function independently in any important area and regional and global cooperation is a growing reality in many spheres (communication, health, environment, economics etc.) If all of us continue to do our best—as you are doing—I believe we will win the race between civilization and disaster.

Gertrude joins in sending warm greetings to you and Susan.

Appendix V
Mr. R. Ward Harrington's Letter
of Oct. 11, 1989

I had the pleasure of becoming acquainted with you, at a meeting in Dr. Lisinka Ulatowska's residence in New York City a month or so ago, and I have received the copy of your book, "One World" with the follow up, "Two Years After". A heavy schedule of work has slowed my progress in studying your work, but I will push on, and give you my comments later. I have read with interest your letter of 8/29/88 to Lucille Green, and have some comments to offer with respect to that.

It is very gratifying to see the clarity of your conviction of the need for an authentic world order under an effective governmental institution, but there are some questions in my mind about the choice of means by which you anticipate moving toward the realization of that goal.

You urge the establishment of "one party", to bring into unity all of the organizations and people who are striving for some solution to the problem of anarchy, injustice, and the threat of nuclear extension. Serious doubts arise in my mind as to the efficacy of such an approach. The crux of the problem, I feel, would be that the influence of major elements in many of these organizations would hold back any action of an effective nature. Strong elements in many of these groups draw back from "world government now". They prefer slow incremental movement that would offer the prospect of world government with no disturbance to prevailing privileges of establishment groups. The clarity of the focus and commitment which you bring to the matter, would be blocked by those who, rather than "revolutionists", are bootlickers of the prevailing establishment figures.

You very properly identify a key part of the problem as the independence of the nation, (with its absolute assertion of sovereignty). Your solution is not really a solution. It is merely a 'wishing away of the problem'.

You do not solve the problem of independently sovereign nation-states by saying, "Merge all nations into one world". The "sovereign and independent nations" will merely say, "We refuse", and since they are independent and sovereign, their pronouncement will prevail. There is a need for you to accept the full implications of your recognition, that the task before us involves *revolutionary* change. How can we overthrow the existing "independent and sovereign" nation-state institutions in a non-violent manner. Revolution by non-violent means lays a very demanding burden on us, but that is what has to be achieved. A mass movement with all the other organizations that have some interest in this, is the *least* likely way to accomplish the needed revolution. It seems clear that if a revolution is to be achieved, then there must be a "lean and mean" outfit that will seek the ways to achieve non-violent revolution. You will not achieve revolution by assuming the behavior appropriate for an English tea party, but that is the behavior that a very large part of the "world federation" movement seems to prefer.

The progress of human civilization has entailed and required the construction of increasingly larger and encompassing political institutions. Now we are at the point where we must make the last great leap in institution-building. We must construct the political institution for world order, which can establish justice and security for all people. We should have no illusions about the power that must exist in the world government authority. Some provisions of the U.S. Constitution may serve as some guide for this. Article XIV of this constitution states, "No State shall make or enforce any law which shall abridge the privileges and immunities of citizens of the United States; nor shall any State deprive any person of life, liberty or property without due process of law; nor deny to any person within its jurisdiction the equal protection of the laws."

Article VI says, "This Constitution and the laws of the United States, which shall be made in pursuance, thereof . . . shall be the supreme law of the land; and the judges in every State shall be bound thereby, anything in the Constitution or the laws of any State to the contrary, notwithstanding."

When we have world government established with power in these terms set forth, with respect to nation-states, then we shall have peace, order, justice and human dignity. We have a big job, achieving that goal and we will not achieve it by "nice words" or "gentle persuasion".

P.S. A *convoy,* in wartime, may provide a useful analogy for the concern I feel about your proposal to gather all organizations together. A convoy moves at the speed of its slowest members. Time presses on us. We should, rather, develop an agile and speedy "attack force".

Part Three

OUR WORLD

A Solid Base for Unity

Translate a Passage of the Chinese Poetry I Composed Recently as the Foreword

I have worked hard for
  a peace on earth forever
  and a happiness for mankind everywhere,
As the goals of the doctrine of *One World*
  I have developed earnestly for years.
There are two major obstacles remaining on the way:
    the independence of the nation as an original evil,
    and the national sovereignty as a modern curse.
Although more efforts are needed to wipe them out,
The outlook is bright and clear.

John Kiang
Oct. 1, 1990

抄近作念奴嬌詞一節代序

為萬世開太平,
生民立命,
費盡了心血。
多年來努力提倡,
"天下一家"學說。
獨立成灾,
主權作孽,
理想待貫徹。
放眼遠京,
秋水長天一色。

姜　逸　樵

226

I. Great Background

1. The Universe

The physical substance of our world is the Planet Earth, which belongs to the solar family with the sun as the center. In the solar family, the sun is larger than the earth by hundreds of thousands of times. Yet the sun is just a minor star at the edge of the Milky Way.

As a vast rotating system of billions of stars, the Milky Way is itself just one among billions of other galaxies in the universe with distances exceeding billions of light-years.

Thus in the universe the earth is just like a particle of sand. But it is huge when compared with the Moon. It is the mother planet around which the Moon revolves as her satellite.

The diameter of the earth is 7918 miles, about 4 times that of the Moon. The surface area of the earth is 196,950,769 square miles, about 13 times that of the Moon. Above the surface of the earth, there is an atmosphere very important to the existence of life. It is an insulation of temperature, protecting the earth from unbearable cold at night and unbearable heat during the day. The atmosphere extends up at least 1000 miles, and has four main layers. The lowest layer contains a shield of ozone at a height of 20 to 30 miles. It absorbs a lot of the ultraviolet rays of the sun and is the major defense of the earth against the sun's harmful effects.

The lowest part of the lowest layer is very agreeable air, up to about 50 miles above sea level. It contains water vapor and twelve gases. All of them help to make the earth a livable place. The most abundant of these gases is nitrogen, 78% of the total. It is in constant demand by bacteria in the soil as plant food. Next abundant is oxygen, 21% of the total. It is in demand by every living thing that breathes. Without it, there would be no plants, animals, or any living thing. Carbon dioxide is the most important of the other gases. It is the basic ingredient for making sugar and starch needed by animals and plants to keep them healthy. It is also the air that serves as the carrier of the water and the filter of the sunlight.

2. Long Life of Earth

According to geological marks, the earth has been over four and a half billion years old. This long time is generally divided into fifteen periods, each shorter than the one before. The later the stage, the greater its variety of land formations and life, and the more abundant the fossils. The earliest one is called Cambrian Period starting from 500 to 600 million years ago, and the latest one is called Holocene Period starting 10,000 years ago. These periods include more than six Ice Ages, each with cold and warm episodes.

The long living character of the earth is well maintained by its elementary recycling: Minerals become part of plants as the plants grow. Plants become part of animals, when animals eat them. When plants and animals die, they are slowly turned back into minerals. This process is at work all the time.

How long will the earth be living in the future? Scientific vision is that some billions of years later, the sun will have evolved into a luminous red giant and have a radius much greater than at present, perhaps reaching the orbit of Mercury. The oceans will have disappeared and the atmosphere will have lost its protective ability, and life as it is known today will have become impossible if only because of the intense heat. Under such circumstances the earth may not only cease to be a living place, but may even go out of existence itself in accordance with the stellar evolution. This will not happen, however, until billions of years later.

228

3. The Oceans

There is plenty of water on the earth. Of the total area of the earth, water surface has about 71%, amounting to 139,480,841 square miles.

The total amount of water the earth has is estimated to be 326 million cubic miles. The oceans contain about 97% of the total. Another 2% is frozen in glaciers and ice caps. This leaves about 1% in lakes, rivers and underground. So the oceans are great water reservoirs. Their water is too salty for direct drinking or irrigation, but is continually evaporating great amounts back to the land as fresh water to meet all actual needs. It is an ever-working hydrological cycle.

The oceans contain a tremendous wealth of minerals too. Each cubic mile of their water is estimated to contain more than 160 million tons of minerals. There are more than twenty varieties of these minerals. They include gold, silver, magnesium, as well as common salt. At the present time, the floating gold alone is enough to make four billion millionaires.

Not so intangible like the floating minerals is the great mineral wealth lying on and beneath the ocean floor. Already many undersea oil and gas fields have been found. It is beginning to look as though the ocean floor is even richer in these fuels than the land area of the world. In addition, large areas of the ocean floor are known to be covered with stones containing iron, copper, cobalt, nickel, manganese, and other metals. All of them are in great and growing demand, and are becoming harder to find in the land area of the world.

The oceans also contain tremendous stocks of plant and animal life. Among the marine animals, fish alone have more than 30,000 species. Most of the marine plants and animals are usable for food or products.

4. The Land

Of the total area of the earth, land surface has about 29%, amounting to 57,469,928 square miles. It includes all the continents and islands. The area of the continents in square mile is: Africa, 11,699,000; Antarctica, 5,100,000; Asia, 18,685,000; Australia, 3,201,000; Europe, 2,085,000; North America, 9,420,000; and South America, 6,860,000. The highest point is Mount Everest, 29,028 feet above the sea level; and the lowest point is the shores of the Dead Sea, 1286 feet below the sea level. About 10 percent of the land surface has good soils, and almost all of them have been cultivated to produce various crops as the most important resource of food. There is also a good portion of land which is used for pasturing to produce meats, milks and other food stuff.

Forests cover about 30% of the land surface. They produce material primarily for houses, furniture, paper and many other industries.

On and beneath the land there is fresh water. It is the most common and also the most precious natural resource, because it is indispensable to all forms of life. It makes possible for the land to be the home of hundreds of thousands of species to live together with a close relationship. Water resource has been developed for irrigation and lately for hydroelectric power.

Under the ground the land contains natural gas, oil, and coal for fuel and uranium for nuclear energy. It also contains more than 70 noteworthy nonfuel minerals for industries. Rocks are made up of minerals, and minerals themselves are composed of one or more of the 90-odd natural elements in the earth's crust. More than 1,500 different kinds of rock have been found so far.

There are deserts which cover over one third of the land surface. They are not useless either. They are the source of dry air which makes most of the other areas more agreeable for living. Hot deserts such as the Saharas are not an endless stretch of sand completely devoid of vegetation. Shrubs and grasses are part of their scene, and there are large areas of oasis, some covering hundreds of square miles, where land is extremely fertile. Cold deserts are all the Arctic and Antarctic regions, including ice caps and the tundra. If all the ice and snow in these deserts were to melt into water flowing down to the oceans, it would raise the sea level everywhere by about 200 feet to drown most of the lower and good lands.

5. Origin of Mankind

When and where did man start to appear in the long history of the earth?

According to evidences so far archaeologists and anthropologists have found, as early as four million years ago, man had appeared on the scene in eastern and southern Africa. One of the sites is known today as Olduvai Gorge. It is in the country of Tanzania.

In early times the Olduvai Gorge was probably a bit like the Garden of Eden pictured in the Bible. It was well watered. The rainfall was heavier and the dry seasons were shorter then they are today. They were lakes where now there are salt flats. There were deep rivers with mountains nearby. It was warm during the day and chilly in the evening. Due to favorable weather with adequate water supply, this area had plenty of vegetation and animals to provide food for the early man.

However, the Olduvai Gorge was not a perfect paradise. It was located too close to active volcanoes and too low to be free of flash floods. Hence, the people of Olduvai moved gradually, over thousands of years, from Africa into Europe and Asia. By about 500,000 years ago, men had lived in northern China and in Indonesia. The size of the brain and the bone structure of the face of the Peking Man and Java Man place them between Olduvai men and modern men.

Exactly when man reached the Americas is still the subject of debate. For a long time it was believed that some migrants walked from Siberia to Alaska across a dry Bering Strait between 20,000 and 16,000 years ago in the last glacial period when a great deal of water was locked up in the ice sheets and the sea level was over 300 feet lower than it is now. However, recent evidences indicate that man had been there earlier.

Finally man had succeeded in "island-hopping" from Indonesia to Australia by about 12,000 years ago.

6. Control of Fire

Thus, man wandered to the far corners of the earth. The only help the early people had for the long journeys was a few simple tools, and later, a magic fire.

The terrific energy of fire is the source of heat and light. Its control by man for service is an extremely old technical attainment, though the time, place, and original method will probably never be learned. The earliest evidence derives from a living site near Nice, France, that may have been occupied as early as a million years ago. About 500,000 years ago in European and Chinese sites, evidence for fire has been found in abundance. The movement of man into the northern cold areas was probably a direct consequence of his control of fire. By the last Ice Age fire is universally attested by the hearths within the living sites everywhere.

Fire helped man to conquer not only the vast cold regions, but also other animals everywhere from subduing big flesh-eating beasts by flame to chasing small infectious mosquitoes by smoke. Fire helped man too to eat fish and dry grains through cooking so as to increase the sources of subsistence greatly, and to develop agriculture by burning jungle and clearing fields.

It was fire too which helped man to produce pottery and glass, and to draw metals out of minerals through the art of metallurgy. Most of the increased available energy in modern times has come from heat originated by fire, such as that produced from coal, steampower and electricity.

Since its heat and light could provide comfort and protection, fire has become the center of family, focus of group activities, and signs of ceremonies such as smoking incense, memorial flame, torchlight and candle.

In short, fire was the first great discovery, perhaps the most important one man ever made. It is the deep foundation of his career and the general agent of his civilization. It is the mysterious power of fire that has distinguished man from all other creatures on the way up ever since.

7. Development of Tools

The control of fire was the beginning of a series of energy conversion by man for his own use. This series includes the application of wind power to sailing ships and windmills, the employment of water power for waterwheels, and the utilization of the power of dog, horse, buffalo and other animals for driving, riding, farming and hunting.

Along with the series of the conversion of energy there has been a significant development of tools.

Tools may be regarded as extensions of the body's physical endowment. The hammer, for example, is the lengthened arm with a harder and heavier fist at the end. Without tools, man would not be able even to survive, because physically he is inferior to many of the other creatures in strength, speed and some other qualities, and he could not compete with them in the struggle for existence.

The use of tools is not an exclusively human trait. Some insects, birds and certain mammals have used some naturally shaped tools. However, tool-making is almost by definition human, and the development of tool-using and tool-making in quality and quantity has enabled man to be the master of nature.

Since the development of tools is so essential to the rise of man, that to the most important materials used for tools has gone the honor of furnishing names for the ages of history of his civilization, five in order: Old Stone Age, Young Stone Age, New Stone Age, Copper Age, and Iron Age.

In the Old Stone Age, which may be traced back to several million years ago, man first appeared as a naked animal, and had practically nothing except some rough stones and perhaps a wood or bone stick as tools. The ability to use fire was limited, and no animals had been tamed for working. For these reasons, he could only maintain a very simple food-gathering life.

By the beginning of the Young Stone Age, probably 30,000 years ago, sharper stones were used for cutting. Rough hooks and lines were devised for catching fish. Better hunting tools were developed. Man started "taking to the air" by throwing spears and culminating in the invention of the bow and arrow. Dog was domesticated for chase. Better methods for using fire had also been discovered. Man then enjoyed a good hunting-fishing life.

Down to the beginning of the New Stone Age, about 12,000 years ago, stone tools had been notably improved, and of special importance was the appearance of the hoe and sickle sharpened from stone or bone, together with the earthern pot. These tools made possible for the development of a hoe-cultivation life. However, there still appeared no plow, nor any animal domesticated for wide and deep tilling. This is the main difference between hoe-cultivation and agriculture which did not develop until several thousand years later.

The Age of Copper began about 7,000 years ago. This age brought in for the first time the use of a metal called copper to make handy and efficient tools for the domestication of animals in taming, hiding, cooking, as well as for wool-works. Its quality was improved and application was extended when it was mixed with tin as bronze. More durable vessels and containers could be made with bronze, or by pottery, to store meat and dairy products in larger quantities for longer times. An animal-raising life for man was thus developed.

Finally came the Iron Age about 3,000 years ago. Iron is a metal, not only harder and more durable, but also more economical than copper or bronze for making heavy-duty tools possible to utilize animal and natural energies, such as the plow and harrow drawn by the ox or horse for field work, the rotary quern driven by the ass, the mill turned by water or wind for grinding grain, and the water-raising wheel for irrigation and drainage. This was the time favorable for man to grow an agricultural life.

It is remarkable that the development of tools with five ages has led the change of economic life into five modes: food-gathering, hunting-fishing, hoe-cultivation, animal-raising, and agriculture, and this change has had consequently a tremendous impact to the expansion of group life of mankind all the time everywhere.

8. Increase of Knowledge

It is amazing that man has worked his way up through the conversion of energies and the development of tools. How could he convert energies and develop tools? Basically it is through the increase of knowledge which is the key to the taming of energies and the making and use of tools.

Then, how can he increase knowledge? Generally speaking, there are three important ways: Invention, accumulation, and diffusion. Invention is the original and infinite resource of knowledge. It can make new things, perform labor in a more efficient way, and lessen the burden of mankind in its economic and cultural tasks. In a broader sense, it includes discovery and even development.

The importance of the accumulation of knowledge is next, if not equal, to that of invention. Scholars remind us that man would do well to realize that knowledge has been an accumulative process from which he is the chief beneficiary, and that all of his wonderful achievements would not be possible if it were not for this rich legacy; or that emergent novelty becomes truly significant only through accumulation.

Diffusion in its broad sense means the spread of knowledge through the factors of imitation, borrowing, suggestion, or migration, alone or in combination. Since diffusion can be carried by more people through more ways than invention, there have been schools of thought which emphasized diffusion over invention in the increase of knowledge.

In early times, man like other animals was largely occupied with the procurement of the most basic necessities of life, and had little time to think and act for anything else. Invention depended on accident, accumulation depended on memory, and diffusion depended on imitation. Since accident was unpredictable and unlikely to result in anything elaborate or complex, memory was usually gone with time and death, and imitation was limited by the little contact between the sparsely scattered and always hostile peoples, it was obviously very difficult to increase knowledge, and consequently very difficult to convert energies and develop tools. For this reason, it took some million of years for man to get through the Old

Stone Age, and more than 20,000 years to get through the Young Stone Age.

At last came the time when man's life was improved by utilizing some energies gradually converted and some tools gradually developed. He was able to gain some time to do some inventions. Meanwhile population grew roughly from 10,000,000 in the Young Stone Age, through 15,000,000 in the New Stone Age, up to 155,000,000 in the Copper Age. Trade and other contacts between peoples became frequent leading to a fast accumulation and wide diffusion of knowledge. As a result, knowledge increased remarkably, shortening the New Stone Age to approximately 5,000 years, and the Copper Age to approximately 4,000 years.

Later man's life was further improved. He was able not only to gain some time for invention, but even to save some money to stimulate it through specialization and competition in trade. At the same time, progress was made in the accumulation of knowledge by the use of writing to keep data and records, and by the formulation of theories for application. The Aristotelian school, for example, produced eight books on physics, four books on the heaven, and many on other fields. This progress made it possible not only to accumulate knowledge on a permanent basis, but also to diffuse it to more people and wider areas, thus to increase knowledge greatly since the early Iron Age.

However, great speed in the increase of knowledge had yet to wait until modern times.

II. Current Affairs

1. Machine Age

As stated above man has passed five tool ages: Old Stone Age, Young Stone Age, New Stone Age, Copper Age and Iron Age. He is now in a new age: the Machine Age, which replaces the Iron Age, since the simple tools made of iron are no longer adequate to characterize a time under the domination of complex machine.

Machines may be distinguished from tools in that the latter are relatively undifferentiated and may be used for more than one kind of operation, always under the control of the worker, whereas machines are designed to perform one particular function, with an accuracy, speed, or regularity not readily attained by the individual worker.

Simple machines have been in use since the potter's wheel, but it remained for modern man to develop them into a very complex structure, and also to convert more and more energies from water, coal, petroleum, and nuclear materials to actuate them. This conversion has been very drastic especially in some leading nations. For instance, "In 1850 work animals and human beings accounted for over 94 percent of the energy in the United States. Mineral fuels and water power accounted for the remaining 5.8 percent. In that year wood accounted for more than 90 percent of inanimate energy and coal for the remainder. The petroleum industry had not come into being. Wood largely disappeared as a source of energy during the latter half of the 19th century and is no longer considered a significant energy fuel. Coal became the most important source of mechanical energy and continued in that lofty position until it was replaced by petroleum and natural gas about 1950. The work animal has ceased to be a significant source of energy, and human beings accounted for less than one percent of the energy used in industry. The shift from muscular energy derived from food and feed to mechanical energy derived from mineral fuels and falling water is almost complete," according to *Zimmermann's World Resources and Industries.*

With the drastic conversion of energies from water, coal, petroleum, and nuclear materials to actuate machines, the world energy production has increased rapidly. According to the *United Nations' Statistical Yearbook,* in million metric tons of coal equivalent, it was 1,778 in 1929; 2,365 in 1949; 4,050 in 1959; 6,512 in 1969; and 8,027 in 1973.

Of the converted energies, only a small portion is for domestic use, most of them go to factories for production through assembly lines, automation, and robots. In assembly lines, parts are automatically transferred to, into, and out of a series of machines which perform successive operations on them. The only limiting factor on the productivity of the machine is the speed of the machine itself, since loading and unloading mechanisms are geared to the machine cycle. Thus the full productivity of the machine is realized, and the heavy manual effort formerly associated with many metal-working operations is reduced to a minimum.

Automation goes somewhat further or beyond the assembly lines in a production system that uses electronic computers or related equipment to regulate and coordinate the quantity and quality of what is produced. Automatic control of production is achieved in factories by transfer machines, which move a product from place to place for successive operations. Computers, transfer machines, and related equipment use the principle of "feedback" in which the input of machines is regulated by the machines' own output. "Feedback" is a new development truly unique to automation.

Robots go somewhat further or beyond automation. A robot is a mechanical device that can perform a task of manipulation or locomotion under automatic control. Industrial robots already are beginning to make a significant contribution to several manufacturing processes, such as loading and unloading punch presses, tending die-casting machines, spot-welding automobile bodies, and handling materials. Robot technology is crucial to the performance of modern missile guidance systems. Robots will surely play a major role in planetary exploration and in the exploitation of the ocean floor, and will eventually appear in the household.

Complex machines powered with energies have gone not only to the factories for industrial production, but also to the fields for agricultural production. Giant gasoline tractors, large gang plows, pulverizing harrows, and grain drills enable farmers to plow, harrow, and sow grain in one process. Likewise, at harvest time a combined header, thresher, cleaner, and bagger permits the execution of the harvesting process in a single operation.

So also go the complex machines powered with energies for transportation, communication, building and printing. In printing, for instance, a latest press can print, cut, fold and count no less than 1,000 thirty-two-page newspapers per minute.

In short, machine has almost gone everywhere for everything. It is indeed a Machine Age.

2. Science and Technology

In modern times, the increase of knowledge signifies the advance of science and technology. These two spectacles are the driving force of the Machine Age, and are the mysterious power that makes machines.

Science is viewed as an attempt by man to understand the physical world; technology is the attempt by man to control the physical world. This distinction may be briefly put as the difference between the "know-why" and the "know how". But technology for much of its history had little relation with science, for man could and did make various devices without understanding why he did. In modern times, however, science has been generally regarded as the big brother of technology.

The mother of the two brothers is invention.

The importance of invention was not duly and formally recognized until in 1474 when the Republic of Venice enacted the first patent law. Since then the idea of protection of invention by patents spread gradually through Europe to other countries. "The Patent System added the fuel of interest to the fire of genius," once remarked by Abraham Lincoln.

Later on, invention has been not only protected widely by some international agreements, but also promoted in various ways:

First, it is usually encouraged by various grants and awards. There are hundreds of foundations which make grants to invention every year. Of the awards among the famous ones are the Nobel Prizes.

Second, it is usually supported by official agencies, such as the U.S. National Research Council and Academy of Sciences, with public funds. There are a good number of countries a good portion of whose budget is directly or indirectly allocated for this purpose.

Third, it is usually well planned and systematically executed to produce the expected result. This is the way to make the so called "systematized invention", such as the semiconductor, and lately the super-conductor if successfully worked out.

Fourth, it is usually done in a well-equipped industrial or academic research laboratory. The basic difference between industrial research and academic research is that the former is much more than the latter to emphasize immediate and practical purposes of the invention.

Fifth, more and more specialists are organized into groups to work for it. Recently many important inventions are the result of collective efforts by super-teams. Hence "the inventor" as a peculiarly gifted personality with a special insight for seeing further into problems than other men becomes an anonymous member of a group of specialists.

Finally, better and better scientific instruments are produced to work for it. Top on the list are microscope and telescope which help the human eye tremendously for making invention. Successively many other important tools are developed and improved to meet research needs. In order to probe more deeply into the heart of the nucleus, for instance, smashing devices as long as up to several miles have been in use. Yet a super-collider of 53 miles long will be built soon with an estimated cost of $5.9 billions.

For these reasons together with strong competition, pressing demands, and many high incentives, the spirit of invention has been skyrocketing in recent years. Hundreds of inventions now come out each day in contrast to one in hundreds of years in earlier times.

In addition to invention, science and technology are also advanced by the accumulation and diffusion of knowledge through various ways. First is through modern library service which has been improved to help the study of science and technology with many efficient tools, such as indexes which indicate the place in a book in which particular information is to be found and classification schemes and subject headings which arrange books and other materials into a systematic order for easy access.

Second, through audiovisual media: In the United States, for instance, by the mid-1960s, in addition to 250 AM and 32 FM educationally-owned and operated radio stations, there were 109 educational television stations on the air. These media are especially effective in instruction for science and technology.

Third, through scientific and technical training: A great number of students complete their scientific and technical training at higher educational institutions every year. According to UNESCO Statistical Yearbook, for instance, there were in 1970 in sixteen representative nations, 176,267 in natural sciences; 224,335 in engineering; 113,975 in medical sciences, and 51,686 in agriculture.

Fourth, through international conferences: There were, for instance, approximately 1,300 international meetings on science and technology in 1969, as listed in the *World List of Future International Meetings,* by the U.S. Library of Congress.

Fifth, through publications: "Estimates of the total number of scientific and technical journals published throughout the world have run as high as 100,000. However, more realistic estimates seem to point to a world-wide publication of

241

about 15,000 significant journals, and one million significant papers per year,'' said *American Documentation*.

Sixth, through international trade: It was estimated that the trade of commercial countries in 1700 was about $125,000,000, which doubled in 1750. The increase has accelerated since the beginning of the 19th century. For instance, it was $1,400,000,000 in 1800, $20,100,000,000 in 1900, and $68,619,000,000 in 1929, according to experts. Most of the goods and services in the international trade are good representatives of science and technology.

Above all, there is a new tool that has facilitated the accumulation, diffusion as well as invention for science and technology to an extent beyond the limits of imagination. This new tool is computer. More will be told about it as a modern wonder.

3. Modern Wonders

As the driving force in the Machine Age, science and technology have brought forth many modern wonders, and among the most interesting are electricity and computers.

Electricity is a form of energy that occurs everywhere in nature—in space, in the atmosphere, in living creatures, in bulk matter, in chemical bonds that hold atoms together in molecules, and in the atoms themselves. Lightning bolts are an example of a large-scale display of an electrical effect. On a much smaller scale, weak electrical impulses are transmitted from one nerve cell to the next in animals, providing signals for the brain and other parts of the organism.

In modern times man has developed many techniques for harnessing electricity and putting it to use. Almost all industries have been drastically transformed by the ability to generate electric power and transmit it over long distances. Electric power runs motors in factories, provides building and street lighting in cities, and makes appliances and lights working in homes. Electrical phenomena are the heart of telephone, radio, television, and radar systems. In short, electricity is at work almost everywhere for everything. Its importance to man and his civilization may be ranked only second to fire. It is indeed a power wonder.

Computer is a device that performs calculation and processes data. Modern computer is the culmination of a long line of devices used as aids to calculation, including fingers, tallying pebbles, the abacus, and the adding machine.

There are two basic types of computer: analog and digital. The analog computer was introduced in the 1940's. It can add, subtract, multiply, divide, and perform more complex mathematical operations. The digital computer is designed to process discrete numerals. It functions fundamentally as a numerical transformer of coded information. It came later but has gone faster than the analog computer, and has had the most profound influence on science, business and industry. Scientific and mathematical research have been vastly accelerated by the use of computers; in business, management practices have been revolutionized by computer methods, and in industry, computers play the vital role of control in automation. In addition, computers have proved matchless as repositories and correlators of the massive amounts of data generated by a more and more complex society in every wake of life.

The rapid progress of computers in recent years may be viewed in the increase of their capability, speed, storage, and in the minimizing of their size. A scientific problem that took an hour on a big 1950 machine at 1000 operations per second can be run on the fastest computer of the 1960's in less than half a second. Computers of the 1970's operated at internal speeds up to 100 times of the speeds of their counterparts of 10 years earlier with the storage volumes increased up to twentyfold. The miniaturizing breakthrough in the 1970's came with the invention of the microprocessor. A piece like one half of a chewing gum can contain up to 3,000 transistors, equivalent to a room-sized computer of 10 years ago. With the size drastically minimized, so also the cost. Computers can be used in every office and even in a kitchen.

In less than 50 years, computer has progressed to be good quickly and precisely not only for calculation and data processing, but also for memory, control, guidance, plan, design,

243

and many other functions that usually require a lot of thinking. It is indeed a brain wonder.

4. Modern Wonder Works

In addition to modern wonders, science and technology have also accomplished a great number of modern wonder works, especially through biology, chemistry, and bio-chemistry, in food, clothing, housing and medicine.

In food: Man has been doing such unheard-of things as doubling the rate of growth of pigs and other meat animals; increasing animal products, such as making a hen to lay 100 more eggs a year, and a cow to produce 200 more gallons of milk a year; producing tasty and nourishing foods out of such odd things as wood, seaweed, and pond scum; growing crops in deserts and other places where none grew before; and making four large corncobs growing where only two small ones grew before. Most significant, however, is the increase in yields of the principal crops. In the decade of the 1950s, they rose about 25 percent for the whole world. Since then more progress has been made by the Green Revolution in a number of developing countries through the adoption of new high-yielding varieties of wheat and rice with the use of chemical fertilizers and pesticides.

In clothing: In the thousands of years before the last century, man developed only three basic fibers for clothing: silk, wool, and cotton. Now man-made fibers have become so numerous that it has been necessary to classify them into generally 17 basic classes, determined by their chemical base, and each of them must be labeled as belonging to one of the basic classes for identification. Various beautiful clothes made of synthetic fibers with less expensive prices are pouring into markets by the millions every day.

In housing: Man has learned how to double the timber crop of forests for house-building and furniture-making in recent years. In addition, he has been able to produce plastic materials having the hardness of stone, the transparency of glass, the elasticity of rubber, or the insulating ability of mica.

In combination with suitable fillers, these materials are readily molded into products characterized by strength, lightness, dimensional stability, and resistance to moisture, moderate heat, sunlight, and other deteriorating factors. These materials have made construction works much easier and better.

And in medicine: In the last century, Louis Pasteur developed the germ theory of disease, Joseph Lister carried out pioneering studies of infections and antiseptics, and Robert Koch made early findings of specific agents causing diseases, which led in time to the production of immunizing substances. Subsequently more and more progresses in medicine have been made. They include better obstetrical and child care, the use of vaccines and antitoxins, and the discovery of many effective drugs from aspirin to penicillin. As a result, a number of old diseases have been prevented and even eliminated, and the expectation of life has risen from an average of 25 years in the middle of the 17th century to over 70 years at the present time in many regions, and is predicted to pass over 100 years in the next century. Lately with the help of effective anesthetics significant progress in surgery and genetic engineering is most amazing. Artificial organs have been used to replace real ones, and transplantation has been carried out for many organs including kidney. Some doctors have tried to transplant heart, not just with human heart, but even with animal heart.

5. Modern Evils

It seems in some cases that man has outplayed God. But he is still living under the shadow of the tree of knowledge that produces good and evil at the same time as designated by God. So, coming along with the wonders and wonder works brought forth by science and technology in modern times, there have been a lot of evils, and most common among them are pollutions in the air and water, and the solid waste.

Air pollution contains vast quantities of various pollutants: Carbon monoxide from gasoline, diesel, and jet engines, sulphur oxides from factories, apartment houses, and power plants; and other compounds including nitrogen oxides and hydrocarbons. Automobiles alone are pumping more than 500,000 tons of carbon monoxide into the air every day. All of them are poisonous. They damage virtually everything that exists, corrode machinery, and deface buildings. The most dangerous constituents of air pollution is carbon monoxide. It is a colorless, tasteless and odorless gas, and is a merciless killer. In addition, billions upon billions of specks of dust, particles of ash, and minute flakes of paint and varnish are constantly rising into the air. Most of them remain suspended for days and weeks, sometimes for years. Mingling with the poisons, they form the witches' brew so called smog, fouling the air and causing diseases.

Waste heat is a special form of air pollution and is the final product of all uses of energy. It blows out with smoke and gas into the air from chimneys and various exhaust systems and has had a great effect on weather in some regions.

Waste heat also is a special form of water pollution. It is introduced into streams and lakes by the water which is used by power plants for cooling purposes. It is estimated that at the present time more than 200 trillion gallons of water is flowing through the power plants of the world each year to keep them cool. This is not only a waste of huge quantities of energy, but also a threat to aquatic life. Since heated water holds less oxygen, fish suffer loss of appetite, digestive problems, difficulty in breathing, and reduced rates of reproduction.

The transfer of dangerous elements of air pollution into water is another source of water pollution. But more serious are the sources from agricultural waste, municipal waste and especially industrial waste. For a long time, streams and lakes have been used as dumping grounds for industrial wastes. Industrial wastes also put poisons into the water. Mercury is only one example. Over the years much mercury has found its way into the sea and through the food chain has made its way into the bodies of such predator fish as swordfish. Many are now no longer fit to eat.

Other serious sources of water pollution include coal mining and oil leaks. In the United States, for instance, it is estimated that by 1973, 13,000 miles of streams and 145,000 acres of lakes and reservoirs had been adversely affected by acid mine drainage and siltation from coal extraction. Oil leaks in great quantities have occurred from time to time especially on the sea. In 1967, for instance, an oil tanker Torrey Canyon was wrecked off the southwest coast of England. More than 117,000 tons of crude oil were spilled. The oil spread out over a wide area of the English channel and the bordering coasts of England and France. More than 50,000 sea birds were killed, either by the oil or by the detergents used to clear the oil from the beaches. It would be several years before the marine life of the area was back to normal. Lately on January 28, 1989, about 250,000 gallons of diesel fuel have spilled off the cost of Antarctica from a sunken Argentine oil ship. It is estimated that 30,000 penguins, many other birds and mammals, mainly seals, were in peril; and also on March 24, 1989, the Exxon Valdez, a 987-foot tanker owned by Exxon Shipping Co., struck Bligh Reef about 25 miles from Valdez, the northernmost ice-free port in the United States, spilling an estimated 270,000 barrels or 11.3 million gallons of oil into the Pacific Ocean. It is the biggest oil spill in the United States. Soon the oil had floated over a 3,000 square-mile area and killed thousands of birds and sea otters along the central Alaskan coast.

Most lately there were three accidents of oil leaking occurring on the same day—June 23, 1989 in three states of the United States. One was a Greek oil tanker that spilled more than one million gallons of fuel drifting at least 20 miles and washing onto Rhode Island shores. One was a Uruguayan oil tanker that spilled about 800,000 gallons of fuel in the Delaware River near Wilmington, Delaware; and the third one was a tug-driven barge that spilled about 250,000 gallons of fuel in the Houston Ship Channel at Galveston Bay, Texas.

The dirtiest source of the air and water pollutants is solid waste. In addition to the common trash and garbage, solid waste includes such familiar things as worn-out TV sets, refrigerators, automobile bodies, and empty cans, bottles, jars, and their caps. The United States alone every year in the 1960's had to junk 7 million automobiles, and to dispose 125 million tons of urban solid wastes including 55 billion cans, 26 billion bottles and jars, and 65 billion metal and plastic caps. How to dispose the ever-increasing solid waste? If burned, it greatly contributes to air pollution. If dumped at sea, it pollutes the water and creates "dead seas". If put into open dumps, it prepares a breeding ground for rats, flies, and other such disease-carrying pests. If dumps are covered with dirt as landfills, water percolating threatens people living around, and also contributes to the pollution of streams and lakes.

The difficulty to dispose solid waste was clearly demonstrated some months ago by the garbage barge Scow with a fruitless search down and up the Atlantic Coast and across the Gulf of Mexico for a place to unload 3,100 tons of non-toxic waste, about one seventh of that produced every day by New York City. The Scow returned in desperation.

As solid waste increases rapidly everywhere, the difficulty of its disposal has developed to be one of modern evil legacies which will be discussed after a quick look into a hazardous condition of the nuclear power plants.

Nuclear power plants have been developed rapidly since the 1960s in most of the industrialized countries. They are producing electricity for peaceful use. Although there are various safety measures and regulations for their process, they are still under a hazardous condition. In the nuclear power plants of the United States in 1987 alone, for instance, there were nearly 3,000 "mishaps," 430 emergency shutdowns and 104,000 incidents in which workers were exposed to measurable doses of radiation, according to *Public Citizen's* report.

The well known cases on the danger of the nuclear power plants in recent years are the accidents of the Three Mile Island, near Harrisburg of the United States and the Chernobyl, near Kiev of the Soviet Union. The Three Mile Island case occurred on March 28, 1979 when one of the two reactors lost its coolant, causing the radioactive fuel to overheat and a partial meltdown. Some radioactive material was released. The cleanup work is still going on after ten years, and the cost is expected to reach $1 billion before it is completed.

The Chernobyl case occurred on April 16, 1986, when explosion and fire in the graphite core of one of the four reactors released radioactive material, spreading over part of the Soviet Union, eastern Europe, Scandinavia, and later Western Europe. Some people were killed immediately, and the threat to the wide areas is still not quite over.

6. Modern Evil Legacies

In addition to the difficulty of disposing solid waste, there have been a number of other modern evil legacies, such as "dead sea", "acid rain", "greenhouse effect", "threat of ozone", "nuclear waste" and "computer virus".

Pollutions have not only made some rivers, such as the Hudson of New York, so unclean almost like city sewers, but also caused some lakes and seas to be slowly dying. Pollutants have led to a drastic reduction of commercial and sport fishery in Lake Erie. For example, in 1925 about 25,000 pounds of cisco were harvested while in 1960's only about 1000 pounds were harvested a year. A steel plant has discharged into Lake Michigan every day 13,750 pounds of nitrogen that enhances algae growth, and 54,000 pounds of oil that is damaging aquatic life and waterfowl. As a result of heavy pollution, the concentrations of numerous salts in Lake Ontario have been rising exponentially with severe declines in the catches of most commercially valuable fish. Increasing accumulation of organic waste in the Baltic Sea, where water circulation is minimal, has resulted in a steadily decreasing oxygen concentration in the water. In some areas, especially in deeper waters, oxygen concentration is zero and almost no forms of aquatic life can be supported. The "dead sea" phenomenon may lead, as some scholars warned, to the death of the whole ocean.

"Acid rain" is the pollution of sulfuric acid which is a dangerous chemical. Even a drop of it falling on skin could cause a very painful burn. Recently each year more than 400 billion pounds of its water content are dumped upon the surface of the earth, mainly from fossil fuel burning and coal mining. It sinks into the ground, stripping away or leaching precious calcium from the soil. Since tree growth is correlated with the calcium content of the soil, trees suffer. Further more, it destroys fish, people, and the structures.

"Greenhouse effect" is the trapping by the atmosphere of the heat energy radiated from the sun. The effect is named after the solar warming observed in greenhouses below a ceiling of glass. A normal level of the effect is necessary for a normal climate of the earth, but such level has been threatened by the increase of the carbon dioxide content of the air through the burning of coal, oil, and gas, and the heat waste. On a worldwide scale the carbon dioxide content of the air has been increased by about 25% in the past 100 years. Lately scientists have been concerning the destruction of the Amazonian rain forest which is believed to have played a key role in maintaining the normal level of the greenhouse effect of the world. This forest has been destroyed by cattle raising, slash-and-burn agriculture and the predatory extraction of hard timbers. It is estimated that in 1987 manmade fires destroyed 70,000 square miles of the forest, an area roughly the size of West Germany, and in 1988 an even bigger area went up in flames. At this pace, this largest remaining tropical forest will be destroyed by the end of the century. The fires contribute at least one-tenth of global emissions of carbon dioxide which is affecting the greenhouse effect. Other gases, particularly methane and nitrogen oxide, drift high into the atmosphere. It is possible that they are helping to create an alarming hole in the ozone.

Ozone, as noted early, is a shield at a height of 20 to 30 miles in the lowest layer of the atmosphere. It absorbs a lot of the ultraviolet rays of the sun and is the major defense of the earth against the sun's harmful effects. In 1974 two scientists first warned that the ozone shield was being eroded by industrial chemicals called chlorofluorocarbons for producing refrigerant, plastic foamer, computer chip solvent and fire extinguisher. A hole has been found in the ozone. Even as critics contend that much of the hole is naturally occurring, and will expand and shrink over time, strong evidence has made the erosion of ozone a fact irrefutable. It is a serious threat to life on earth, and if not stopped quickly it is projected that 130 million extra cases of skin cancer alone will occur over the next century.

Nuclear waste is the spent, used, or old fuel from nuclear reactors which are now hundreds in number over the world. It is literally hot and still radioactive dangerously. Some of the radioactive elements in the old fuel will decay to safe levels in a matter of hours or days. Others take centuries. One form of plutonium loses half of its radioactivity only after 24,000 years, and some will remain for 280,000 years.

Storing nuclear waste is harder than keeping just about anything else devised by man or created by nature. It needs to be isolated for at least 10,000 years, which is three times longer than the tomb of Tutankhamen in Egypt has lasted.

Now we come to the last topic—computer virus. In only a very short time computers have become the bedrock of how the developed world operate. They handle the bank transfers, half a trillion every day in the United States alone; they guide planes through the air and back to the land; they monitor hospital patients, predict weather, run phone systems, and store any data imaginable from household accounts to military operations. But a virus has developed in them. It works the same way as how other viruses invade humans, replicating or infiltrating until the body is overwhelmed. When a computer gets sniffles, a whole system can catch pneumonia. The computer disease caused by the new virus can spread at the speed of light. "There is a potential risk that matches the destructiveness of a nuclear attack," warns Donn Parker, and authority on computer crime. A computer virus broadly believed to have programmed in early November, 1988, by Cornell University student Robert Morris as a "hacker", within hours fouled up some 6,000 interconnected computers in a defense-university network. Estimates of the damage done together with repairing costs run from $20 to $95 million. What Donn Parker fears most is that a "hacker" may be a terrorist who can introduce a virus to get a whole computer network fatally stricken at any minute.

7. Endangered Earth

The 130 million extra cases of skin cancers as mentioned above are just a sample of the consequences of the ozone erosion if it is not stopped quickly. More general and more serious is that according to computer projections, the combined force of the erosion of ozone and the development of the greenhouse effect "could drive up the planet's average temperature 3° F to 9° F by the middle of the next century. That could cause the ocean to rise by several feet, flooding coastal areas and ruining huge tracts of farmland through salinization. Changing weather patterns could make huge areas infertile or uninhabitable, touching off refugee movements unprecedented in history." This was warned by the *Time magazine* of New York in its issue of Jan. 2, 1989.

For this and some other good reasons, *Time magazine* has meaningfully named the "Endangered Earth" as the planet of the year in order to call for a "universal crusade to save the planet."

The Planet Earth has been endangered in many ways, but there is a common symptom: the upsetting of the balance of its ecosystem.

In an overall view, nature can be thought of as a giant ecosystem composed of four groups of constituents: nonliving elements, such as the climate, rocks, and water; the green plants as the producers; animals as the consumers, and bacteria as the decomposers. As a dweller on earth, dependent upon it for foods, raw materials, and space for activity, man himself is an integral part of the ecosystem, and his welfare necessarily depends on its balance. But man has threatened this balance ever since he appeared on earth in various ways deliberately or through ignorance. The most deliberate way is the removal of resources in order to use them, such as hunting, fishing, lumbering and mining. The other way is to damage resources through use, such as the effect of farming on the soil. A more ignored situation is the injury resulting from damage to native vegetation, such as when the destruction of trees hastens the runoff of rain water and thus reduces the amount that soaks into the ground, thereby aggravating erosion and the effects of drought.

As a result of the threat by man, the ecological balance of the earth has been very difficult to maintain since the early time in some areas. For example, soil erosion had begun to be serious in southern Italy long before the end of the Roman Empire. The over-grazing of the upper Hwang Ho valley had made the land red and bare and the water "the muddiest great river in the world" hundreds of years ago. The famous cedars of Lebanon have shrunken to a tiny grove, and the soil cover of the Judean upland has worn so thin that bedrock is at the surface everywhere.

Yet, in early times, the threat by man to the balance of ecosystem was limited by smaller numbers of population and simpler tools. Now in modern times, population has increased by hundreds of times, and machine has increased the tool power also by hundreds of times, so has been the increase of the threat by man to the balance of ecosystem. The increase of this threat may be exemplified by quickening soil erosion, vast mining extractions, the serious menace to wildlife.

"Perhaps the most serious single threat the earth now faces is the widespread loss of topsoil," warned an expert. Because of this loss in recent times nearly a million square miles of new deserts has been created, and much greater areas are fast becoming deserts. Beginning as the sapping of soil fertility, a process of erosion will end in what can be described as a new, man-made cataclysmic geologic era, in which the fertile food-producing soils are being swept in the rivers and the seas. In "The State of the World 1989," the Worldwatch Institute reports: "The Earth is losing 24 billion tons of topsoil a year—as much as covers Australia's wheat belt—chiefly from overtilling."

The situation of mining extractions may be reviewed with some interesting comparisons. As long as two thousand years ago when Alexander the Great took Susa and Persepolis, he is reported to have seized precious metals valued at $190 million, the accumulation of a thousand years or more. The gold mines of the South African Rand have produced that much in less than a year. It is estimated that modern mines could equal the entire output of the Athenian silver mines in Laurion in less than a year. Modern blast furnaces would take less than one day to produce the world's total output of iron in 1750. Six million acres in the United States have been destroyed by strip mining. That is two Connecticuts. The work goes on at the rate of 4,650 acres per week, or one more Connecticuts per decade.

As regards to the menace to wildlife, it is estimated that since 1600, 359 species of animal life have become extinct. The rate accelerated in the last century, largely due to man's destruction of suitable habitat. It is also estimated that 100 species of mammals have become extinct in the last two thousand years, 75 of these having become extinct in the last two hundred years. Thus the rate has accelerated, from one species about every 70 years to one about every 3 years. At the present time, about 500 species of wildlife are so rare that they are in peril of becoming extinct. Among them are such birds as the California condor, the Eskimo curlew, the monkey-eating eagle of the Philippines, and the short-tailed albatross in some western Pacific islands; and such land animals as the Florida panther and Key deer, the white rhinoceros and giant sable antelope of Africa, the Tasmanian wolf, and the Australian banded anteater. One of the sea animals in danger is the world's largest mammal, the blue whale. When fully grown, it weighs more than 100 tons and is more than 100 feet long. During the 1930's more than 14,000 were killed every year. Today, probably not more than 600 are left in the oceans.

8. Imperilled Man

In addition to the many species which are in peril of becoming extinct, there is an important one. It is man himself. For many other species, the major extinguisher has been man. Now in his own case, too, the villain is himself. A species is deemed to be imperilled when its habitat is imperilled. Now, by upsetting the ecological balance of the earth with power tools and increasing population, together with modern evils and their legacies, man is not only fouling his own nest, but even destroying it, thus, he is imperilling himself badly.

Man is also imperilled by his new tool—machine in a particular way as warned by "The Empire of Machines" appearing in the *Yale Review*, Oct. 1933. For thousands of years, man's status as a super creature has been achieved and assured by using tools. Now this very status is being threatened by a powerful tool itself. This tool is modern machine, which brings man into the grip of forces beyond his control and of purposes not his own. It does not necessarily threaten his physical life, but it does threaten his supremacy, his freedom of will, and his control of his own destiny. It is driving man, lashing him onward at a racking pace towards some goal which he cannot even foresee, and leaving no choice for himself. Meanwhile he is more and more depending on the machine and more and more losing self-reliance; and the more he gets from the machine, the more vulnerable he becomes. For instance, a break in an electric power line by a thunderstorm can not only bring production to a halt, but can also stop the cooking of food and ruin vast quantities of provisions in deep-freeze lockers. Blackout has occurred very often in many cities and in many areas by accidents.

Under the dominance of machine there is a craze growth in economy. It begins with mass production which is brought forth by modern machine. Mass production needs more raw materials, more markets, and more consumers to consume more; and for earning more, it needs a fast flow of products from raw materials through markets to consumers. Hence, various temptations including enormous advertising through news media, come into play to make more sales for more profits. This is the way leading to the rise of economic growth. All drive and optimism are bound up with this growth, and this growth has become synonymous with hope. An addiction of this growth is the unwritten and unconfessed religion of modern time. Yet, it is a craze growth, a growth without equilibrium for the whole and without foresight in the long run. It is imperilling man by leading to some kind of explosion sooner or later, as warned by experts.

Along with the craze growth in economy is the current lifestyle in favor of great quantity: more clothes, more houses, more cars, more highways, more urban centers, and more in some special cases, such as 50 toys for an average kid, 3000 pair of shoes for a certain first lady, and almost a quarter of a million calories in energy consumption per person per day in some areas against only 2000-3000 calories per person per day for the ancient man before the use of fire. The craze growth in economy together with the fancy lifestyle has made modern man the great abuser of resources on one hand and the great producer of wastes on the other. He is imperilling himself in both roles.

Finally man is imperilled by a wide gap between material achievements and social reform, or say, between advancing technology and traditional ideology. This is a cultural lag, and is nothing new, since man throughout history has been a genius at solving technical and physical problems while a near-idiot in making moral and social adjustments. But the cultural lag has assumed its most dangerous role in modern times, because the gap between the two major segments of civilization is so wide that it appears to be advancing and changing, at the speeds of a super-sonic jet and of a horse and buggy respectively. This wide gap is imperilling man more than anything else.

It is sad that man is in double trouble: he is imperilled and his planet is endangered along with many modern evils and modern evil legacies. Yet there are more of his headaches to be discussed separately.

III. More Headaches

1. Rapid Growth of Population

The rapid growth of world population in modern times is a sharp contrast to its slow development in the long past. According to estimates, in the Olduvai times about four million years ago, the world population was no more than a million. At the culminating time of the Old Stone Age about 32,000 years ago, it was about 5,000,000. At the culminating time of the Young Stone Age about 12,000 years ago, it was about 10,000,000, and at the time of Rome Empire around 2,500 years ago, it was approximately 150,000,000. The rate of increase in the period from the Olduvai times to the culminating time of the Old Stone Age averaged about one person per year, in the period from the culminating time of the Old Stone Age to that of the Young Stone Age, about 160 persons per year, and in the period from the culminating time of the Young Stone Age to the time of Rome Empire, about 14,000 persons per year.

At the beginning of the Christian era, it is estimated that the world population was 200 to 300 million, and during the first sixteen centuries of this era, it increased about 250 million, representing a doubling in 1,600 years. In 1650 at the dawn of the Industrial Revolution, the world population was about 500 million, and in the 320 years up to 1970, it increased sevenfold, to nearly 3.6 billion. In 1650 it was growing at a rate of approximately 0.3 percent per year. That corresponds to doubling time of nearly 250 years. In 1970 the rate of growth was 2.1 percent per year, and its doubling time is 33 years. Thus, not only has the world population been growing exponentially, so also has been the rate of growth.

1970 the world population increased by six million per month. That is one metropolitan Chicago, much more than the whole of such countries as Israel, Denmark, Finland, Hunduras, or New Zealand, and even more than the total of a number of smaller countries. Yet today that rate of six million per month is accelerating, not slowing.

If the rate of 33 years' doubling time stayed constant—stayed constant and did not increase at all—in 800 years the world population would be about 60 million billion. Such a population could be housed in a continuous 1,000 story building covering the entire planet earth, with 3 to 4 square yards of floor space per person. The ultimate fantasy is that at the current growth rate would be only a few thousand years, before the visible universe would be filled with people, and the mass of humans would be expanding at the speed of light.

Now, back to the reality and not looking ahead too far, the world population has reached the mark of 5.1 billion in 1988, up by 90 million in 1987 alone. That totals 1 million births than deaths every four or five days. With the actually moderated rate of growth, the world population would be more than 6 billion in 2000, more than 12 billion in 2050, and more than 24 billion in 2100. If this kind of growth is not checked drastically and effectively, a food crisis alone will soon set a red light to the future of mankind.

2. Food Crisis

Food is the most commonly needed material with the most generally limited resources. It produces calories for human body to maintain life and activity. According to experts, 2,700 calories a day are generally needed by a person doing active work, with 3,000 as high standard and 2,200 as minimum. Estimates tell that before 1940, slightly less than half the people of the world lived with minimum calories. By 1955, the number of people receiving less than 2,200 calories had risen to 66 percent. There is simply no question that today as many as 10 to 20 million people are slowly starving. It is often said that at least 10,000 people a day die of starvation directly or die because an inadequate diet does not protect them from disease. On this basis, malnutrition accounts for about one in every 13 of the world's deaths today.

It is significant that most of the people receiving less than 2,200 calories a day belong to the developing countries. The main reason for this is that these countries have more population, while produce less food. For instance, of the 3.3 billion world population in 1965, only 1 billion, or 31% were in the developed countries, nearly 2.3 billion, or 69% lived in the developing countries. As regards food production, cereals are the predominant food grown in most of the developing countries, but they produced only 40% of the world cereal supply while the developed countries produced 60% in 1965. On a nutritional basis, the per capita cereal production in the developing countries averaged less than 0.2 tons that year, equivalent to 1,860 calories per day, whereas in the developed countries, each person's share was more than 0.5 tons, equivalent to about 5,000 calories per day.

Much more serious than the phenomenon of disproportion in the distribution of population and food supply, however, is the limitation of farmland. According to experts, of the 35,700,000,000 acres of the earth's land surface, only 2.5 to 3 billion acres, or about 7 percent, are good farmland with all the essentials necessary for food production and almost all of them are already under cultivation. In addition, drawn from the drier, colder, wetter, more rugged or less fertile lands are some 6 billion acres of pasture, which are generally weighed by some experts as having 20 percent of the productivity of good farmland, making a total of about 4 billion acres of good farmland, or its equivalent. This total has to provide not just for food, and too, for houses, clothes, roads, airports, industrial sites, power lines, etc. The big trouble is not only that there is little hope to get rid of the limitation of good farmland, but also that there is a sharp decrease of its per capita share in proportion to the rapid increase of population of the world. By 1830 when the population reached the first one billion mark, every person had as much as four acres of good

259

farmland. By 1930 when the population doubled to two billion, every person had two acres, and by 1975 when the population doubled again to four billion, every person had only one acre.

Opinions on how much good farmland is needed per capita vary from 2.5 to 1 acres, and no one assures that less than 1 acre is enough. If the population continues to grow as predicted before, the per capita share of good farmland would drop to one half an acre in the 2020's, and to a quarter in the 2070's. This means that the good farmland, if taking no more out for other uses, will have to produce food twice in the 2020's and four times in the 2070's, as much as it did in the 1970's.

It is true that significant increase in the yields of crops, especially through the Green Revolution, has been achieved since the 1950's as noted earlier. But the momentum of the increase has lost in the 1980's, and its driving force—the heavy use of chemical fertilizers and pesticides for the soil and crops, has threatened the environment in various ways.

It is also noted earlier that there are wonder works in food production in modern times. Their contribution to the whole food output is not significant, however. New ideas such as to grow crops with soiless technique of hydroponics, and to convert petroleum into a pure protein, have not proven to be practical either.

Surely, there exists a kind of food which is not limited by the land. It is fish from the sea. Some believe that this resource could supply mankind with more than enough food, since fish is rich in protein and the sea is immense in scope. Actually it is a resource mostly confined to areas of shallow water, about 5 percent of the oceans, or less than 2,000,000,000 acres. Even in these limited areas, edible fish yields are low. For instance, in the English Channel which is one of the world's rich fishing spots, the catch has been estimated at only about five pounds per acre. Overfishing would result in a drop in both the daily catch and the size of the fish. For these reasons, sea fish has not become an important food resource. The world harvest from the sea increased about 6 percent from 1950 to the mid-1960's. In 1968, 60.5 million tons were harvested, less than one percent of total world food production. Experts say that the maximum that can be hoped is about 100 million tons, or up to 150 million tons according to some optimistic opinions. Even the highest figure cannot help very much to brighten up the gloomy outlook of the food situation of the world.

3. Energy Shortage

The Machine Age is characterized by using more and more machines, and also by consuming more and more energy, because the more machines are used, the more energy is consumed. According to statistics, for instance, by the mid-1960's, the annual world consumption of fuels was equivalent to about 4.7 billion metric tons of coal, compared to about 900 million metric tons in 1900, a rise of 500% in more than 60 years. Are there enough energy resources to meet the rapid increase of energy consumption?

Some optimists say quite enough. They believe that controlled thermonuclear fusion is enough for from one to two billion years. They also see the possibility of using the immense gas from the zone around Saturn.

Thermonuclear fusion is the greatest power of the universe. It drives the sun and stars. Various efforts have been made to research on controlled thermonuclear reaction, the quest to harness the hydrogen fussion process. If perfected, reactors using this process could literally generate power forever because the virtually limitless hydrogen from the oceans would be the fuel. But it will be some time before any type of fusion reactor can be worked out, according to experts. lately on March 23, 1989, researchers of the University of Utah and the University of Southampton in England announced that some kind of success in fusion reaction has been achieved. Their announcement has not yet been verified.

Spacecraft Voyager II's discovery of a doughnut-shaped zone around Saturn containing gases 100,000 times hotter than the surface of the sun may one day help scientists develop a revolutionary new source of energy on Earth. At the present time, however, this is a prospect just as remote as Saturn is to earth.

So, in reality, most of the world's available energy today is from fossil fuels: coal, oil and gas. Unfortunately the reserves of the fossil fuels are awfully limited. Experts estimate .17 Q (a Q is 1 quintillion British thermal units, equivalent of 40,000 million tons of coal) as the 1970's annual level of the world consumption of energy. At this level alone, the world's known reserves of fossil fuels will be exhausted in 132 years; and their estimated reserves, in 2832 years. But if the rate grows to 2.8 Q per year as they assumed to meet the adequate need of a population of 7 billion, the known reserves will be exhausted in 8 years, and their estimated reserves in 173 years.

Most critical among the fossil fuels is the situation of oil. This resource is not only unevenly distributed, but also is very limited. It is estimated to be only 3 percent of the total reserves of fossil fuels, while its output has recently accounted for about one half of the world's energy consumption. The prospects for its potential supplements, such as oil shale, tar sand, and vegetation, do not appear very bright too. None of them can be feasible in great quantities nor at low prices. Their resources are not renewable either, except for the plants growing on the land. But the world needs the land to produce food and materials for clothing and housing much more urgently than to utilize it in yielding gasoline.

Gas among the fossil fuels is a twin sister of the oil, with an even smaller reserve, about over one half of that of oil.

The reserve of coal is accounted for over 90 percent of the total resources of fossil fuels. It has been taken out from the coal mines very fast in modern times. During the second half of the 19th century, the annual world production of coal rose from about 180 million tons to nearly 930 million tons. In the first half of this century, it rose to more than one billion. Now it is more than 2 billion and is still rising.

Coal is too "dirty" for a clean environment. Its burning produces oxides of sulfur and solid waste particles, and the mines themselves empty waste into the atmosphere. The techniques needed to extract and utilize this fuel, such as better more economic ways for gasification, liquefaction and artificial oil, remain to be developed.

Recently the fission power of nuclear energy has attracted wide attention. However, its resource, uranium, is not unlimited. According to experts, if a world of 7 billion population needs 2.8 Q of energy a year for adequate use, the known reserves of uranium available at a cost of from $5 to $30 per pound will last only 4 years, and the estimated total reserves may strech the time to 8 years. The picture looks better only when the price of the uranium is raised much higher. Currently the problem on using the fission power of nuclear energy concerns not so much about its resource, but about its hazardous nature, especially after the accidents of the Three Mile Island of U.S.A., March 28, 1979, and the Chernobyl of the Soviet Union, April 16, 1986.

In addition there are energy resources of natural forces. Well-known among them is water power. It is widespread, especially in Africa. Surprisingly enough, its total amount is accounted for only 1.8 percent of all existing power resources, and its limitations are probably much more than commonly supposed.

Other energy resources of natural forces include ocean tides and currents, geothermal steam, windmill, and solar heat. Up to date, however, none of them can be feasible in great quantities nor at low prices in general, like the potential supplements to the fossil fuels.

It is no wonder under these circumstances and for these reasons that the warning of an energy shortage has been heard here and there.

4. Shortages of Other Resources

The warning of an energy shortage concerns its availability rather than its resources. There are many other resources which may sooner or later run into shortage, however. Among them most important are non-fuel minerals, forest, and water.

Non-fuel minerals are the most important raw materials for industry. Their vital role in the development of civilization is implied in the terms used for the major periods of history, such as Bronze Age and Iron Age. Today, an industrial economy requires more than 70 different non-fuel minerals from which metals and inorganic chemicals are derived. Among them, most common and most important is iron, the principal machine material. Others include copper, aluminum, lead, tin, chromite, manganese, bauxite, cobalt, mercury, tungsten, zinc, platinum, nickel, molybdenum, gold and silver, in addition to various nonmetallic minerals such as sulphur, phosphate and potash.

The production and consumption of the non-fuel minerals have increased enormously since the Industrial Revolution. During the 370 years from 1500 to 1870, for example, the world's iron output increased from about 50,000 tons to approximately 12,000,000 tons every year. A single Lake Superior iron mine in the 1930's produced every two weeks a volume of ore equivalent to the great Pyramid of Egypt, which required the toil of vast hords for several decades and has been long regarded as one of the most stupendous works of man. In 1929 the United States produced more zinc than all the world did in the first fifty years of the last century. The copper production of the world in 1929 was more than twice as great as the estimated production for all history up to the 19th century. The world's consumption of iron now doubles every 10 to 15 years, copper every 12 to 15 years, and aluminum every 9 years. During the period from 1950 to 1970, the world consumed almost half of the zinc which had been produced until that time. At present, Americans use steel at the rate of more than one half ton per person per year. If everybody in the world consumed steel at this rate, the world's known reserve of iron ore would be exhausted in about 20 years. If everybody in the world consumed copper at the present American rate, the known reserve of copper ore would be exhausted in less than 10 years.

True, prospectors will continue to find some new deposits of these resources, scientists will continue to find some substitutes for them, and technicians will continue to find some

264

better ways to extract them. But is would be very difficult to match them with the vast demand of industrialization for the growing population, and ultimately, there is only so much of them in nature's bag. Man is using them up faster and faster and is getting closer and closer to the bottom of the bag. He may run out of them completely someday, and not just get into the trouble of their shortage.

Forests cover about 30 percent of the land surface of the world, or about 10 billion acres, and about 2 acres per capita at the present time. The products of the forest are the primary material for house, furniture and paper. While in the face of a probable reduction of forest lands, the rate of wood removals has increased remarkably, up about 50% between 1945 and 1965. It is estimated that the world demand for wood will increase two or even threefold in the next several decades in view of the tremendous needs for building many million of new homes for decent settlements over the world.

What is more, the range and variety of the products of wood are widening all the time. In addition to various papers, wood can now be turned into textiles as light as feathers and as soft as silk and into plastics as heavy as lead and as hard as iron. Unbreakable eyeglass frames and rigid hammer heads can be made out of it as easily as brittle toothpicks and bendable hair combs and brushes. While most woods are highly inflammable when dry, some of the products derived from them, including some of the paints, are fireproof. There are also some wood products which contain poisons, such as wood alcohol, and moisture-absorbing surgical cotton.

With the heavy demand for its products and also with the continuously decrease of its acreage per capita in proportion to the rapid growth of population, a shortage of forest may become a real threat in the near future, if there are no effective measures taken to prevent it from further drastic depleting and to manage it efficiently.

A shortage of water may become a real threat too. There is indeed plenty of water, but about 97 percent of its total is salt and contained in the oceans, and about 2 percent is frozen in glaciers and ice caps. The rest is only about 1 percent. Yet, of this 1 percent, 95 percent is underground. In the United

States, for example, there is about 20 to 30 times as much water underground as in all lakes, streams and rivers combined.

Consequently, all life on the land is supplied by only a small portion of water in the recycling process of rain and snow. About 875 cubic kilometers of water are evaporated from the sea each day. Of this, 715 cubic kilometers return to the sea through precipitation, while 100 cubic kilometers are blown over the land precipitated there. About 100 cubic kilometers of water are evaporated from the land each day, and they are also precipitated mainly over the land. Half of the total water precipitated over the land, whether its source is land or sea, runs off into the sea through rivers and streams. Thus the maximum available if the runoff could be fully utilized would be 200 cubic kilometers a day, while almost everything needs a lot of it. For instance, producing a pound of dry wheat requires 60 gallons of water; a quart of milk, some 1,000 gallons; a pound of meat, between 2,500 to 6,000 gallons; and an automobile, some 100,000 gallons. Each American, directly and indirectly, uses up almost 2,000 gallons each day. Given the existing rate of water consumption, 100 years from now the United States will be overspending its expected rainfall income by 100 percent.

Meanwhile the demand for water is growing everywhere at an accelerating pace, not only because of population increase, but also because of the vast needs of industry and agriculture. Thus, besides the fresh water from the recycling process of rain and snow, man has had to use much ground water, of which the reserve is being depleted all over the world. It is estimated that the people of Europe have been taking out 3 times as much water from the underground reserve as is returned by the water cycle and that Americans are taking out twice as much.

So, water shortage is something not imaginary anymore, it is real now.

5. Natural Calamities

As a matter of fact, water shortage has occurred here and there. For instance, in 1988, in the United States, a three-month drought baked the soil from California to Georgia, reducing the country's grain harvest by 31 percent and killing thousands of head of livestock. In the 1930's the Great Plains of this country received only from 10 to 15 inches of rain yearly, much less than usual. The surface soil dried out, caked and cracked. The worst of the drought area was the central and southern plains, in parts of Kansas, Oklahoma, Texas, Colorado, and New Mexico. This area was wheat bowl, now it became a dust bowl, and its good soil had "gone with the wind."

Great as the Dust Bowl was, nearly all the people survived, but such is not the case when drought strikes a heavily population region where people are completely dependent for each year's food supply on the crops produced in that year. In recent history, a single drought-produced famine had cost the lives of a million people in India and several million in China. Lately in Ethiopia, drought enlarged a terrible famine in 1984–1985 and another one in 1987.

Closely related to water shortage are forest fires such as caused by lightning. In the area near the equator, there are several thousand lightning storms a day. But it is rare for any of them to start a big fire, because the ground and vegetation are damp and even if a fire starts, it is almost alway doused by the heavy rain that accompanies the storm. It is a very different matter in other areas where sometimes are very dry. For instance, in the United States, lightning caused 11,068 forest fires in 1960 alone. In the fall of 1988, parched by the lack of rain, the western forests of this country including Yellowstone National Park, went up in flames for several weeks. With rainfall in March and April of 1987 less than 50 percent than normal, forests in the western portion of Heilongjiang Province in northeaetern China became dangerously dry. A fire was first reported on May 6, and not until rain began falling on May 24 was it brought under control. In this period high winds and dry weather combined to spread the fire over more than 2.4 million acres of land, 70 percent of which was forest. The fire destroyed three towns and several villages, and forced the evacuation of 60,000 people. Some 200 people died in the flames.

Ironically, there are floods here and there too. This phenomenon does not prove that there is too much water rather than not enough. It occurs primarily because the weather distributes the precipitation in the recycling process of rain and snow unevenly and often in the wrong place or at the wrong time. For this reason, floods have been one of the greatest trouble for mankind since ancient times as told by the Bible that a great flood once covered the earth and destroyed all living things except Noah, his family, and the form of life he saved with a great ship Ark; by Mesopotamian flood stories, and by the first recorded flood of the Yellow River of China in 2297 B.C. It is also noticeable that floods have occurred as a natural disaster more widely and more frequently than any others. No region is spared from flood damages, not even the deserts where sporadic floods form fearsome walls of water that rush down normally dry channels and wash out roads and bridges. Flooding destroys crops, disrupts the life of cities, and takes a toll in lives. Floods in the United States, for example, cause an average annual loss of 80 lives and damage of about $1 billion. Just 100 years ago at the end of May, 1889, a flood swept Johnstown of Pennsylvania away and took over 2100 lives. Last year a flood devastated Bangladesh and killed up to 20,000 people.

Weather is also responsible for terrible storms, such as tornado, hurricane, cyclone, and hailstone. Tornado is a small extremely intense whirlwind formed by a severe thunderstorm. It occurs in all parts of the world. It can break trees many feet thick and lift cattle and even automobiles high into the air. It kills thousands of people and destroys property valued at about a billion dollars every year over the world. In the United States, about 700 tornadoes are reported each year. Fortunately not very many of them touch down the ground to make big destruction.

Hurricane develops from minor tropical depressions over most of the warm oceans. A full-grown hurricane may reach speeds of 150 to 200 miles an hour, last 12 to 15 days and travel more than 3,000 miles. Five to eight big hurricanes occur every year. Their great size and intensity make them the most dangerous and destructive of all storms. For instance, on

Sept. 21, 1934, a hurricane killed more than 4,000 people on Honshu, Japan; from Oct. 2–7, 1963, Hurricane Flora killed up to 7,000 people in Haiti and Cuba; and on Sept. 20, 1974 in Honduras, Hurricane Fifi struck northern section of the country, leaving about 8,000 dead and 100,000 homeless.

Cyclone is a type of hurricane characterized by a whirling storm that tends inward around a center of low atmospheric pressure. It occurs often in the Indian Oceans and inflicts heavy damages there. On Oct. 5, 1864, most of Calcutta was denuded by a cyclone, about 70,000 killed. Lately, on Oct. 16, 1942, a cyclone devastated Bengal, about 40,000 lives lost; on May 11–12 and June 1–2, 1965, cyclones killed over 47,000 people of East Pakistan; on Nov. 13, 1970, in East Pakistan, about 200,000 were killed by tidal wave driven by a cyclone from the Bay of Bengal, over 100,000 missing; and on Nov. 19, 1977, a cyclone struck Andhra Pradesh State of India, killing about 10,000. Elsewhere on Dec. 25, 1974, in Darwin, Australia, a cyclone destroyed nearly the entire city.

Hailstones are balls of ice, falling separately or in lumps, usually associated with thunderstorm, with sizes up to larger than a baseball. They can be very destructive, injuring persons and animals, breaking glass panes, and severely damaging crops by beating them to the ground. For instance, on April 20, 1989, hailstones hit Sichuan provine of China, killed about 87 people and injured 4,200 in 10 cities. More than 90,000 homes were damaged in Luzhou, 60,000 in Gulin County, and 4,300 in Zigong City; and 52 air force training aircraft stationed in Luzhou were impaired.

In addition to the natural calamities related to weather, there are still others such as avalanches, volcanic eruptions and earthquakes.

Avalanches are still more or less related to weather. They are mass of snow, ice, mud, etc, which slide down steep mountain slopes, and make sudden killings and damages. For instance, on Jan. 10, 1962 in Peru, an avalanche down Huascaran, an extinct Andean volcano, killed more than 3,000 people; on Oct. 9, 1963 in Italy, an avalanche of landslide down into the Vaiont Dam, causing flooding and about 2,000 people were killed; and on Oct. 21, 1966 in Aberfan, Wales, an avalanche of coal, waste, mud, and rocks killed 144 persons, including 116 children in a school.

Early record of volcanic eruption showed that on Aug. 24, 79 A.D. in Italy, the eruption of Mt. Vesuvius buried the cities of Pompeii and Herculaneum, killing thousands. Recently, on Aug. 26–28, 1883 in Netherlands Indies, the eruption of Krakatau destroyed two thirds of the island, and killed about 36,000 people; on May 8, 1902 in the West Indies, Mt. Pelee erupted and wiped out the city of St. Pierre, killing about 40,000 people; and on Nov. 14–16, 1985 in Colombia, the eruption of Nevada del Ruiz buried most of the town of Armero and devastated Chinchina. An estimated 25,000 were killed.

Earthquake is a shaking of the ground caused by the breaking and shifting of subterranean rocks under immense pressure. Its great vibrations may cause most terrible destructions, big fires in the cities and rapid waves in the oceans. Earthquakes are numerous. On the average each year, there are a great one, 10 major ones, 100 destructive ones, and 1,000 damageing ones. Only a few great ones in recent history are reported here as samples. On Jan. 24, 1556 in Shensi, China, a deadly earthquake killed up to 830,000; on Nov. 1, 1755 in Portugal, a severe earthquake leveled Lisbon and killed up to 20,000; on Jan. 13, 1915 in Avezzano, Italy, a big earthquake left 29,980 dead; on Sept. 1, 1923 in Japan, a big earthquake desproyed one third of Tokyo and most of Yokohama, and killed over 140,000; on Dec. 27, 1939 in northern Turkey, earthquakes destroyed the city of Erzingan, killing about 100,000; on May 31, 1970 in Peru, an earthquake left about 50,000 dead and 17,000 missing; on July 28, 1976 in China, a big earthquake devastated 20 square miles of the city of Tangshan, estimates vary from 240,000 to 700,000 dead, and on Sept. 19–20, 1985 in Mexico, earthquakes devastated part of Mexico City and three coastal states, killing about 25,000.

6. Uneven Distribution

It is known that most of the natural calamities are caused by weather and the way the weather to do damage is mainly through an uneven distribution of heat and precipitation. This uneven distribution also has a great effect on the daily life of everything, since both heat and precipitation are indispensable to all forms of life, and they are things for which no substitutes exist.

The uneven distribution of heat can be exemplified by some typical places. For instance, Singapore, at the southern tip of the Malay Peninsula, has an average yearly temperature of 80° F; Manaus, Brazil, and Bombay, India, each have 81° F; and Khartoum, Sudan, has 84° F. while the average yearly temperature of the coldest inhabited places is between 10° F, such as Barrow, Alaska, and 3° F, such as Verkhoyansk, Russia.

The distribution of precipitation is just as uneven as the distribution of heat. For example, the average yearly precipitation in Cherrapunji, India, is 457 inches, or more than 38 feet. On the other hand, there are places like Yuma, Arizona, that have only 3 inches a year. Yet, there are places drier. For example, in Salah, Algeria, and Arica, Chile, the average yearly precipitation is close to zero. By the way, Arica held the world record for the longest period with no rainfall: 14 consecutive years.

Closely related to the uneven distribution of heat and precipitation is the uneven distribution of vegetation. The most vigorous growth of natural vegetation is in the rain forests of the tropics. Here thousands of species of plants flourish in wild, colorful profusion. As there is little seasonal change in this hot moist region, each plant has its own individual time schedule, so that there is continuous shedding of leaves, budding, flowering and fruit bearing.

In contrast are the trees of the seasonal forest which extends from the tropics to the temperate and polar zones, both north and south. Many of the trees become dormant during part of each year, while others lose all their leaves in one season.

Twenty percent of the earth's land surface is covered by dry deserts where conditions are too harsh for vegetation to develop except in some cases. Few of them are actually rainless, however. Shrubs and grasses may be seen here and there.

271

In addition to the dry deserts, there is a wide cold desert which lies far to the north known as the tundra, covering a strip across Alaska, northern Canada and northern Europe. With long cold winters and short cool summers, its natural vegetation is limited to ground covering of grass, lichens, and stunted brush. This is so much alike above the tree line of the high mountain ranges in other regions.

There are also great grasslands that stretch across the inland basins of the temperate zone in northern Asia, northern America, Australia, southern America and southern Africa They have long provided food for grazing animals from buffalo and wild cattle to domesticated cattle and sheep.

It is natural that the uneven distribution of vegetation makes some difference in economic life of the people in the various regions, but it is not as much as the difference made by the uneven distribution of fossil fuels and minerals since the Industrial Revolution. Before this Revolution, the world economy was essentially agricultural, and its basic prerequisites are soil and water. Although soil as well as water is not evenly distributed, they are widely scattered, the differences between regions were not essential, and therefore, no great inequality existed in the world economy. Modern industry is founded on iron, which is the principal machine metal, and coal, which is the primary provider of power to run the machines. The main deposits of these two minerals occur concurrently in a belt which extends from the Mississppi Valley of North America through Central Russia. Their combination has prompted this belt to be known as the industrial heart of the world, and has made the countries in this belt to have developed generally ahead of others and to be richer than others.

Of the two minerals, the known reserves of the coal are even more unevenly distributed. Asia has almost one half of the world total of 5,113,899 million tons. North America has about 34 percent, Europe has about 13 percent, Africa and Oceania each have about one percent, and South America has only about one third of one percent. It would prolong the inequality of the world economy, if coal remains as a major resource of energy in the long future.

Currently oil has emerged as a very important resource of

energy. This fuel is much more limited and unevenly distributed, however. More than 60 percent of the world known oil reserves are in a small area of the Middle East. Most of the other countries have nothing at all.

It is the Industrial Revolution too that makes the distribution of population more uneven, because in general, people in the industrialized countries are more conscious in controlling the growth of population, probably due to the desire for leisure, education, advancement, and material goods, while people in the developing countries pay less attention to the increase of population. Thus at the present time, North America, Europe, and some part of East Asia, have an annual rate of population growth of 0.8 percent, while in Africa, the Middle East, Indian subcontinent, Southeast Asia and Latin America, the annual rate of population growth is 2.5 percent.

With the rapid growth of population, these countries need more and more food, and with the price for oil going up, most of them need more money to purchase it for minimum use. For these and other reasons, the distribution of wealth has become more uneven in recent decades. The poor countries have to live on aid and loan from the rich ones. As a result, the external debt of the poor countries has grown to roughly $1.3 trillion, with an increase of some $60 billion a year. Interest payments of about $80 billion a year have reversed the traditional net flow of capital from the industrial to the developing countries, leading to a net capital transfer from poor to rich countries nearly $30 billion annually. This burden has sapped the poor countries of their economies, lowered their living standards, and increased their political unrest.

7. Drug Abuse

As the distribution of wealth becomes more and more uneven, some people of the poor countries themselves directly or indirectly, are selling abusive drugs to the rich countries, so as to make easy money.

There are many abusive drugs. Very well known are opium, cocaine, and marihuana. Opium is the basic drug for narcotics which include purified alkaloids obtained from opium, such as morphine and codeine; derivatives of morphine, such as heroine; and the synthetic morphinelike drugs, such as meperidine and methadone. More than twenty different narcotics may be found somewhere in the world.

Opium is produced from an annual plant of from 2 to 4 feet high, with white, pink or purple flowers. The plant requires cultivation under special conditions of soil and climate, and is native to Asia Minor. It is probable that opium was used by man before the dawn of written history. In the Odyssey, Homer referred to the power of opium as to assuage grief. In the 9th century, Arabian physicians were aware of the use of opium, and Arabian traders introduced the drug into the Far East.

The major effects of opium are on the nervous system and gastrointestinal tract, inducing a state of indifference to pain and anxiety. For some people, the drug lessens fatigue, alleviates depression, and reduces interest in sexual activity; and for some users, it brings about an unusual sense of well-being. If it is used several times a day for a few days, an addiction develops in the user. More of the drug is needed to get the same effect obtained when it was first used, and if not satisfied, there would appear a lot of trouble, such as running nose and eyes, anxiety, yawning, cold sweating, generalized body aches, and even nausea, vomiting, loss of appetite, and increase in body temperature, blood pressure, and the rate of respiration.

Cocaine is an addictive alkaloid drug known as "coke" or "snow", and its related drugs such as crack known as freebase, and amphetamines, known as "ups", "pep pills", or "speed". Cocaine is obtained from the leaves of the coca tree and related species. The tree is indigenous to Chile, Peru, and Bolivia, but it is now cultivated in other countries as well.

The action of cocaine is to paralyze nerves, especially sensory nerves, and produce anesthesia in the affected areas. When cocaine in small amounts reaches the brain through the circulating blood, it tends to produce a very sudden pleasurable sensation that is often called a "flash" or "rush". This feeling leads some people to become addicted to the drug. Cocaine also increases the constriction of blood vessels. It is too a cell poison, and if it is present in an area for too long or in too high a concentration, it will kill the cells. Its addiction is one of the most difficult drug diseases to overcome. Its effect may threaten pregnant woman and her baby.

Marihuana is a mixture of leaves, stems, and flowering tops of a hemp plant. Although this plant is probably indigenous to Central Asia, it now grows wild throughout most of the world and can be cultivated in any area that has a hot season. It has been used in medicine for some thousand years in many areas and later for pleasurable effects. There have been some new drugs related to it, including LSD, DMT, DOM or STP.

The most consistent effect of marihuana is a change in mood. It usually produces a good feeling, enhanced self-esteem, and relaxation. These mood changes are frequently accompanied by changes in sensory perceptions. Distances may appear greater, and time intervals may seem longer than they really are. Sensory stimuli may also take on a more novel quality so that ordinary sounds or objects may seem aesthetically more pleasing or interesting, leading to a "high" level of intoxication. All the effects are actually visual and auditory illusions that are often accompanied by agitation, feeling of panic and other psychotic symptons, and sometimes, cause a decrease in emotional control, giving rise to impulsive behavior. It is said that thirty percent of heavy marihuana smokers will lose their physical capabilities to function as a sex partner, and one hundred percent of males who smoke marihuana over a long period of time will lose their desire for sex.

The three major abusive drugs—opium, cocaine, and marihuana, together with their related ones, are working vigorously to find their ways to wherever money is available. Necessarily, the rich countries are their destination. They have not only spoiled many people of the rich countries, but also have ruined the morality, vitality, and social order of these countries. According to a 1988 U.S. Justice Department study, for instance, half to three-fourths of the people arrested for serious crimes tested positive for illicit drug use. Drugs can lead to crime, such as murder, assult, prostitution, robbery, theft, and burglary. Drugs and crimes often go hand in hand.

As more and more abusive drugs are trafficking into the rich countries, drug abuse is spreading widely in the streets, schools and sports fields and is creating an epidemic of addiction. In 1980 there was an article entitled "Drug Abuse: America's $64 Billion Curse" and in 1988 the auther, Carl T. Rowan, wanted to change the subtitle to $150 billion curse.

As the amount of money involved in drug abuse is so astounding, it is no surprising that more and more people are entering into the illicit drug business. In the United States, for example, an average of 2,568 arrests are made daily for possessing, selling and making drugs, according to a recent report of the FBI.

Along with the daily arrests are daily drug seizures. But the seizures announced by law enforcement authorities with fanfare are barely denting the street supplies. It is said that the supply of heroin alone in New York City amounts up to 200 tons a year, worth about $360 million. Yet all seizures of this drug through this country in 1988 were no more than 8 tons. Dealers of the abusive drugs absorb the seizures simply as a cost of doing business, and they regard arrests merely as a way of life.

There are supply centers of the abusive drugs in the Middle East, South Asia, South and Central America. Most notorious is the "golden triangle": the northern portions of Burma, Thailand, and Laos. It is a lawless region, and satanic realm.

To smuggle the abusive drugs from their supply centers to the black market are networks of various gangs and cults with kingpins as their leaders. They are ever involved with mysticism. Lately on May 4, 1989, in Matamoros, a border area between Mexico and the United States, a drug cult was discovered and its ringleader was slain, after 15 people were killed as human sacrifice in a series of its satanic rites, making the scene like a human slaughterhouse, according to eye witness.

276

8. Terrorism

The horrible scene as reported above has been created by terrorism much more often than by drug cults, however. Human slaughter is not a regular business of the drug cults. It is their occasional satanic rite. But terrorisim demonstrates human slaughter to be its professional work. It is actually a satanic business.

Terrorism may have originated from political assassination which has been a staple of political life since Brutus stabbed Caesar. In the 50 years between A.D. 235 and 285 in the Roman Empire, for example, there were 26 emperors. Only one of them died a natural death, while all the rest died by intrigue or counter-intrigue through some sort of terrorism. In the Middle Ages, kings and princes were often kidnapped and held for ransom by terrorists.

Since early modern times terrorism has flourished in the Middle East. Under centuries of the Ottoman rule, not only the Jews but also other groups used violent means to counteract Turkish control. In 1918 the British united with the Arabs to free the Holy Land from Turkish rule. Jewish and Moslem terrorism continued under the British mandate. The Jewish terrorist group Irgun was active until the founding of the state of Israel in 1948, which gave rise to the Palestinian terrorist movement supported by some Arab and Moslem states. Consequently modern terrorism soon developed to world wide. People were riveted to their televisions and radios awaiting news from the Olympic village at Munich, Lod Airport in Tel Aviv, and the embassies in Bogota and Teheran.

Most deplorable in modern terrorism is that its victims are usually innocent and civilians including women and children, mainly because of its changes in weapon and strategy. The greatest change in weapon is from the early stab for individual attack to modern bomb to hit indiscriminate target. Bombing was used in the 19th century by Russian nihilists and by anarchists in Europe and America. Now more sophisticated bombs from hand grenade to car bombs with timing and remote controlling devices have been used widely.

The new strategy adopted by modern terrorism is sophisticated too. It tries to make show aiming at the people watching rather than at the actual victims. The main goal is to acquire a soapbox for expressing a position on a controversial issue, or is in attempt to advance a certain obscure political cause. A side goal is to provoke the opposition into violent reaction, thus providing an excuse for further terrorism. Along with the new strategy there has appeared state-planned terrorism, leading to state-directed violent retaliation against terrorism, such as U.S. bombing of Libyan cities in April of 1986.

As a show and for more exciting and attracting, modern terrorism picks up famous persons for kidnapping, big airplanes for skyjacking, and dangerous targets for shootoutings. Terrorists are encouraged by the great adventures. A major hostage seizure is a sensational television production. Persons sidetracked by life suddenly see themselves or their news on the screens. In the 1970's there was an average of one incident of international terrorism each day, and in 1985 alone there were 812 cases. In Northern Ireland since 1969 there have been more than 2400 deaths and over 27,000 injuries due to terrorist activities in this period with over 30,000 shootings and more than 11,000 actual or attempted bombings. The more active area for terrorism in modern times is Lebanon where terrorist shootings and bombings have become almost a daily routine affair. Lebanon had been a beautiful country, but now it is a real hell.

Since terrorist news are so numerous that sometimes there appear several in a page of a daily paper. For instance, there was nothing but reports of terrorist activities in the full page no. A4 of South Bend Tribune, Dec. 27, 1987. The headlines are quoted with some excerpts as fellows:

"Grenades in Spain USO club wound 6 Navy men: A lone assailant threw two hand grenades into a Christmas-trimmed USO club Saturday evening and wounded six U.S. Navy sailors on shore leave, one of them seriously."

"3 bomb blasts kill 1, harm 40 in Pakistan: Three car bomb blasts rocked two downtown shopping areas within seconds Saturday, killing one person and injuring 40 on the eve of the eighth anniversary of Soviet intervention in neighboring Afghanistan. About four blocks of shops were damaged, including some of the most expensive and fashionable in Islamabad.''

"Terrorist call mother, newborn hostages healthy: A Frenchwoman reported to be a hostage of Palestinian extremists has given birth to a daughter. She was among a group of eight Europeans reported kidnapped at sea by Palestinian terrorists.''

"Grenade accident in Nicaragua hotel kills 2: A hand grenade accidentally exploded in a Matagalpa hotel while a Canadian woman was handling it, killing her and an army officer.''

"West Bank, Gaza quiet after wave of violence: Israeli soldiers kept a heavy guard on Christmas pilgrims in Bethlehem Saturday, but life was returning to normal in much of the occupied territories after a wave of violence in which at least 21 Arabs were killed.''

"3 guerrillas captured by Israeli troops: Three Palestinian guerrillas wearing Israeli army uniforms crossed the border from Jordan, but were intercepted and captured by Israeli troops after a brief firefight that wounded one guerrilla . . . The army said the three belonged to the Palestine Liberation Front. The Front is a PLO faction headed by Mohammed Abbas, who engineered the 1985 hijacking of the Italian cruise ship Achille Lauro.''

Yet, experts on terrorism fear more bloodshed may be in store. They are concerned about "techno-terrorism," the use of hard-to-detect plastic explosives, and hand-held missiles. They think the effect of a terrorist attack on some energy facility would be more serious than a major earthquake. And they even worry that terrorists may be able to get some small nuclear weapons, such as the newly developed 58-pound nuclear "backpack" bomb that can be carried by one person, smuggle it into a big city, and detonate it to destroy the whole city and kill all its people.

IV. War as Cancer

1. War Fever Up

As terrible as terrorism is, it is yet just a trivia when compared with war, which has been a cancer threatening civilization ever since, and its fever has been going up and up in recent centuries along the drastic development of modern weapons, as demonstrated by the increase of the intensity, extensity, magnitude, severity, and cost of war, according to *A Study of War* by Professor Quincy Wright.

The intensity of war is reflected in the duration of battles, their number in a war and their total in a century. A battle consists of the fighting during a period of time in which hostile forces are uninterruptedly in contact with each other. This period has through most of history been limited by the rotation of the earth and the consequent difficulty of operation at night. So the duration of a battle has always been for a few hours in the daytime, and fighting at night has not been very common. But this has been less true in recent wars, owing to changes in military technique. While in the 17th century, 96 percent of the battles lasted for a day or less, in the 18th century, the figure was 93 percent, in the 19th century 84 percent, and in the early 20th century only 40 percent.

The average number of battles in an European war has grown from less than two in the 16th century, about 4 in the 17th century, about 20 in the 18th and 19th centuries to over 60 in the first forty years of the 20th century. The total number of battles fought by the principal European nations in a century has increased from 87 in the 16th century to 892 in the first forty years of the 20th century. It is worth to note that Napoleon fought more battles than Alexander the Great, Hannibal and Julius Caesar combined.

The extensity of war may be measured by the number of belligerents in a war and by the area covered by a war. The number of belligerents in a war has risen from less than 3 in the early modern times to 33 in the first World War and up to 57 in the second World War. The spread of the war area is manifested by the fact that the European nations fought no important battle outside of Europe from 1550 to 1750. But from 1900 to 1940 alone there were 248 extra-European battles.

The magnitude of war may be fairly represented by the size of armed forces. Before the 16th century in Europe, armies were mercenary, and they seldom exceeded 20,000. In the 17th century, arimies often reached 50,000, even 60,000; and about three in a thousand of the European population were under arms. In the 18th century, Marlborough, Prince Eugene, and Frederick the Great had armies of 80,000 or 90,000 men. Napoleon had as many as 200,000 men in certain battles, and at times he may have had 1,000,000 men or 5 percent of the French population mobilized. There was some diminution in the size of armies after 1815, but in the later half of the 19th century, the armies of the great nations grew again. Before the outbreak of the first World War, there had been about 5,000,000 men in the armed forces in Europe. During the war, the total mobilization reached more than 63,000,000, about 12 percent of the population of the actual belligerent nations, and 36 percent of their active male population. Twenty years later in the second World War, the total mobilization amounted to more than 92,000,000.

The severity of war has been greatly enhanced by the rapid development from a limited war to a total war, and even to an absolute war. A total war has been defined as armed conflict between nations, sponsored and waged by a society in arms. "As modern military techniques develop, at least a dozen people must be engaged to production and transportation services behind the lines to keep one soldier supplied. As a result, almost the entire working population have to take part in direct or indirect war services," according to an expert. A total war actually diminishes the distinction between combatants and non-combatants and between the frontier and rear, giving reason to destroy the transportation, industries and population centers far behind the front lines; and leading to an absolute war which is described as aiming at "the utter destruction of the vanquished nation and its final and complete disappearance from the stage of history." "To introduce into the philosophy of war a principle of moderation would be absurd. War is an act of violence pursued to the utmost," said Karl von Clauseqitz, a famous military philosopher.

The cost of war in both human and economic aspects has increased greatly in modern times. In human cost, for instance, it was estimated that the war deaths in Europe in the 15th century were 285,000; in the 16th century, 863,000; in the 17th century, 3,454,000, and in the 18th century, 4,635,000. The figures of war deaths per 1,000 population for these periods were 10, 15, 37 and 33 respectively. As regards the economic cost, Julius Caesar spent about 75 cents to kill a man, and Napoleon almost bankrupted France because he used almost $3,000 to kill an enemy in his day.

2. Cost of Two World Wars

The cost to kill a man in the battlefield rose to $21,000 in the first World War and to approximately $50,000 in the second World War.

The rise of economic cost from the previous century to the two World Wars may be reviewed in a general calculation. It was estimated that the expenditures in the second half of the 19th century in Europe of the five major wars—the Crimean War, the War of 1859, the Austro-Prussian War, the Franco-Prussian War, and the Turkey War, were about $6,000,000,000. This aggregate number becomes a dwarf before a giant when compared with the costs of the World Wars in the first half of the 20th century. The first World War was estimated to have direct costs of $186,000,000,000, and indirect costs of $152,000,000,000, making a total of $338,000,000,000.

In order to help understanding, the *Scholastic* made an effort to translate the costs of the first World War into terms in constant 1919 dollars a common people can visualize: it is sufficient to furnish (a) every family in England, France, Belgium, Germany, Russia, the United States, Canada and Australia with a $2,500 house on a $500 one-acre lot, with $1,000 worth of furniture; (b) a $5,000,000 library for every community of 200,000 inhabitants in these countries; (c) a $10,000,000 university for every such community; (d) a fund that at 5 percent interest would yield enough to pay indefinitely $1,000 a year to an army of 125,000 teachers and 125,000 nurses; and (e) still leave enough to but every piece of property and all the wealth in France and Belgium at a fair market price.

More profoundly, Dr. Nicholas M. Butler, a prominent scholar, spoke of the cost of the first World War, "We are pouring out not only the world's earnings, but the world's savings, savings for a thousand years, and those savings are not illimitable. In the last war, there was destroyed a value equal to that of five countries like France plus five countries like Belgium."

The second World War was estimated to have direct costs of $1,154,000,000,000, six times more than that of the first World War; and among the indirect costs, property damage alone amounted to $230,000,000,000, excluding China. Other indirect costs were not calculated. If the total amount of indirect costs is somewhere close to that of the direct costs as manifested in the calculations for the first World War, the total economic cost of the second World War would be far above $2,000,000,000,000.

Actually property damage is only one side of the story of the havoc wrought by war. The other side is the absorption of materials into the manufacture of war implements. It is a net waste of resources. This kind of waste has increased tremendously in modern times. For example, in medieval age, a knight and his steed carried no more than 200 pounds of iron and steel. In 1943, for each man in the American fighting force, the industry poured forth some 24,000 pounds. In order to meet the need of the war industry, the United

States in 1942 alone mined 126,527,159 tons of iron ore, and from January, 1942 through July, 1945, its steel industry produced 60,335,000 tons of finished steel for war equipment and supplies.

In addition to steel, modern war also wastes many other minerals, such as copper, alumunum, and magnesium, and even materials from vegetable sources. For example, a battleship and its equipment require seventy five tone of rubber, and a 28-ton medium tank needs an amount of rubber which is the equivalent of that required to manufacture 120 automobile tires. Out of the total cotton crop in the United States in 1943, about one million bales of cotton linter, each weighing about 630 pounds, went for munition. Cotton is the basic propelling charge used in all battle weapons.

The economic costs of war also has serious legacies, such as war pensions, war debts, and depression. War pension has appeared in many nations as a standing expenditure of the government and a permanent burden of the people. The United States, for example, had not completely liquidated the pensions of the veterans of the first World War when the second World War broke out, and in the seven years after the second World War, it spent more than 42 billion dollars for the benefits and services of the veterans.

More permanent in character has been the burden to pay the interest on war debts. In modern times almost all the great nations have had a great amount of debt raised for war emergency or for the preparation of war. The United States, for example, had only 1.193 million dollars of debt in 1913, and through the years of the first World War, this number rose to 22,964 million in 1922. It was 45,890 million in 1939, and in 1946 it had reached 269,898 million. This means that at the end of the second World War, every American family had a debt of about $7,200. As the debt speedily grew, its interest increased enormously. Since the second World War, the United States has had to pay every year more than five billion dollars for the interest on the public debt.

There have been three severe depressions since the beginning of the 19th century, each following an important war. The most familiar one was the great depression from 1929 to 1939 caused by the first World War. The symptoms of post-war depression usually are: disorganized production, breakdown of credit, vanishing world trade, unemployment, and social distress. Their deteriorating elements can penetrate deeply and extensively into every life, and no people, victor, vanquished, or even neutral, could escape from them. So, economic depression has been labelled as the ultimate cost of war. It was generally diverted after the second World War only by multiple efforts, including the Relief and Rehabilitation by the United Nations, and Marshall Plan for western Europe and the Mutual Economic Assistance for eastern Europe.

Most important are human costs, of course. In the first World War, almost 17,000,000 men of the armed forces perished. This number exceeds the total of war deaths in Europe from 15th century to 19th century. Civilian deaths from military action, massacre, starvation and exposure in this war were estimated at 12,618,000. In addition there was a great number of indirect deaths caused by war-distributed disease, raising the total of human costs up to 40,000,000. The second World War brought death to over 22,000,000 directly and caused other deaths to over 34,000,000,000, raising the total of human costs to far above 56,000,000.

3. No Remedies

While war has definitely been getting bigger and worse, there were early in this century some experts who tended to believe that recent developments in military techniques in favor of defense had increased the probablity of a deadlock in war, which would lead eventually to its disappearance. In fact, however, it has been proved not only that their belief was wrong owing to the application of new offensive weapons, especially the bombing airplanes, but also that all the methods designed to cure the rising war fever by maintaining peace have been of little use.

Best known among these methods has been the balance of power which means such an equilibrium in power among nations as will prevent any one or group of them from becoming

285

sufficiently strong to change the status quo by force. Its success depends mainly on the measuring of the actual and potential military power and the keeping of its balance. Actual military power means land, naval, and air armament. It includes personnel material, organization, and morale of the armed forces, It also includes railroads, motor vehicles, civil aircraft, and other means of transportation and communication which, though used in normal times for civilian purposes, are immediately available for military purposes. Potential military power consists of available population, raw materials, industrial skill, and industrial plants capable of producing military hardwares. With the wide variety of factors involved, obviously the task of measuring military power is very difficult. Meanwhile, all these factors are subject to dynamic changes every minute, and strictly speaking, to keep them in a stable balance is impossible. When things were rather simpler in the 19th century, the balance of power played a certain role in maintaining order in Europe. But it has had to struggle for existence since the early 20th century, because the increase of uncertainty in military power has made it more and more difficult to measure it and keep it in some lasting equilibrium.

Another well-known method for maintaining peace is collective security. It claims that nations generally increase their armaments and go to war either because they are in fear of aggression or because they trust that aggression will succeed without too great a risk. If the community of nations could provide its members with security through collective action, the main motive for war would disappear. It implies legal rules and procedures to maintain the security of all. By establishing commitments of legal rules and procedures before aggression occurs, it seeks to make the system preventive and not merely remedial. It assumes that common action will be taken against any member of the group that is found to have committed an act of aggression within the group as defined by the legal rules and procedures that all have accepted.

Theoretically, the assumption of the collective security is different from that of the balance of power, because it rests on interpretation of law rather than on calculation of power. In fact, however, none of the practices of the collective security did not depend on the balance of power, and none of them succeeded in subordinating the system of the balance of power to their juridical and ideological postutates. It had been tried several times in modern Europe before being adopted by the League of Nations, and again by the United Nations. Its history has repeatedly showed that it is not able to survive serious disturbances of the balance of power.

Collective security always puts emphasis on the peaceful settlement of international disputes by consent or sanction. While consent may be reached in settling minor disputes, sanction, if not supported by balance of power, tends to be either an ineffectual procedure, or leads to war itself, such as the cases of Manchuria and Ethiopia, which led to the second World War, and the case of the Korean War in the early 1950s.

Various efforts have been made to seek the outlawing of war in order to maintain peace. They were crowned in the Paris Pact of 1928, originally signed by 15 leading nations and later joined by 48 others. Except for certain moral and legal influence, however, they have not gone beyond the collective security, which, again, depends on the balance of power.

Back to the balance of power, which has not only had more and more difficulties for measuring and keeping, but has also never had wholehearted devotion from any of the great powers. Instead they have tended to wreck it with arms race, because each of them considers the balance of power good for the others but not for itself, each tends to augment its own military power, and tries to establish a hegemony over the others. Consequently, there has been, among the great powers under the balance of power system, a continuous armament race which is always a serious cause of war and threatens the very existence of this system itself.

Necessarily, then, disarmament has been sought as a method for maintaining peace. Its rudimental form was the proposals for holidays in naval building, army building, or military appropriations appeared in the 19th century in Europe, and some principles were first laid down in the Covenant of the League of Nations. It is generally divided into two categories: quantitative and qualitative. The former implies a general reduction of armaments to a special level, and the latter means the elimination of certain types of weapons deemed to be particularly valuable for aggression. Expert commissions have often been set up to work on the technical problems involved, and have gotten nowhere, as commented by a famous author: "It was as foolish to expect a disarmament convention from such a commission, as a declaration for atheism from a commission of clergymen." The main reason for this is that each great power has attempted to take a strategical advantage over the others. Different attitudes towards weapons are well depicted by the parable of the disarmament conference of the animals. The lion wanted to eliminate all weapons but claws and jaws, the eagle all but talons and beaks, the bear all but an embracing hug.

The last resort for maintaining peace is the recognition of the right of self-defense against aggression. Actually this recognition is nothing new in history, but is not only casts distrust upon other security methods, but also leaves open loopholes through which any kind of war could be carried on, because there is no clear demarcation which can be made between defense and aggression, and also because whether the circumstances required to enter into war for self-defense are to be decided on by each nation itself, as qualified by Briand's statement attached to the Paris Pact.

4. New Monsters

As the war fever has been rising higher and higher, the various methods devised to cure it by maintaining peace have proved to be less and less effective, it is clear that war has been dragging mankind and its civilization closer and closer to a total destruction. "Utterly futile are all efforts to restrict, to regulate, to localize, to humanize warfare as trying to regulate a prairie fire," said Oscar Newfang in 1924. "Once the conflagration has broken out, it will be driven by the gale of human passions until it burns itself out; and with the ever-increasing destructiveness of methods and the space-annihilating inventions of the present day, it will eventually reach the remotest corners of combatant nations and will totally destroy the mechanism of civilization."

288

However, it may take a long time through more great wars to reach the horrible conclusion if nuclear weapons have not entered into the picture. The new weapons can do the job of total destruction much easier and faster than the conventional ones. They have been waiting for the chance since their first baby atomic bomb, dropped by an American airplane on August 6, 1945, annihiliated the city of Hiroshima, Japan, and killed almost one half of its 200,000 population. It was a uranium bomb, cylindrical in shape, 10 feet long with a diameter of 2 feet 4 inches, weighing about 9,000 pounds. Its explosive power was equal to 20,000 tons of TNT. Three days later another baby atomic bomb, this time of plutonium, was dropped over another Japanese city, Nagasaki.

An atomic bomb's effects differ from those of conventional bombs in three important respects: first, the amount of energy released is about a million times that of the same weight of high-explosive bombs; second, the atomic explosion is accompanied by the immediate release of penetrating, harmful, and invisible radiation; and third, substances remaining in the area long after the explosion are radioactive and harmful to living organisms.

Five year after the dropping of the first baby atomic tomb in Hiroshima, the United States decided to develop a hydrogen bomb with thermonuclear reactions. The first detonation was carried out on Eniwetok atoll on Nov. 1, 1952. The energy release of the hydrogen bomb exceeds that of the atomic bomb by the same ratio as the blast of the atomic tomb exceeds the conventional high-explosive bomb but more widespread. The atomic bomb is a fission device, and the hydrogen bomb is a fusion device. There has developed a fission-fusion-fission device, which is the most compact and the dirtiest bomb.

As the explosive power of the nuclear bombs is so great that the unit of megaton has been generally used for their measurement. The explosive power of one megaton nuclear bomb is approximately equal to that produced by one million tons of conventional high explosive, or 1,000,000 tons of TNT. This much high explosive would fill more than 10,000 railroad cars. Only a total of over three megatons of nonnuclear explosives was used in the second World War from 1941 to 1945. Today, nuclear bombs with various megatons are poised for action. For instance, some American submarines have carried missiles with warheads of about one megaton. The American land-based missiles throughout 1960s carried one warhead of about three megatons, and the American B-52 bombers generally carry bombs in the range of 10-to-20 megatons.

In addition, a neutron bomb has been developed. It would make mass killing, but would not be so destructive to structures. And also there have been shells for atomic cannon made as small as one kiloton—that it, having the energy equivalent of 1,000 tons of TNT. Lately a 58-pound nuclear "backpack" bomb has been devised as a killing toy. It can be carried by one person to be detonated any place.

Meanwhile, the development of MIRV—the acronym for multiple, independently targeted re-entry vehicle—has been going fast. Instead of one nuclear warhead on the tip of a missile, there are two, three, or more, each of which can be directed at a different target. The consequence of this development is first, of course, greatly to increase the number of warheads that can be delivered from a given number of launching pads. More important, however, is that MIRV greatly complicates the problem of achieving an effective antiballistic missile defense.

There have been two important tools for delivering nuclear bombs in long distances. One is the long range air bombers, such as the American B-52, and the other is the ICBM—intercontinental ballistic missile. The United States has three major ICBMs: Titan II and Minuteman II, each with a range of 7,000 miles, and Minuteman III with a range of 7,500 miles. These missiles and others from submarines or moving bases, can carry nuclear warheads to hit any place in the world. They could travel through the long distance in about 30 minutes. Warning time at best would be 15 minutes. Each of them is equipped with a guiding device operated by computers and this device can guide the missile to locate its target automatically.

In this respect, the most striking news is the coming of an American Stealth bomber. Shrouded in secrecy for more than ten years, the radar-deceiving bomber was unveiled publicly in the fall of 1988 and flight tested in the summer of 1989. It resembles a thin-winged black and gray insect, and is virtually invisible. With a crew of just two, the sinister-looking craft is designed to evade any of the world's current air defense. If it works, the plane would make the radar detection system largely obsolete, because it could penetrate beyond early warning stations before being noticed. It could be zeroing in on enemy command centers with a relatively small payload unofficially reported at 16 nuclear-tipped missiles.

It is no doubt that all the new delivering tools can carry chemical or biological weapons to targets too. The well-known chemical weapons are tabun, sarin and botulin. Their formidable agents are nerve gas and mustard gas which kill rapidly by inhibiting the action of the enzyme cholinesterase, resulting in lack of muscular control and in respiratory paralysis. Biological weapons use viruses, rickettsiae, bacteria, and fungi as their killing agents. Lately a new poisonous substance has been developed as weapons. It is so deadly that a tiny drop, small enough to fit on the head of a pin, touching the skin of a human being will produce death in ten agonizing munutes. Estimates on the current stockpiles of chemical warfare agents are: Soviet Union, 50,000 tons and the United States, 30,000 tons. Some other nations including Iraq also have a great quanity.

Furthermore, the United States and the Soviet Union have been accelerating an arms race in space. Their satellites spy on each other and on other nations with high revolution cameras. Ships, submarines and planes navigate by satellite. Military leaders communicate around the world by satellite. Other satellites hang in space to warn of enemy rocket launches as infra-red sensors detect their heat. It is said that the superpowers have introduced the first tactical space weapon—a hunter-killer satellite capable of blasting enemy's payloads out of the sky. They have also developed satellites to carry high energy laser weapons that could fire destructive beams of light at other satellites hundreds of miles away. Lasers can be used also to burn holes in an enemy vehicle or spaceship. They too may form the basis for "disintegrator" of death-ray weapons.

5. Race for Doomsday

Four years after the dropping of the first American baby atomic bomb on Hiroshima, the Soviet Union set off an atomic explosion, probably in September, 1949. A few months after the first detonation of a hydrogen bomb tested by the United states in Nov. 1952, the Soviet Union used the thermonuclear principle in their nuclear tests. After the American and Russian tests, thermonuclear explosions were produced by the British in 1957, the Chinese in 1967, the French in 1968, and the Indians in 1974. Each addition to the number of nations armed with nuclear weapons drives its neighbor toward acquiring similar arms. They feel themselves threatened and the pressure to compete is great. As the knowhow for producing nuclear weapons becomes easier and wider and their cost is going down and down, it has been estimated that tens of nations could have nuclear weapons in the near future. The newcomers probably include Pakistan, Argentina, Brazil, Japan, West Germany, Israel, Italy, South Korea, North Korea, Egypt and Taiwan.

With the rapid increase of nuclear arsenals, Fred Warshofsky, an *American Science* editor, pointed out some years ago that the United States could totally destroy every Soviet city of 100,000 or more population 36 times over, and that the Soviet Union could do the same to similarly sized American cities 12 times over. Yet, 25% of all American and Russian scientists and engineers have kept working on the development of weapons. For the whole world as it is known in 1982 there had been 50,000 nuclear warheads, equal to 20 billion tons of TNT, or 1,600,000 times the yield of the American first baby atomic tomb dropped on Hiroshima. This amounts to over 3 tons of TNT per person of the world population, and we all know that a pound will suffice. Meanwhile, five more nuclear weapons have been produced every day as if there were a shortage.

Going along with the contrast for more nuclear warheads has been that for more of their delivering tools. In order to match with American long range guided missiles Titan II, and Minuteman II and III, for instance, the Soviet Union has produced SS-9 Scarp with a range of 7,500 miles, SS-11 Sego and SS-17, each with a range of 6,500 miles, SS-18 and SS-19 Mod 2, each with a range of 6,300 miles, and SS-19 Mod 1 with a range of 7,000 miles.

In addition to the building up of nuclear arms, there are various side-ways to increase the tempo of the race for doomsday. There include the cold war, limited war, and arms trade.

The cold war means a perpetual tension between the two blocs of nations, Communist led by the Soviet Union, and anti-Communist led by the United States, of such unique intensity that one may question the adjective used to describe it. Yet it is regarded as "cold" rather than "hot" because there are no overt hostilities on a large scale. These hostilities are prevented by an historical phenomenon as unique as the cold war itself. Both sides have nuclear weapons which could erase the distinction between victor and vanquished by destroying all participants, hence neither side has been tempted to initiate a total war, and they had to adopt a policy to fight by cold means—ideological, political, economic, and limited military action.

In the cold war a limited military action is usually aimed at protecting a bloc from defections whenever these occurred. Thus, for instance, the United States aided in the overthrow of an alleged pro-Communist regime in Guatemala in 1954 and landed troops in the Dominican Republic to forestall a possible victory of pro-Castro followers; and the Soviet Union "filled out" its eastern European zone with a coup d'etat in Czechoslovakia in 1948 and suppressed the 1953 East German and 1956 Hungarian revolts. This kind of limited military action, however, is not generally regarded as a limited war which has to be fought overtly by at least two belligerents.

There have been more than 50 limited wars that occurred after the second World War, more than one every year. As the number of participants is concerned, there has been no year in which there were not a good many nations at war. In 1983, for instance, there were 45 nations, one-fourth of the world's total, fighting in some kind of limited war. Most known of the limited wars are the three wars between Israel and Arabian nations, Korean War, Afghanistan War, Cambodia War, and Iran-Iraq War. Few of them were started by the superpowers, but almost none of them was not involved with the superpowers. Wherever there were sides to be taken, the superpowers took them. There were three factions in Cambodia and one for everybody. Mutual suspicion and hostility of the superpowers touched every part of the globe, even the smallest and weakest nations. For instance, South Yemen took aid from the Russians and gave them access to the port of Aden. North Yemen told Washington that South Yemen was about to invade. Washington sent arms and advisers to North Yemen. Finally, several Arab nations mediated the fight between the Yemens, and North Yemen made an arms deal with Russia twice the size of the American deal.

The limited war is limited in scale, not in time. A good number of them have fought for many years. The Vietnam war, for example, lasted more than 7 years, longer than either of the two World Wars. The Iran-Iraq War was brought to an end only after 8 years of bitter fighting with millions killed, and the Cambodia War has made that country a human slaughter house for 15 years without peace in sight. The latest assessment on the limited war was made on May 17, 1989 by the Stockholm International Peace Research Institute who reported that 1988 was a good year for peace, and among the 33 wars existing at the beginning of this year, 5 were over and only 28 are still kept running at the year-end!

The prime source for running the limited wars is the arms trade. Sometime ago, this was the trade of the "merchants of death" like Krupp and Zaharoff, who made and sold arms to any nations that could afford them. It has become a business of government and has been increasing in tempo since the second World War. From 1945 to 1955 it was dominated by the United States and Great Britain with an average yearly rate of $2 billion and $400 million respectively. Then the Soviet

Union entered the picture in a big way in 1955, and soon thereafter, a revitalized France broke into the market. Up to 1976 annually, the Soviet Union has sold $500 million in arms, and France, $400 million. The global arms trade in 1976 was about $10 billion, with new orders running at about $20 billion. There were in this year 95 nations that imported major weapons—tanks, ships, missiles or aircraft. In almost all of these nations there was no other feasible way of obtaining these weapons. By far most of these nations belong to the Third World.

The arms trade has grown even more rapidly in the 1980s' with the Soviet Union taking the lead and China jumping from behind. For instance, its global total in 1988 was approximatelly $34 billion—the smallest number since 1983. Of the total the Soviet Union had a share of 38%, and the United States, 28%. The third was France; fourth, China, and fifth, Great Britain, as reported again by the Stockholm International Peace Research Institute. Other important ones are Italy, North Korea, Czechoslovakia, West Germany, and Israel. Through the arms trade, these governments, as "merchants of death", made a lot of dirty money. But they spent much more for the cold and limited wars. For instance, the United States has expended more money for these wars than for the two World Wars combined.

The great amounts of money the nations spent for the cold and limited wars have been just a part of their military expenditures. They have spent more for the arms race, particularly for new weapons. In the United States, for instance, it cost $5 million for a single rocket, $8 million for a B-52 bomber, and $500 million for a nuclear powered carrier. It would cost more than $35 million for a single Atlas ballistic missile placed in a firing position, more than $500 million for a Stealth bomber, and more than $1 billion for a Trident submarine, bristling with 24 deep-striking missiles. 38,000 people were employed to work for a model of the Stealth bomber; 5,000 different firms and 1,500,000 people were required to build the DEW line radar fence, and the new MX mobile missile system carries a price tag from $31.5 billion to $33.8 billion, depending on how it is deployed. Consequently their military budget has

295

risen all the way up to $300 billion for the United States, and $118 billion for the Soviet Union as Mr. Gorbachev disclosed in this summer, for 1989. For the whole world, the military budget rose from 1900 to 1976, at least 30 times at constant prices. The world military budget of 1976 was about 100 times larger than the actual capital of the World Bank, and about 5.5 percent of the world income in that year.

The rise of the military budget has spread, like an epidemic disease, over the whole world. In recent decades the underdeveloped nations have followed the the developed ones in this respect with even a faster pace. In the ten years from 1970 to 1980, for instance, the world's developed nations increased their military expenditure from $156 billion to $424 billion, while the underdeveloped ones, from $24 billion to $117 billion.

All the money of the military budgets of all the nations have gone to fuel the race for doomsday, although as Dwight D. Eisenhower, President of the United States, said in 1953, "Every gun that is made, every warship launched, every rocked fired, signifies in a final sense, a theft from those who hunger and are not fed, those who are cold and not clothed. This world in arms is not spending money alone. It is spending the sweat of its laborers, the genius of its scientists, the hope of its children."

6. Nuclear Holocaust

Under the vicious and insane race mankind is certainly drawing closer and closer to doomsday.

What will doomsday look like?

There have been a few films in attempt to depict the horrible scene. For example, *The War Game,* made by British filmmaker Peter Walkins, is a harrowing documentary of England under nuclear attack; and later, *The Testament,* is about a suburban housewife in Hamlin, California, who watches her family and community die from the lethal radiation generated by a nuclear strike on San Francisco; and *The Day After,* a made-for TV movie, chronicles the demise of the town of

Lawrence, Kansas, following a nuclear attack on Kansas City, forty miles away. All the horrible scenes depicted in the films are limited to a small area within a short time. It is impossible for them to show any more of the whole situation.

There is a tense description made by Mr. John F. Kennedy, President of the United States, in a television speech on June 26, 1963: "Three times in the last two and a half years I have been required to report to you as President that this nation and the Soviet Union stood on the verge of direct military confrontation—in Laos, in Berlin, and in Cuba . . . A full scale nuclear exchange, lasting less than 60 minutes, could wipe out more than 300 million Americans, Europeans, and Russians, as well as untold numbers elsewhere. And the survivors, as Chairman Khrushchev warned the Communist Chinese, would envy the dead."

Many scientific estimates have been made of the probable effects of nuclear attacks. One of them, reported in the 1957 hearings before the Special Subcommittee on Radiation of the Joint Committee on Atomic Energy of the Congress of the United States, was for an attack on population and industrial centers and military installations in the United States with 250 bombs totaling 2,500 megans. The estimate of casualities presented in the testimony, corrected for the increase in population since 1957 to 1964, is that sixty days after the day on which the attack took place, 98,000,000 of the 190,000,000 American people would be dead, and 28,000,000 would be seriously injured but still alive, many of the remaining 70,000,000 survivors would be suffering from minor injuries and radiation effects. This is a small nuclear attack, made with the use of about one percent of the existing nuclear weapons in 1957.

A major nuclear war might well see a total of 30,000 megatons, one tenth of the generally estimated nuclear stockpiles in 1959, delivered and exploded over the populated regions of the United States, the Soviet Union, and the other major European countries. The studies of Hugh Everett III and George E. Pugh of the Institute of Defense Analyses, reported in the 1959 hearings before the Special Subcommittee on Radiation, led to an estimate that sixty days after the day on which such a war was waged, 720,000,000 of the 800,000,000 people in these countries would be dead, 60,000,000 would be alive but severely injured, and there would be 20,000,000 other survivors under very miserable conditions.

The World Health Organization concluded in the conference "The World After a Nuclear War" in Washington, D.C., Nov. 1983, that a major nuclear war between the United States and the Soviet Union could leave 1.1 billion dead from immediate nuclear effects of the blast, fireball and radiation. Another 1.1 billion would be injured. Since medical facilities would be almost wiped out, most of the injured will die. The ultimate toll within a few months will be more than 2 billion people, or roughly half of the world's population. The corpses if laid end to end would reach from the earth to the moon.

When a nuclear bomb explodes, it scoops up great chunks of earth so that a huge crater is formed in the ground. Dirt and debris are blown high into the air and crushed to smithereens, then descend as dust—radiated dust, with Strontium-90, and plutonium in it; also carbon-14 and other deadly poisons. The dust mingles with the clouds and then falls with rain. And through this way it spreads over everywhere and penetrates onto everything.

It is well known that any amount of nuclear radiation affects the gens, so that the effect is carried into future generations. The poison of Strontium-90, for instance, has a "half-life" of 28 years. That means that 28 years after it enters the human body, half of it is still there; and 28 years after it enters the human body, half of it is still there; and 28 years after that, half of that amounts is still there. What is more, it is cumulative so that the amount which enters the body today is added to what was absorbed yesterday. Strontium-90 has an affinity for calcium. When it enters the body it finds its way into the bones. Once it gets there, it stays. You cannot eliminate it. You cannot neutralize it with medicine. It stays there indefinitely and is passed on to future generations. Strontium-90 is known to cause leukemia and bone cancer. It does not exist in nature. It is produced by atomic explosion.

298

Plutonium does not exist in nature too. It is converted from uranium to make high-yield nuclear bombs. As a deadly poison, it has a "half-life" of 24,000 years and is poisonous for at least 280,000 years. Many evidences of the dangerous effects of the nuclear weapons have been presented by their tests.

In 1954, actors John Wayne, Susan Hayward, Agnes Moorehead and producer Dick Powell filmed *The Conquerer* on the sandy dunes outside St. George, Utah. A number of atomic bomb tests had been conducted in Nevada about 150 miles away. For three months the filmmakers were breathing the dust laced with radioactive plutonium fallout. Twenty five years later John Wayne, Susan Hayward, Agnes Moorehead and Dick Powell had all died of cancer. Of the 220 people in the cast and crew, 91 had contracted cancer by late 1980, and half of the cancer victims had died of the disease, according to *Killing Our Own* by Harvey Wasserman and Norman Solomon.

Between 1945 and 1963 several hundred thousand soldiers were marched through areas where the Nevada atomic weapons tests were conduced. The rate of leukemia among these men had been 400 times the national average, as reported by *Shut Down* of the Book Publishing Co.

In 1958 a Russian nuclear installation exploded at Kyshtym. Radioactive clouds devastated the countryside for hundreds of miles. This area of the Ural Mountains is now a wasteland that cannot be safely inhabited for millennia. It is interesting to note that the government of the United States hid this CIA report for almost 20 years. It only came to light in 1977 under the Freedom of Information Act.

Furthermore nuclear explosions endanger not only humans, but also other animals and even plants. They send millions of tons of dirt and debris high into the air to mingle with the huge amounts of smoke from the rampaging forest and city fires, and cover up the sky for months. The earth will be almost dark even at noon, and temperature will drop to freeze even in July. This kind of ecological change will make it much more difficult for the surviving humans and other animals tosustain, and for the plants to grow, and will deprive vast lands of food corps and other harvests for several years.

Meanwhile nuclear detonations would destroy a large part of the atmospheric ozone layer that screens the earth from ultraviolet rays of the sun. The ultraviolet rays of the sun are the ones that cause skin burns. They can also blind eyes that are exposed to them for any period of time. Animals that have eyes depend on the ozone for protection. What happens when a nuclear weapon explodes is that a very large number of nitrogen oxides are generated by the radiation that flies out from the explosion. A one-megaton nuclear weapon can generate 10^{32} molecules of nitrogen oxides. They are lifted up with the fireball, and can reach the altitude above 50 thousand feet where the ozone is, and will start eating up the ozone. When the dark and cold days are over, the loss of some ozone will start to take effect. The United States National Research Council Committee predicted that a reduction of half of the ozone would increase the rate of skin cancer 10 percent in mid-latitudes for 40 years. If 70 percent of the ozone were wiped out, a likely possibility, the ultraviolet rays of the sun would be so intense that a person would get a severe, blistering sunburn in 10 minutes.

With respect to the effect on eyes, only 20 percent depletion of the ozone will allow enough ultraviolet rays of the sun coming through to blind all eyes of humans and other animals on earth except those protected with glasses. In other words, almost all fauna on earth be blinded and eventually die as a result of a major nuclear war and the depletion of a small portion of the ozone. This is the large-scale ecological catastrophe one can imagine. Virtually the entire ecosystem will collapse, according to a videotape of a symposium of physicians and scientists held in Nov. 1980, *The Last Epidemic: The Medical Consequences of Nuclear War* from Physicians for Social Responsibility.

In view of such devastating effects, Dr. Philip Handler, President of the United States National Academy of Sciences warned that no distant other nations could ''survive a major nuclear exchange unscathed and, thereby inherit the earth . . .

300

The economic, social and political consequences of the result-ant worldwide terror are entirely unpredictable.''

A declaration signed by 52 Nobel laureates at Mainau, Lake Constance on July 15, 1955 warned that ''by total military use of weapons feasible today, the earth can be contaminated with radioactivity to such an extent that whole peoples can be annihilated. Neutrals may die thus as well as belligerents.''

The *Russell-Einstein Manifesto,* July 1955, warned that ''No one knows how widely such lethal radio-active particles might be diffused, but the best authorities are unanimous in saying that war with H-bombs might quite possibly put an end to the human race.''

7. The Dead End

Indeed, there have been various attempts to erect anti-ballistic missile systems against nuclear weapons. But it is very difficult for such systems to be perfected technically. The fundamental reason for this is that all anti-ballistic missile sys-tems have to depend on radar and computers. The attacker can take a number of steps to confuse or blind or ''blackout'' the defending radar. No matter how many missiles an anti-ballistic missile system is designed to handle simultaneously, the at-tacker could always send in enough missiles to throw the com-puters into confusion. The newly developed American Stealth bomber could make anti-ballistic missile systems almost use-less with radar-deceiving equipments.

On July 31, 1967 the *U. S. News & World Report* pub-lished a ''Scenario'' in which it was assumed that 100 nuclear bombs were directed at the United States, defense efforts de-stroyed most of them, and only 18 managed to penetrate. What would be the result? The author, Rep. Craig Hosmer, a member of the Joint Committee on Atomic Energy of the United States Congress, concluded: ''Three of every five Americans were dead and the nation's military-industrial back was broken.''

Nevertheless, there are still continuous attempts to set effective defense systems against nuclear attacks. In the early 1960s, for example, Secretary of Defense McNamara announced that the United States would build what he called a limited defense system of ABM—Anti-Ballistic Missiles with $5 billion. But Dr. Simon Ramo who was the chief designer of the Air Force missile program remarked that he did not think the $5 billion would be enough, and that by the time this system finished its installation, it has become obsolete, because the other side would have taken sufficient additional measures to nullify its effects.

A recent development in this respect is the well known Strategic Defense Initiative or what has been popularly dubbed "Star Wars." It was described by President Reagan of the United States in a speech in March, 1983, as a research program to "render nuclear weapons impotent and obsolete" with a cost of $33 billion for the first five years and much more to continue. It is projected to build a shield in outer space to intercept and destroy the incoming nuclear missiles before they attack the target. How effective can it be? According to a noted expert Richard Garwin, a technical consensus has been reached that neither cities nor populations would be immune to low-flying cruise missiles, stealth, submarine-launched, and alternative delivery means for nuclear weapons. It cannot "render nuclear weapons impotent and obsolete" as President Reagan hoped, but even a likely "introduction" to a war on earth, as Garwin sees it. Furthermore, it is likely that nuclear radiation with Strontium-90, plutonium, carbon-14 and other deadly poisons will sooner or later find its way to earth and kill all lives on it, should many nuclear missiles be exploded in outer space in a great Star War.

To face this kind of arguments, the United States government had to acknowledge that an impenetrable defense is impossible, that the Strategic Defense Initiative "is not a protection of the people. What it is doing is essentially defending missiles and command-and-control centers;" and "providing a better, more stable basis for enhanced deterrence is the central purpose." Then the government emphasized that "The U. S. goal has never been to eventually give up the policy of deterrence. With defenses, the U. S. seeks not to replace deterrence, but to enhance it."

So, we are led back from the new fiction of Star Wars to the older trick of deterrence. The original form of deterrence is the balance of power that depends not just on a nation's own power, but also that of allies, even of some third force. Now a nuclear war can occur between the superpowers at any minute, and destroy both in hours. It would be too quick for even allies to help much immediately in such a war, not to mention a third force. Allies cannot be counted on for immediate help. On the contrary, they may actually decrease a nation's security.

Deterrence is a military strategy under which one major power uses the threat of instant, overwhelming reprisal to effectively exclude nuclear attack from an adversary power's available alternatives. It is a function of the terrible striking power of nuclear weapons. An essential element of deterence is the maintenance by the adversaries of a high level of assured destruction capability. This element cannot assure us of safety however, because the power potential of the nuclear weapons is not just their tonnage and number. Twenty cartridges in the hands of a hesitant moralist are no good against an enemy who does not hesitate to hit his mark although he may have only a couple of cartridges in his belt.

Historically, the way to amass armaments as a force of deterrence is not quite new. It has been tried before, and has never worked. The result, as it is well known, is to stimulate other nations to increase arms for themselves in turn. For if one nation builds armed strength thinking thereby to deter attack, other nations will think the first is preparing an aggression against them. When one nation has the power to attack, other nations cannot but fear that that power will be used, and they will arm to defend themselves against it. In the nuclear age, the stimulation of arms race is much more serious and critical than before, and may lead to "if not the detonation of nuclear armaments to destroy the world, the cost of paying for the awesome arsenal might well ruin the world economy," as warned by a famous author.

In fact, the strategy of deterrence adopted by the superpowers in the early Nuclear age has created a nuclear dilemma under which even a surprise attack would not be certain to grant immunity to the attacker from retaliatory measures of such destructiveness that the conflict might well make any distinction between victor and vanquished irrelevant. In order to lessen the tremendous pressure of the nuclear dilemma, a policy of "detente" has been advocated. It means in general to ease the international tension, and militarily it includes such measures as to freeze nuclear weapons, to promise not to use them first, arms control and disarmament.

It is a good idea to deal with the nuclear threat by freezing nuclear weapons, by promising not to use them first, rather than by deterrence. But how to make such a freeze to be true and how to make such a promise to be real? Since military techniques are developing so rapidly in modern times and government personnel is changing so frequently under various political systems, how to keep such a freeze stable, and how to keep such a promise lasting? There have been no answers to these questions. Even if there is a divine power to hold such a freeze and such a promise in effect permanently, nuclear threat will still remain in the world.

A nuclear war may be started by human errors, emotional impulses, limited wars, third nations, mechanical mishaps, or electronic accidents. For instance, on November 9, 1979, a reportedly fail-safe computer responded to a war games tape by turning on all American early warning systems around the world. On June 3 and again on June 6, 1980, computer mistakes in American warning system began a rapid chain of events that could have ruined the earth. In another case, the failure of only a 46 cents computer part in American warning system produced a false signal that Russian missiles were on the way.

There have been a number of accidents in nuclear arms which may have triggered a a nuclear war or some other kind of nuclear disaster. Daniel Ellsberg, an assistant to the former United States Secretary of Defense McNamara, revealed of an accident in 1961 when an Air Force plane carrying a 24-megaton bomb crashed in North Carolina. On crash impact five of the six interlocking safety mechanisms on the bomb failed. Only one switch kept the bomb from unleashing the equivalent of 120 Hiroshima-type explosions.

Retired Admiral Gene R. LaRocque of the United States Navy once reported that an American best missile submarine, George Washington, ran right into a Japanese ship and sank it in the early 1980s, and that the United States has lost two nuclear attack submarines, the Scorpion and the Thresher. They sank in the ocean of unknown reasons. Other well known accidents include: an American submarine carrying nuclear missiles collided with a Russian ship; by mistake, an American airplane dropped in the sea near Spain four plutonium bombs which fortunately did not explode, and a Russian airplane carrying a nuclear weapon crashed in the Sea of Japan.

According to data compiled by the Greenpeace Environmental Movement in early May, 1989, the United States and the Soviet Union together have littered the ocean floor with at least 48 nuclear weapons and 11 reactors. Newly disclosed was the loss of a B-43 bomb aboard an A-4 attack plane off the American aircraft carrier Ticonderoga not too far away from Okinawa, on Dec. 5, 1965. Also newly disclosed was the loss of a Russian Yankee class submarine that sank on Oct. 6, 1986, off the coast of Bermuda. It is believed to be carrying 16 SS-N-6 ballistic missiles, with two warheads apiece, and powered by two nuclear reactors. The most recent Russian loss was a Mike class submarine off the coast of Norway on April 7, 1989, with two nuclear reactors and probably some nuclear weapons aboard.

Less illusive than freeze and promise are arms control and disarmament, but their practical value again does not mean much.

Disarmament was tried before and after the first World War with little success. In the charter of the United Nations, there have been provisions for it. An Atomic Energy Commission and a commission for Conventional Armaments were established in 1946. The two commissions were combined into a single Disarmament Commission in 1952. Disarmament conferences were held in 1960 and 1962, both in Geneva, but achieved almost nothing. In the early stage of negotiation, when the Soviet Union had not reached a strong position in nuclear power, it insisted on the prohibition of the atomic bomb first, and the United States supported a somewhat quantitative disarmament. Obviously, both wanted to hold a favorable position in their own temporarily dominant technique or strategy. Later, the two superpowers agreed in principle on the need for fixing numerical limits to armed forces and armaments, and each sponsored plans for destroying stockpiles of fissional materials, for terminating their production, and for destroying nuclear delivery vehicles. But these goals could not be implemented since they maintained opposing views on verification.

Since disarmament has gotten nowhere, a theory of Arms Control was developed. Arms control is not supposed to go as far as disarmament, but to make it easier to work out something hopefully leading to disarmament. It is an attempt to find a turning on the dread road of arms race. Its first achievement is the test ban treaty of 1963, banning nuclear weapons tests in the atmosphere, in outer space, underwater, and in any other environment if the explosion would cause radioactive debris outside of the nation conducting the explosion. It was negotiated by the United States, Great Britain and the Soviet Union. Its effect has been greatly depleted by the refusal of China and France to go along.

The second achievement of arms control is the nonproliferation treaty of 1968 under which nations party to the treaty that did not possess nuclear weapons when the treaty was concluded may not acquire them in the future. While the treaty affirms the right to develop nuclear energy for peaceful purposes, the non-nuclear weapons nations must accept inspection by the International Atomic Energy Agency to insure that nuclear materials are not diverted from peaceful to military uses. Unfortunately more than 20 important nations have not been party to the treaty, and they could produce nuclear explosives any time if they wanted to, and even the party nations can do so through some loopholes.

Very significant are the Strategic Arms Limitation Talks (SALT) between the United States and the Soviet Union. Three treaties have been concluded. The SALT I treaty, includeding the ABM agreement, Interim Offensive agreement and a Protocol, was signed on May 26, 1972, in Moscow by the United States President Nixon and the Soviet Union leader Brezhnev. In the ABM agreement, the two nations agree to limit the building of ABM system, no more than 100 ABM launchers and interceptors at certain area, and not to transfer the ABM system to other countries. The development or testing of air-based, space-based, or mobile land-based ABM is prohibited. The interim agreement prohibits both parties from starting construction of additional fixed, land-based ICBM launchers after July 1, 1972. Actually these agreements did nothing to curb the already extravagant power of nuclear weapons of the two nations.

The SALT II treaty was signed in Vienna, on June 18, 1979, by the United States President Carter and Soviet Union President Brezhnev. It sets equal overall ceilings on major categories of strategic nuclear weapons, and reduces the ICBM launchers to 2,250 from 2,400 allowed by SALT I treaty. It also limits to 1,200 the number of ballistic missiles that can be armed with multiple, independently-targeted-warheads. The treaty was opposed by the United States Senate, and following the Russian intervention in Afghanistan in Dec., 1979, Carter delayed ratification efforts indefinitely. He had warned early when he signed it, "the threat of a nuclear holocaust still hangs over us."

The SALT III treaty was signed in Washington, on Dec. 8, 1987, by the United States President Reagan and the Soviet Union leader Gorbachev. It eliminates the superpowers' intermediate-range nuclear missiles from 340 to 3,000 miles. It has been hailed as a history-making agreement and a breakthrough work. Actually it "will retire fewer than 4 percent of the worldwide inventory of nuclear warheads, and these retiring ones are too vulnerable to be valuable" according to a well-known columnist George F. Will. Even with the complete implementation and verification of this agreement, the threat of nuclear war to the world remains as serious as before.

Before the ink was dry on the signatures of the SALT III treaty, Reagan and Gorbachev were talking of another more sweeping pact. It is the proposed Strategic Arms Reduction Talks (START) to slash by up to half the number of the superpowers' longer-range nuclear missiles. There are still serious obstacles, especially the American project of Star Wars, to the proposed talks. Even if the talks successfully achieve up to the highest goal—half the number of their longer-range nuclear missiles to be slashed, again, the threat of nuclear war to the world remains as serious as before, because the remaining nuclear weapons are still many times the power to annihilate mankind and its civilization.

Meanwhile the knowledge to produce nuclear weapons has been becoming more and more common, and the material to produce them has been spreading through various ways. Under these circumstances, even if all the existing nuclear weapons were destroyed all at once by some arrangements of miracle, they can be reproduced easily and quickly with advanced techniques, when demanded by great and bitter wars for desperate use by war-mongers or fanatic zealots, or even by nice gentleman like the United States President Truman at the end of the Second World War. So, as long as the chance for war exists, the threat of nuclear war to the world will not disappear.

Further, there have been several hundred nuclear power plants in the industrial nations over the world. They are producing electricity for peaceful use, but they can be exploded by conventional bombs. If Europe had nuclear power plants during the second World War, the bombs from both sides could have exploded them to devastate the whole continent with deadly poisons of nuclear radiation and make it inhabitable for thousands of years. Thus, as long as the chance of even if only the conventional war exists, nuclear threat to the world will not disappear.

Now, against all misleading, confusion, illusion and ignorance, the hard facts stand sternly: Mankind has been living under a "balance of terror" as termed by Sir Winston Churchill, "a continuous hell-condition" as viewed by Pope John XXIII, "the constant threat of sudden annihilation" as told by Albert Einstein; on the "edge of oblivion" as noted by Saul Pett, and as "despairing hostages" with a "perpetual nightmare" as described by E. L. M. Burns. "The end of the world is as near as the next 30 minutes," as warned by Howard Brembeck, and there is "no place to hide" as indicated by the title of two books, one by David V. Bradley and the other by Seymour Melman.

The ancient Greeks had a legend about a nice guy named Damocles who sat down to enjoy a great feast. The table was loaded with all known delicacies. Everything was perfect, except for one thing. Suspended above his head was a sharp-pointed sword held by only a single hair. The peculiar situation mankind has today is quite similar to Damocles had in the Greek legend.

8. Quest for War Abolition

Under the threat of war accelerated by nuclear weapons, it is undeniable that the doom of mankind is near and there is almost no way to escape. However, there still is a hope, the only hope. It lies in the abolition of war. If war is abolished, all weapons are destroyed or converted to peaceful use, and all systems for war are eliminated, mankind will be assured with not only a survival, but also a permanent peace. If war is abolished, all costs and expenditures for war are transferred and all human wisdom and labor for war are devoted to the promotion of humanity, environments and world economy, mankind will be assured with not only a survival, but also a general happiness. With a permanent peace and a general happiness mankind will be assured with a great future forever. Hence, the abolition of war is not only the hope for the survival of mankind, but also the key to our great future.

The idea of abolition of war is not new. The words of Isaiah came out about 2700 years ago: "They shall beat their swords into plowshares, and their spears into pruning hooks; nation shall not lift up sword against nation. Neither shall they learn war anymore."

About 300 years later, Mo Ti, a Chinese philosopher, taught that universal love and mutual respect would be infinitely superior to war, which he regarded as the greatest crime men could commit. He reasoned that the killing of one man was a crime, that the killing of a hundred men increase the crime a hundred times, and the greatest of all crimes is the invasion of a country resulting in the killing of hundreds of thousands of human beings. He urged that this large scale killing of human beings should not be praised and called right; and he wanted one standard of morality for individuals and states. He also condemned the economic wastefulness of war since neither the invading country nor the invaded lands profit by war.

The earlier idea of the abolition of war has encounted no serious opposition in theory except the opinion of some evolutionists that war is an effective instrument for evolution. They hold that out of the armed conflict emerges a selection whereby old and effete societal forms are eliminated, new forces are set free, and the process of development enters into its next phase. A simple but profound comment on this opinion is that "a trouble with war is: while it may cure the disease, it is likely to kill the patient." Further, with nuclear weapons, war will not only surely kill the patient, but even bring an end to the evolution itself.

It is not in theory, but in practice that the problem of the abolition of war remains unsettled ever since. In other words, the real problem is how to abolish war.

There have been few noteworthy opinions about how to abolish war positively. One is by abandoning weapons. It is asserted that most of the warlike peoples in history were those who possessed better weapons, that the development of warfare has always followed the progress of weapons, and that the present situation in which war has been getting bigger and worse results from the invention of new weapons. It is true that weapons are a great stimulus to war, and that their progress always intensifies the development of warfare. But there are no evidences that can prove that weapons were the roots of war. On the contrary, history indicates that it is weapons that exist for war, not war that exists for weapons. It is well implicated in a conclusion on disarmament: "The solution of the problem of disarmament cannot be found within the problem itself, but outside it. In fact the problem of disarmament is not the problem of disarmament. It really is the problem of the organization of the world community.''

In contrast to the opinion of by abandoning weapons, there are people who have believed that war would be abolished through the invention of more devastating weapons. 200 years ago, Thomas Jefferson thought that submarines, when invented, would prove so powerful that they would prevent wars. Victor Hugo in 1842 predicted that balloons would end war. Later Alfred B. Nobel, the inventor of dynamic and the smokeless fire powder, wanted to invent a substance with such terrible power of mass destruction that war would thereby be made impossible forever. The nuclear weapon might be the ultimate weapon Nobel wanted to invent. Thus, when Dr. Robert Hutchins supervised the development of the atomic bomb at the University of Chicago in 1942, he called it "the good news of damnation," contending that it would frighten people into banding together to avoid world suicide and achieve world peace. All these beliefs and predictions, however, are just theorized vaguely and are yet to be elaborated and verified.

Another opinion is to abolish war by eliminating the private property system which according to this opinion, is the root of war. Some socialists, including some anarchists and communists, have held this view. Some communists further blended it with capitalism, stressing that under capitalism there was an inevitable struggle for the control of market and raw materials leading to war, that so long as capitalism endured this struggle and the chance of war would continue, and that the only way to get rid of war was, therefore, to get rid of capitalism. This particular point of view was refuted by Norman Angell among others, who shows that war does not win markets but is likely to lead to their forfeiture, and in most respects the capitalist is adversely served by war.

Generally, if the private property system is the root of war, it is hard to explain why in primitive times when most of the peoples lived a life of communist economy, war raged between them, and why the chances of war are existing between modern communist nations, somewhat like between capitalist ones. In fact, the greatest and most important property war

311

has always been fought for is territory, which Plato found "at the root of all wars." But territory, in general, belongs to the public. It is not private property under almost all political and economic systems.

On the other hand, some people have held that man was basically a killer, or that war is something contained in the nature of mankind and is an end desirable in itself. Accordingly, they concluded that war is likely to last forever, or that the process of eliminating warfare is a painful uphill battle of surpressing human natural instincts and striving for a higher spiritual and ethical enlightenment. No wonder again and again one hears people say that warfare will be eliminated only when mankind "evolves into some higher form."

To support the opinion that war is related to human nature with a different approach is the view of some evolutionists, who asserted that man was the product of the brutal process of natural selection, evolving over the millenia under the influence of the "kill or be killed" law of the jungle. It was only to be expected, therefore, that mankind would be a brutal, bloodthirsty and destructive savage.

However, there has never been any convinced evidence in biology, psychology, or any other field that human beings have a natural or acquired killing instinct toward each other. They go to war usually by order, under plan, with collective action, not through individual instincts. In fact and at any rate, they go to war not merely for the joy of killing each other. Consequently the opinions of these naturalists and evolutionists could not set a deadlock to the search for an answer to the question of how to abolish war.

In addition, there has been some idea seeking to abolish war through the elimination of its very causes. Unfortunately, the very causes of war are something like a many headed hydra which, according to a Greek story, can grow more new heads as soon as old ones are chopped off.

V. A Road to Heaven

1. War and Group

Professor Quincy Wright and some other authorities define war as a violent conflict between groups. Although war is always mixed up with personal ambitions and other interests, it is essentially an affair of groups. In general, war is fought by groups and also for them. There has been no war without groups as central actors, and there is nothing which is more important and more inseparable with war than groups. It is necessary, therefore, to direct the search for an answer to the question of how to abolish war into the groups and their relationship with war.

In the long course of social evolution, mankind has had a series of groups, from the early single family, through a primitive community, clan, tribe, and the nation. They are the groups that have fought almost all the wars. Most peoples of the world have advanced along with this series, but not always at the same pace. Some started early, some make leaps, and some are still lagging behind in various stages under different conditions. Thus, actually throughout the world today it is possible to find examples of all these groups. This phenomenon offers a unique opportunity to review the actual situation of their development along with historical records, anthropological studies, and archeological remains.

The single early family dominated several million years through the Old Stone Age. Some samples were still found in modern times, such as the detached Indians in the Rocky Mountains and the African Bushman in certain isolated areas.

They have "no settled dwelling-place, but spends the night in a cleft in the rocks, bends down a bush as shelter and protection, or hollows out a trench in the ground into which perhaps two adults and several children squeeze," according to an eyewitness in the early last century.

The primitive community dominated the Young Stone Age, beginning probably 30,000 years ago. It may be composed of several adult pairs and their dependents, camping together or living in one locality, regarding themselves as a unit and operating as such. It has also been called "camp", "band" and "horde" by social anthropologists, because it often moved together from place to place when it became necessary in the food quest.

Down to the beginning of the New Stone Age, about 12,000 years ago, the tightly organized clan replaced the loose primitive community as the dominant group. Clan is an exogamous group, the number of which are held to be related to one another by some tie. It may be belief in descent from a common ancestor, a species of object, animal, plant, or inanimate, called totems. Most frequent are animal totems. Early the term "clan" was used only for the matrilineal group which traces its descent through the mother. The patrilineal group which traces its descent through the father, was called "gen". Later, the term "clan" has been generally used to included both and also other similar groups since the theory of the matrilineal system always preceding the patrilineal system has lost most of its support, and most of the authorities have believed that both systems are equally early and equally primitive and some peoples have evolved the one, others the other.

The tribe appeared to be the dominant group when the Age of Copper began about 7,000 years ago. The term "tribe" has been widely used for any kind of group of primitive peoples, their subdivisions, or their federations. But in a properly defined sense, it is "a group of simple kind, nomadic, or settled in a more less definite locality, speaking a common dialect, with a rude form of government, and capable of uniting for common action." It differs from the clan by the characteristic that it is "an inbreeding or intermarrying group" while the clan is normally exogamous. It is better

314

organized politically, unlike the primitive community which usually lack any cohesion.

The nation started to emerge with the Iron Age about 3,000 years ago. But is did not distinguish itself as a dominant group until in modern times. The word "nation" stems from the Latin verb *nasci*, "to be born," and originally meant a group of people born in the same place. It was used as synonymous of clan, tribe, or other kinds of human group in the early literature. Its modern definition was first proposed by John Stuart Mill some time ago as a human group whose members place loyalty to the group as a whole over any conflicting loyalties. Other experts emphasize its common culture and consciousness, and note that it is something quite new in history. Antiquity was not acquainted with it, and ancient Egypt, China and Chaldea were in no degree nations.

It may be noted that the word "city" was sometimes used as a human group. It was actually a special form of clan or tribe in some areas, such as the ancient southern Europe. It is not a special class of group. It may also be noted that "state" and "empire" are different in status from the early single family, primitive community, clan, tribe, and the nation. The state is a political machinery, or the government of a group. Thus there are tribal state, national state. While the state may represent a group or act as its agent, as it always does, it is nevertheless not the group itself. Neither is an empire, which is virtually a state, but extends its control over more than one groups. There have been national empires, such as the French Empire under Napoleon I, and the British Empire in the last centuries. There also were clanish or tribal empires, such as the Empires of Sumer, Babylonia, Egypt, Assyria, Persia, Macedonia and Rome in the ancient western world; the Inca Empire in South America before the Spanish conquest; and the dynasties of Shang and Chou in ancient China.

The significance and importance of the elements, such as sex, blood, kinship, language, religion, custom and habit, attached to the five typical groups—the early single family, primitive community, clan, tribe, and the nation, vary from period to period and from area to area. Culturally, nevertheless, they are overall groups in their respective stages. This overall character is usually signified by an independent nature by which a group normally recognizes no other group as superior to itself, and not willing to be regulated, interfered with, or controlled by any other group; and internally, it can act as its will. It is this nature that ties these groups with war, because it enables them to wage war with necessary manpower and other resources. It is also this nature that requires them to protect it. It is therefore that the independent nature of these groups is the basic factor of war. In other words, the independence of these groups is the root of war.

The independent groups have fought war since very early times, and have been the successive fighting organs with traditional and legitimate rights to wage war. There were in history some wars originated by church or class, but neither church nor class has really been a fighting organ. There were also wars fought by fractional forces within a group as "civil war," but most major wars in history were waged by the independent groups.

War in primitive times between the early single families, primitive communities, clans or between tribes, might be not so devastating as that between the nations in modern times, owing to different military techniques and weapons. But it was certainly much more frequent as found by social anthropologists. For example, "it was war, war, incessant war between the natives of New Caledonia," "Raid and foray, massacre and pillage, were the order of the day in New Zealand," "The history of the African peoples has been, in the course of the millennia, undoubtedly a frightfully bloody one," "The Berbers show a state of eternal warfare existing among themselves," "The Aru Islanders are rarely without fighting somewhere," "In Timorlaut, there are incessant fights and no one dares go beyond the palisades without spear and bow," "All of Nauru is a scene of war," "Between the different tribes in the area inhabited by the Jibaros of Ecuador, there exists almost perpetual enmity, and destructive wars are often carried out," "In South America, the Botocudos are in constant war with neighboring peoples," and "among the Araucanians armed raids were constantly made on the neighboring villages, and thus a continual state of warfare was kept up."

316

"In the 18th century it was assumed that the primitive state of mankind was one of Arcadian peace, joy, and contentment. In the 19th century the assumption went over to the other extreme—that the primitive state as one of universal warfare. The proper course, if one is looking for the truth and not defending a thesis, is to go to the facts instead of inferring or meditating. So doing, one finds that there are very few people who do not quarrel and use violence and that these few are generally, if primitive, in such isolation that there is no one to fight or so poverty-stricken that they have nothing to tempt aggression," concluded by the authors of the great book—*The Science of Society.*

Fortunately there has been a ray of light shedding into the darkness of war everywhere. It is a process of the extension of peace along with the expansion of group.

2. Group Expansion and Peace

The extension of peace is based on the fact that there is usually a peace within an independent group and when the group expands, peace extends. This is why the independent groups have often been called peace-in groups.

The expansion of group is based on the fact that there is a great difference between the independent groups in their normal size of population and territory, as found by social anthropologists and other experts.

The early single family usually consists of an adult couple with a few kids. "Lives of extreme privation and hardship in this stage made it very difficult for the early single family to become big. Women always had trouble carrying and feeding babies. Hence, children were usually limited in number and wandered away when grown." The territory of the early single family is usually confined to the area within walking distance of their temporary dwelling place. For example, "the march of a native Australian family spreading over a front of half a mile to a mile and a half, for the purpose of collecting food."

The primitive community usually consists of a few scores of people. For example, a community among the Bushmen contains "on the average from fifty to one hundred persons," among the Bergdama, "from ten to thirty persons," among the Eskimo, "from twenty to sixty persons each, and this is about the range for the Chukchee peoples of Siberia," and among the Australian, "the average number was sixty, it could hardly have been over 100 or less than 25." The territory of the primitive community is usually up to a few hundred square miles. For example, "the average Bushman community is said to have an area of 200 square miles or more; for Bergdama no figures are available, though other evidence suggests that their territories are much smaller," and in some area of the Andaman each community has a "distinctive hunting territory, the mean area being about 16 square miles."

The clan usually consists of hundreds of people with a territory of hundreds of square miles. For example, "it was estimated that at the time when the white men began to come, there were approximately 297,500 Indians with an area of approximately 902,453 square miles in the five regions—New England, Middle Atlantic, South Atlantic, Central States and Gulf States. All of these Indians lived in independent clan groups of an average of 300 persons, accordingly, therefore, each group had a territory of an average of 900 square miles."

The tribe usually consists of thousands of people with a territory of thousands of square miles. With respect to population, for example, "among the Banton in south Africa, there are probably well over a thousand separate tribes. They vary greatly in population. Some have only a few hundred members each, others several thousand, and others as many as the Swazi of Swaziland with 204,000, the Eastern Mpondo with 260,000, and the Sotho of Basutoland with 682,000." As regarding territory, for example, "in Bechuanaland, the Kgatla occupy some 3,600 square miles; the Ngwaketse, 9,000; the Kwena, 15,000; the Tawana, 34,000, and the Ngwato, 42,000."

The nation usually consists of millions of people with a territory of from thousands to millions of square miles. The average population of the 135 nations in the United Nations in the early 1970s was approximately 24,000,000, ranging from the smallest nations such as Tonga with 90,000, Maldives with 110,000, and Iceland with 210,000, to the most populous nations, such as the Soviet Union with 241,720,000, India with 547,368,000, and China with 800,000,000. The average territory of the 135 nations was approximately 300,000 square miles, with some extremely small nations such as Maldives, 115; Malta, 122; and Barbados, 166; and some exceptionally large nations, such as China, 3,705,387; Canada, 3,851,787, and the Soviet Union, 8,649,489.

It is the great difference in the normal size of population and territory that sets the stage for the independent groups to expand step by step. How to expand? Generally, it is not by growth, but through merging: a number of early single families merge as a primitive community, a number of primitive communities merge as a clan, a number of clans merge as a tribe, and a number of tribes merge as a nation. It is hardly possible to find a case in history anywhere in which an independent group expands its population and territory to a very great size by its own growth alone, and not through merging with other groups.

There are many ways leading to merging:

The most natural ways are inter-marriage and inter-group trade. "Trade and the practice of exogamy were the main factors in breaking down the barriers that separated one group from another. It is not by chance that the Latin terms 'commercium' and 'connubium' came to be linked together in a formula; interchange of goods and of wives went along side by side. Followed them was the contagion of ideas or what has been called the cross-fertilization of culture."

Common ways include language and religion. It is well known, for instance, that the written Chinese has played a great role in merging the various peoples of that vast land into a nation. In primitive times relation between hostile and mutual suspicious groups was founded often by rite appealing to what was to be an even higher unity than that of blood. "This rite was religious and resulted in the various taboos on places and times just alluded to: the temple-peace, peace of God, house-peace, market-peace, holiday-peace."

The most unnatural ways are conquest, occupation, and annexation. "Take the case of conquest, where two groups fall into conflict and one overcomes the other; then the ensuing relation is one of dominion. But the classes thus differentiated as dominant and subject tend to amalgamate by inter-marriage and to regard themselves as kin, if not in demonstrable fact, at least through some eponymous ancestor."

Alliance, confederation, and federation are politically con- ventional ways. For example, Switzerland's political development as an alliance, confederation and then a federation streches over five and a half centuries. The first important date was 1291, when the three cantons of Uri, Schwyz, and Unterwalden entered what was known as the first Perpetual League. Then came the Confederation of eight cantons in 1353, the Confederation of thirteen cantons in 1513, the Act of Mediation with nineteen cantons in 1803, and the Federal Pact with twenty two cantons in 1815. But it was not until 1848 that this country transformed itself from a confederation into a federation.

There are still other ways such as adoption, migration and colonization. "The adoption of strangers into the group was a practice so common in the primitive societies that it has been listed as one of the most important privileges of the members of the ancient Grecian clan, the Roman clan, and the Indian Iroquois clan." "An analysis of the decent of the population of every part of Europe proves that intermingling has been going on for long times through migration and colonization. The Doric migration into Greece; the movements of the Kelts into Spain, Italy and eastward as far as Asia Minor; the teutonic emigrations which swept through Europe from the Black Sea into Italy, France, Germany, Spain, and into Africa; the invasion of the Balkan Peninsula by Slavs, and their extension over eastern Russia and into Siberia; Phoenician, Greek and Roman colonization; the roving Normans; the expansion of the Arabs; and the Crusades, are some of the important events that have contributed to the intermingling of the European people."

Through so many ways, merging has kept the process of group expansion working all the way from the tiny early single family to the huge nation, and has reduced independent groups by the thousands in the process. As a result, all these

320

groups soon lost their independence which is the root of war, and the chance of war between them was eliminated. Consequently, peace has been extended from normally inside of the early single family to be nation-wide, while warfare has been subdued from the early times when every man had to be a fighter as well as a hunter for a lifetime to a situation in which only a limited number of people are recruited to be soldiers for a limited time. This is one of the most important achievements in the history of civilization. If the process of group expansion continues to work as it did in the past several million years, all the current nations would be merged into a single group for the whole world, and a single group cannot fight alone, while the independence of the nation would be gone with the wind, and war between nations would pass into history forever. This probably is the only and right answer to the question of how to abolish war.

3. Group Expansion and Happiness

Actually the group expansion has not only done a big job in increasing peace, but has also played a great role in promoting the happiness of mankind.

Man started from an unfavorable position, for he originally lived within a limited habitat, probably a warm jungle. He satisfied his appetite with a narrow and definite range of foodstuffs. He had no natural weapons, such as fangs, claws, or horns; nor was he protected by a thick skin or great speed of movement. He was indeed a very poor candidate for survival. In order to overcome his weakness in the struggle for survival as well as for superior, he had to find and follow two special ways: one is to develop tools, and the other is to extend cooperation.

The great advantage in cooperation is to strengthen the protective power for existence and to increase the productive power for happiness, and the most effective method in cooperation to increase the productive power is the division of labor.

Two thousand years ago Plato in his famous book *Republic* recognized the utility of the division of labor as that the farmer produces more food than he needs, while the shoemaker produces more shoes than he can wear. Hence it is advantageous to both that each should produce for the other, since both will be better fed and better clothed by working together than by each dividing his work for all the various things he needs. This rests, according to Plato, upon two fundamental facts of human psychology; first, that different men have different apitudes and so do some kinds of work better than others, and second, that skill is gained only where men apply themselves steadily to the work for which they are naturally fitted.

There are two major forms in the division of labor: specialization and regionalization. The specialization began when mankind first tried to use his forefeet to hold his prey. By dint of practice he developed a hand-like claw, and after innumerable attempts, he balanced the whole of his body upon the hind legs. A primitive social application was the division of labor between the two sexes, according to which the men went to war, hunted, fished, and made the tools necessary for these pursuits, while the women cared for the shelter and prepared food. The next application was the separation of trades. A further application was the division of a specialized craft into separated processes, and the specialization of detail workers for each process. The classic illustration for this is that of pin-making: One man draws out the wire, another straightens it, a third cuts it, a fourth points it, a fifth grinds it at the top for receiving the head, and so on; the making of a pin is in this manner divided into the above 18 distinct operations and 10 men could make about 48,000 pins in a day, whereas, if they worked separately and independently, they certainly could not each of them have made 20, perhaps not one pin a day.

Regionalization is the division of labor by areas, affected by resources, raw materials, soil, climate, traditional crafts, etc. It is the twin of specialization. When the two sexes began to specialize in their works, regionalization began by the fact that the men worked in the forest, while the women worked in the house; each sex was master of its own field of activity. Later, when handicrafts separated from agriculture, the artists congregated in the cities, while the farmers remained in the country. The advanced form of regionalization is the division of labor between districts, and even between countries. The chief advantages of regionalization come from the opportunities for greater specialization which concentration affords. Where many factories engaged in the same industry are grouped together, the worker has a better chance to use his specialized skill and is encouraged to specialize still further. The industry, moreover, can command a large number of varied services which no single factory could afford and no scattered industry could maintain, such as the special transport facilities, the subsidiary industries, and the use of by-products.

The development of the division of labor, specialization as well as well as regionalization, however, depends mainly on exchange of goods and services. Without exchange, the division of labor may not be able to go much further beyond between the two sexes.

Exchange originates in the mutual dependence which arises from the limited capacity of an individual to supply his own wants, and the natural diversity in the capacities of individuals, which makes individuals able to supply each other's wants. The art of exchange is possessed by mankind alone. There are some other animals, such as ant and bee, which live under a system utilizing division of labor. But there have never been any other animals which make a fair and deliberate exchange. This is why the division of labor can be carried much further than by the other animals. And this is also one of the main reasons why mankind can be superior to all other animals. Through exchange, people are satisfied by giving and receiving the different products of their respective talents. The gains of both sides in exchange are mutual and reciprocal and the division of labor is thus advantageous to the different persons employed in the various occupations into which it is subdivided. And through exchange, people are able to utilize mutually and to enjoy reciprocally the various resources of different areas. Exchange is not only a method of transmitting the advantage of the division of labor to all, but also a condition for the advance of the division of labor itself. Without exchange, every man must have procurred to himself every necessity and convenience of life which he wants. All must perform the same duties, and do the same work, and there could be no such difference in employment as could alone give occasion to a great difference in talents.

The importance of the division of labor as the most effective method to increase the productive power for happiness, together with exchange as the key to the development of the division of labor, was exploited thoroughly by Adam Smith two hundred years ago in his work *An Inquiry into the Nature and Cause of the Wealth of Nations.* He found that the division of labor together with exchange has brought mankind the greatest advantage by increasing and improving products, and held that the history of mankind may be viewed simply the ever-widening application of the principle of the division of labor and exchange.

However, there are always existing many social, political, and economic barriers to the development of the division of labor and exchange between independent groups. Even the highly civilized ancient Greece, for instance, was handicapped by the barriers existing between its independent and small city-states. "In ancient Greece, specialization of craft is found only on the broadest lines; and man could turn his hand to almost any task. The first specialization approaching distinctness was that of the smith, who did almost all the work in metals. He derives his name and the names of his tools from the metal copper, but his operations were not confined to it. He worked in gold, silver, tin, and iron, and his function did not stop even there, for he sewed the leathern parts of shields and otherwise supplemented his main work. There is in Homer no clearly marked case of division of labor in the manufacture of any single product," according to a special study.

In order to keep widening the application of the division of labor and exchange, so as to increase the productive power for happiness, therefore, it is necessary to eliminate the independence of the individual groups, so as to wipe out the various barriers existing between them. This is a big job, but is has actually been done all the time by the process of group expansion. It is indeed a great role the group expansion has played in promoting the happiness of mankind.

As a result of the increase in productive power by the division of labor and exchange through the expansion of group, mankind has progressed from a state of "original destitution" to a much better level in happiness. There is no difficulty to appreciate this progress if we compare modern life in general with that of some peoples who still lag behind in a situation of "original destitution" as witnessed by various writers in the last century.

"The only purpose of life for the natives in Southwest Africa is to fill their bellies with something that looks edible; they eat gum arabic, the pounded roots of trees, steal grass seed from ants, and regard a swarm of locusts as a blessing." "Of certain natives of Borneo, like the animals of the bush they pass a rambling life, caring only for the satisfaction of their subsistence-needs; for food they use all sorts of animals, even the most loathesome, together with sago and wild fruits." "The natives of New Zealand, by no means the lowest of mankind, were pinched for food in the 'grumbling months' of winter. They had no other name for them, being a blank in their calendar, as they could do nothing but sit in their smoky huts, with eyes always filled with tears. Among the American Indians known to the Jesuit fathers, starvation was common, and after eating their skin clothing, and even the lacings of their shoes, the natives ate one another."

4. Group Expansion as Law

In the process of the group expansion through merging, usually the smaller groups give up their independence first and become some kind of autonomous units, which are then transformed into local or custom units, and finally lose all their traces in the larger group. It is a process of amalgamation, and is usually a long and common process: too long to be remembered and too common to be noticed. There are, however, numerous historical accounts by authorities, which serve well as testimonies of this process ever-working every where.

The first Egyptian kingdom was formed about five thousand years ago by several groups which were made up of a great number of villages or clans during a long period of time.

About 2500 years ago, there existed in Greece a large number of cities with economic self-sufficiency and political autonomy. Each of them was formed step by step out of a series of smaller groups similar to one another. Later, some 200 of these cities joined in a confederation led by Athens, while others joined in another league led by Sparta.

Rome was founded by Romulus about 2700 years ago from a community formed out of a hundred small Latin groups around the Palatine Hill. It was later joined by the united people of a hundred small Sabine groups, and later by an alliance of a hundred other surrounding groups. These three hundred groups were thus gathered at Rome, and completely organized under a council of chiefs now called the Roman Senate, an assembly of the people called the comitia curiata, and one military commander, the rex; and with one purpose, that of gaining a military ascendency in Italy.

According to the Bible, Moses organized twelve tribes—Reuben, Simeon, Judah, Issachar, Zebulun, Ephraim, Manasseh, Benjamin, Dan, Asher, Gad, and Naphtali, of the Hebrews as one group called the Children of Israel, with the tribe of Levi as a special unit. These tribes represented a reconstruction of Hebrew society by legislative procurement.

The Celts or Gauls, ancestors of the French people, were a set of loosely organized clans before the Christian Era. It would seem that no one clan ever rose to a complete hegemony over the rest. The victory of Caesar over the Gauls was, above all, the result of the fact that he never had to face a united Gaul, except when, after six years of spasmodic effort, it united for a day round Vercingetorix, only to die heroically at Alesia.

Some other Celts retained the clan system in Scotland and Ireland until a much later time. The clans in the Highlands of Scotland, in particular, did not lose their vitality until the middle of the 18th century.

Up until the Middle Ages, England was still occupied by a good number of separate groups, as were Scotland and Wales. The union of England, Scotland and Wales as Great Britain has only been in effect for about 400 years. The official title of Great Britain was first used in 1604 after James VI of Scotland had succeeded to the English throne, and it was formally adopted in 1707 at the date of the union of the crowns of England and Scotland.

In China, it was said that Emperor Huang divided the land into 10,000 states of 100 lis each 4600 years ago. A Chinese li at the present time is equal to approximately one third of a mile. This legend indicates that in the early times, China was a composite of thousands of primitive communities along the Yellow River. Some 600 years later, it extended its influence southward when Holy King Yu defeated the people of Miau along the Yangtze River and held a convention at Tu Shan. There were still 10,000 states came for the convention with jade and silk as tributes. The number of states was reduced to less than 2,000 when King Wu of the Chou Dynasty took over the hegemony from the Shang Dynasty 3,000 years ago, to less than 200 in the period of the Eastern Chou, to seven in the later period of Warring States, and finally to a single nation 2,200 years ago, when the first emperor of the Chin Dynasty eliminated all the remaining states. Yet, in China today, the ancient clan system can still be traced back clearly. The territory of China as a single nation established by the Chin Dynasty was about one fourth of modern China. All the rest great areas were expanded through the merging of many different peoples in the last two thousand years.

In pre-historic times, Japan was peopled by immigrants from several parts of eastern Asia, mostly of Tungusic origin, and prior to these migrations it was sparsely inhabited by ancentors of the people now known as the Ainu. In the first four centuries, there existed a great number of primitive communities or clans competing with one another, and by the beginning of the 5th century a group known as the Yamato people achieved a position of supremacy in central Japan. But despite the obedience nominally due to the head of the imperial clan, the other clans claimed independence until 1868 when the feudal rule of the islands came to a close. With the easy overthrow of the Tokugawa, Japan took a major step in uniting into a modern nation.

The above historical accounts merely provide some examples. Similar records may be found in the history of any country, and a clearer picture can be seen in the formation of modern federations.

The Germans were impacted into a federation of 25 states by the Franco-Prussian War in 1871. Before the war they had experienced a number of confederations. The first was the Confederation of Rhine set up by Napoleon when the Roman Empire was finally dissolved in 1806. Thirty-nine members in all were admitted. The next one was the German Confederation from 1815 to 1866 with thirty-nine states of widely varying sizes in most of its existing times. The third one was the North German Confederation set up by Prussia after the defeat of Austria in the War of 1866. It included twenty-two states to the north of the river of Main. Before the confederations, it was hardly more than a loose association of scattered German clans governed by their own dynasties, joined together at most by the spiritual crown of the Holy Roman Empire which may be traced back to the 9th century. In the later period of the Holy Roman Empire, there were in Germany more than 1,700 territorial possessions. After the Peace of Westphalia in 1648, these were consolidated into 355 states, and the number shrank rapidly as various unions were formed since then, through the confederations, federation, the Weimar Republic, and the attempt for Third Reich by the Nazi regime. After the second World War, Germany was divided into two, east and west. While the east adopted a unitary form of government, the west was reorganized into a federation of 10 states. Now a reunion of the east and west is likely approaching since the Berlin Wall has been broken down.

To the south of Germany lies the Swiss federation of which the long history has been told early as an example for the merging of alliance, condeferation and federation.

The federation of South Africa is composed of the Cape of Good Hope, Natal, the Transvaal, the Orange Free State, with a combination of black, white, and various other peoples.

Among the blacks, there are 9 major ethnic groups, and among the whites, English and Dutch descent are the major racial origins. There are more than 10 religions in South Africa.

Nigeria is a new federation in West Africa. It has a central government which shares power with 12 regional units. Its population is made up of a wide variety of language and culture groups. Nearly 250 different languages have been identified. The three main linguistic groups are corresponding to its major ethnic groups: the Ibo, Yoruba, and Hausa. Ibo people inhabit the southeastern part of Nigeria. Early there had never been large states or even strong chiefs in Iboland. Their politics were a viable form of village-oriented democracy. Southwestern Nigeria is the homeland of Yoruba. In contrast to the Ibo, Yoruba at an early stage in their history had developed powerful tribe states with kings and bureaucracies. Hausa are the dominant ethnic groups in northern Nigeria. As early as the 13th century they had established major tribe states such as Kano, Zaria, and Katsina. Each state was governed by an emir. Other major ethnic groups in the north include Fulani, Kanuri, and Tiv.

In Asia, an Indian federation of 28 states and territories was formed shortly after the second World War with jurisdiction over an immense population speaking no fewer than 800 languages.

Stretching across Europe and Asia is the huge Soviet federation of 15 major units called Union Republic, and within each of these are a good number of smaller units with various statuses, such as autonomous republic, autonomous oblast, and national okrug. Basically, all the units represent different ethnic groups, which, taken together with the ones not recognized as political entities, exceed one hundred in number.

In the course of 200 years, the well-known federation of the United States of America, which began with 13 colonies through a Continental Congress and a Confederation, has incorporated 50 states, and its population has increased from about 4 million whites and negros including a great number of slaves to more than 200 million from almost everywhere and with almost every kind of ethnic background.

In addition to the seven modern federations introduced above, there are a number more including Argentina, Australia, Burma, Brazil, Canada, Malaysia, Mexico, Venezuela, and Yugoslavia, each formed by a number of units. All the federations at the present time have about 40 percent of the world's population and cover more than half of the world's land.

As testified by historical accounts together with the development of modern federations, it is clear that group expansion has worked with the merging process throughout all of history and over the whole world. Thus, unmistakably, it is an historical law as well as an universal law. It has expanded the size of independent groups from the early single family usually of a few people with a territory of walking distance to the nation usually of millions of people with a territory up to millions of square miles, and has reduced the number of independent groups from about 1,000,000 early single families in the stone ages down to less than 200 nations in modern times. Thus, it is certainly an evolutionary law.

As an historical, universal, and evolutionary law, the group expansion has increased peace by eliminating the independence of the group, from normally within the early single family to be nation-wide, and has promoted happiness by extending the division of labor together with exchange, from the "original destitution" to a much better level in average modern life. Thus, undisputably, it is a law most useful and most beneficial to mankind.

As an historical, universal, and evolutionary law, it is impossible to have been made by human beings. It is a law of nature which "is the accidents and catastrophes of all kinds, happening in every conceivable way, that make it," as Plato put it. It is a law of necessity which is "not the result of any human wisdom, but the necessary consequence of a certain propensity in human nature;" or "a result of the struggle for existence," in the opinions of modern scholars.

Whether it is natural or necessary, the group expansion, as an historical, universal, and evolutionary law, would keep working for the future as it did for the past millenia everywhere, until all nations are merged into a single group for a permanent peace on the earth and a general happiness of all peoples.

5. Conditions for Group Expansion

How soon will all the nations be merged into a single group for the whole world?

The answer to this critical question may be found primarily in the physical conditions to which the law of group expansion is subject. The group expansion is a standing law always ready to move, but it cannot move very far until the right physical conditions are ready for the move. This is why it has been moving slowly over thousands of years, only step by step, and not all the way without interruption.

By far, the most important physical condition for group expansion is economic life, because the size of the group in both population and territory is virtually controlled by economic life: the population is always determined by the subsistence the economic life can provide, and the territory is always limited to the range suitable for the economic life to operate. Thus the group can expand only as far as the economic life allows, and any great expansion depends on the change of economic life.

As remarked earlier that the development of tools with five ages of Old Stone, Young Stone, New Stone, Copper and Iron, has led the change of economic life into five modes: food-gathering, hunting-fishing, hoe-cultivation, animal-raising and agriculture. The change of five modes in economic life has in turn led the group expansion through the five steps: the early single family, primitive community, clan, tribe, and the nation.

The food-gathering people had to live from day to day and from place to place. Their food supply from the wild land was generally meager and irregular. They had to grasp everything available to satisfy their immediate needs. Nature was not under any kind of control. Their life was highly hazardous and subject to the element of chance or luck and to changes in weather and the seasons. It is no wonder, under these circumstances, that the early single family was always limited to a few people confined to the area within a walking distance.

The hunting-fishing people still had to wander about here and there, but their fishing ability began to be a great resource for subsistence. They were also able to gain more and better subsistence by aggressive hunting, especially of big games, such as wild horses, ox, deer, elk, bison. Because of the extension of fishing and hunting, more people were apt to live and work together, and thus to form the primitive community with usually several scores of people in a territory usually of tens of square miles.

In the hoe-cultivation stage, people still more or less depended on hunting and fishing for living. But they started to invest labor in cultivating the land, thus opening a relative reliable sources of subsistence. They also started to domesticate animals for meat. These adventures not only tended to support more people, but also made life more tied to the land, resulting in less wandering. For these reasons, the clan gained ground with usually some hundreds of population and a territory of hundreds of square miles.

There were two kinds of pastoral animal-raising life: nomadic and settled. The nomadic pastoral people moved from place to place, but usually according to a seasonal mass-migration, reappearing in the same regions at regular intervals. The settled pastoral people led a sedentary life, but they wanted a tighter and larger organization to protect themselves and their herds, just as the nomadic pastoral people did. Both pastoral people domesticated animals usually in a great number for more reliable gains in milk and wool rather than merely for meat. They also utilized the land extensively by converting into human food more plants that are not edible by man. Thus they led the tribe developing to consist usually of thousands of population with a territory usually of thousands of square miles.

The agricultural life has been relatively peaceful and stable, depending primarily on longer-term gains. It has naturally led to a much larger group for more security. After all, "the supporting power of the land from agriculture was from 4 to 25 times as much as from pasture," and "meat needs twenty times the land cereals do," according to experts. As a result, agriculture can produce much more subsistence for much more people to live together, thus, leading to the growth of the nation with usually millions of population in a territory usually of millions of square miles.

Transportation and communication are other physical conditions for group expansion. It is transportation that helps the expansion to conquer long distances and to overcome other physical obstacles, such as high mountains, great deserts, wide rivers, big lakes, and immense oceans.

Before the end of the Stone Age, no means of transportation appeared except some crude rafts, canoes on the water, and some sledges on the land. Travel was by walking, and everything was carried by hand, or on the head or back. Contacts between people were very feeble. This is one of the reasons why the group could not expand larger than the clan.

By the Copper Age, tools and energies were beginning to be used for transportation. The most important was the invention of the wheeled vehicle pulled by an animal. The donkey and white ass were probably used as beasts of burden before the horse started to play a great role in transportation, and not much later, the mule was also used. On the water, wind power was first applied to the sail of the boat. All these helped the growth of the tribe.

In the Iron Age, the sailing vessel was greatly improved for the coastlines, the wheeled vehicle was widely used on better roads, the camel appeared as the "ship of the desert", and elephant and reindeer were used in some areas for riding, packing or carrying vehicles. Later the mariner's compass was invented and ships were built for open-sea navigation. All these helped the growth of the nation.

Communication is important to the expansion of group, because it helps to overcome obstacles to understanding and to the dissemination of information. Communication needs speech and writing language as media. Speech led the group expansion up to the clan stage, then writing language boosted

333

the growth of the tribe. The use of papyrus and parchment made communication more reliable over the limits of time and space, thus assisting the expansion of the tribe to the nation. The invention of paper and the application of movable type in printing sped up this expansion greatly.

Another very important medium of communication is money, which has been called "the universal language." Various objects, notably the cowrie shell, were used as money from very early times to the clan stage. Metallic money began to appear about 3,000 years ago, first in the form of tools, then of coins. The silver and gold coins especially inspired confidence, because of their durable and precious qualities with universal demand for them, and facilitated exchange tremendously, thus stimulating the expansion of the clan to the tribe. The rise of the banking system to extend the use of money had a great impact on the expansion of the tribe to the nation.

Weapons also are an important condition for the expansion of group.

Since their first appearance in history, weapons have played an important role in group expansion, because they have facilitated military conquests, occupations and annexations, and have made it difficult for the smaller groups to exist. The influence of this role has grown steadily as their striking power, reaching distance, speed and mobility have continually increased.

Early man probably first used hand-held stones as weapons, then learned to use clubs before starting to use stone-bladed spears and stone axes. The striking power of the club and stone weapons was apparently awkward, their reaching distance limited to several yards, their speed depended on man's hands, and their mobility on man's feet. Notwithstanding, it would be difficult for group expansion to have started through the primitive community without their help.

The transition from throwing a stone as a missile to blowing a blowgun, releasing a sling, or projecting a javelin was a slow journey. But a great leap forward was made with the invention of the bow and arrow. This invention reduced to seconds the time needed to reach a target tens of yards away, and increased the striking power, especially with poison and fire arrows. It was this invention that helped the clan to grow fast.

The substitution of metal weapons for stone ones started about 6,000 years ago. The new weapons had much more striking power, because they were sharper, more durable and maneuverable, and were convenient for developing and training professional skill, such as the use of sword. The striking power also increased when the battering-ram was used. Meanwhile the reaching distance, speed and mobility of weapons were greatly extended by using the horse and chariot on land, and the fighting vessels on water. These developments helped the tribe to reach its heyday.

The most significant development in weapons, however, was yet to be introduced by the invention of black powder and its application in modern times to artillery, rockets, firearms, and naval fleets. This powder strengthened the striking power so formidable as to eliminate almost all the defensive value of feudal castles, heavy city walls, and other fortifications. It also enlarged the reaching distance, speed and mobility of weapons tremendously. Up to the turn of this century, for example, improved guns had been able to hit targets tens of miles away; magazine rifles to fire 15 rounds a minute at 1,000 yards, and naval fleets to carry the far-reaching and high-speed weapons to attack a country across the ocean. These developments helped the growth of the nation to the peak of its history.

6. Ready to Go

Now the problem is: Are all physical conditions ready for group expansion to merge all nations into a single group for the whole world?

Since the beginning of the Machine Age in modern times, the rapid advance of science and technology has enabled machines to make all physical conditions for group expansion moving forward at an accelerated speed. In economic life, agriculture no longer held a prominent position, and had to yield it to a cluster of industries, signifying the rise of industrial life.

335

Led by powerful machines, in conjunction with the extension of the division of labor, the application of mass production and the utilization of new materials, especially those produced by chemistry, such as clothing fibers, plastics and synthetic rubber, industrial life has proved to be able to increase working ability up to hundreds of time, to produce much more commodities and services to support more people, and to rely on much less land for living, thus making it possible to provide adequate subsistence for all peoples of the world to live together as one group, with a reasonable limitation on population.

Actually, the industrial life not only makes it possible for all peoples to live together as one group, but also ties them together as one group by establishing a worldwide economic interdependence. This is mainly because industries do not depend so much, like agriculture, on soil which can be found everywhere. They require various resources which are unevenly distributed over the earth, and no country, even the richest, has them all in sufficient amounts at all times. This uneven distribution, together with local differences in climate, the availability of technical skills, equipment, capital and labor, necessarily intensifies the division of labor and exchange between countries and regions. The result is a quick growth of world economy which inevitably makes all peoples of the world dependent on each other for mutual and common benefits. This interdependence has been clearly demonstrated in world trade, which, since the Industrial Revolution, has increased rapidly in volume, has extended from luxury items to goods for comon consumption and essential uses, and has developed into a network covering all countries, at every level of economic development, and under every economic system.

There is no doubt, therefore, that modern industries have made economic life ready for group expansion to merge all nations into a single group for the whole world. Also ready are transportation, communication and weapons.

In transportation, the steam engine was applied to boat and train early in the 19th century. The gasoline engine was applied to highway vehicle as automobile about 60 years later and to airplane early in this century. In the 1950s the airlines

336

began to abandon gasoline engines in favor of jets which offered new possibilities in speed, and economy of maintenance and operation. Meanwhile huge ships propelled by nuclear power started to appear. They can run for several years around the world for several times without refueling. These new means have increased not only the speed of transportation greatly, but also its carrying ability up to thousands of times. In space as well as in time they have actually enabled transportation to shrink the whole world into a small country.

In communication, telegraph was invented just before the middle of the 19th century. About 30 years later telephone was invented. Early in this century radio was invented, and about another 30 years later television was invented. These new media were soon expanded all over the world, and in the 1960s they started to hook up with satellite transmitters and have made global communication a matter of hours, minutes and even seconds. They have virtually connected all peoples of the world as nearby neighbors. Furthermore, the new comer—computer has made it possible for a central government of the world to manage public affairs of all peoples with necessary information available any time in a small office.

The development of modern weapons described early has been more than ready as a physical condition for the group expansion. Their striking power is so devastating that they can kill millions of people and destroy hundreds of cities with one attack; and their reaching distance, speed and mobility are so great that they can hit targets thousands of miles away in minutes. Actually they have made the entire world a small tactical theater in which no place is safe and not covered by terror, and no nation can be really protected.

So, clearly, all physical conditions—economic life, transportation, communication, and weapons are ready for the group expansion to merge all nations into a single group. For the first time in history, they have nullified the border-lines of the nations, the integrity of their territory, and the existence of their independence; and for the first time in history, they have made possible and also necessary for all peoples of the world to live together as nearby neighbors, and to have a common

337

government to manage their public affairs conveniently like a small kingdom.

In addition, there have been various endeavors to help the building of one world for all peoples. They are not very much new. They had slow beginnings and deep roots in the past, but they have grown very fast with new vigor in modern times. Important among them are geographical exploration, migration, intellectual dissemination, agricultural dispersal, uniformity and standardization, social progress, and developments in international relations and organizations, together with the socialist international movement.

Geographical exploration started to fan out over the oceans in the 1400s with the great success of Columbus reaching the New World. About 200 years later, Captain Cook opened the age of Scientific Discovery, and finally, Peary approached the North Pole and Amundsen the South Pole. The era of great geographical explorations is now about closed. But their accomplishments have been miraculous. They have unveiled the real globe, completed its map, and transformed it from numerous scattered, isolated and unknown parts into an integral body. It is this accomplishment that has cleared the ground for the building of one world.

The most significant migration in modern times has been of an intercontinental type. Mass emigration from Europe to America began in the 16th century. From the late 19th century to the first World War, the annual average was over one million. Negro slaves also were an important element in modern migration. It is estimated that from the 16th century to the middle of the 19th, about twenty million Negroes were brought out from Africa, most of them imported to the tropical and subtropical regions. In general up to the early decades of the 20th century, modern intercontinental migration totaled to sixty million. Meanwhile migration within Asia, Europe and America was extensive too. The contribution of modern migrations to the building of one world has been great, especially in the possession of the globe, redisbution of the population, racial intermarriage, and cultural assimilation.

338

Intellectual dissemination is largely achieved through the migrations of students, scholars, learning and the applications of foreign languages, exchange and translation of foreign publications, screenings of foreign movies, the gathering and spreading of international news, and transmission of information by mail, telegraph, telephone, radio and television to other lands. All these elements have grown very fast. For example, the total number of migratory students throughout the world in 1971 reached 528,774, more than 100 times 100 years ago. All these elements have been working for the building of one world quietly in the long run.

As regarding agriculture dispersal, wheat, for example, was first brought to the New World by the great explorer Columbus. Other plants brought by modern explorers to the New World include coffee, tea, sugarcane, and soybean. In return, they brought corn, potato, and rubber from the New World to their old homelands. As far as domestic animals are concerned, it is significant that almost all the important ones which the New World now has, such as cattle, sheep, pig, and horse, came from the Old World, although some native species of them have existed in the New World for a long time. Prior to Columbus, there existed a wild turkey in the New World, but there was even no common chicken of the Old World. The agricultural dispersal has made various contributions to the building of one world, such as enriching subsistence, distributing natural resources more widely, utilizing the land more effectively, and assimilating tastes, habits and interests in living.

In assimilating tastes, habits, and interests in living as well as in understanding, more contributions have been made by various efforts for universal uniformity and standards. First and most important of these efforts is the adoption of common symbols and the most important adopted common symbols are the Arabic numerals which are now used and understood almost everywhere. Other important and widely adopted symbols are signals for transportation and communication, such as used in road traffic control, maritime and aviation operations. Second is the time system including the adoption of

Gregorian Calendar, Christian Era, the seven-day week, and the division of a day into hours, minutes and seconds with clocks. Third is weights and measures, especially the development of the metric system, and the last is the thermometer with three major scales: Kelvin, Fahrenheit and Celsius which has virtually become the International Temperature Scale.

In social systems, there has been no uniformity or standard reached, but a significant progress has been made in some areas to aid the building of one world. First instance of this progress is the rise of democracy, primarily as a political system. This rise was initiated by the theory of Social Contract, and inspired by American and French revolutions in the 18th century. Since then, it has developed from a term of abuse to a notion of honor and its face value is today almost universally accepted. Next is the promotion of human rights of which the overall principle is that men are equal and free, as declared by American and French revolutions. There have been great achievements including the abolition of slavery and the adoption of women's suffrage in the 19th and early 20th centuries, and the Declaration of Human Rights by the United Nations. The third is the growing similarity of national laws, paving ground for a world law. This is a consequence of the mutual influence of the two great legal systems—Civil Law and Common Law, and the acceptance of the West legal principles by the East countries in modern times. Finally comes the development of international laws—the law of conflicts and the law of nations. The law of conflicts comprises the rules for setting problems arising from the laws of different countries in private international relations. The law of nations comprises the rules which regulate relations between nations, but there has been a tendency to limit the national sovereignty and to claim a direct position for the individual in it. The establishment of international judicial systems from arbitration to world court is important for implementing the international laws.

International organizations are required to be treated separately from social progress because of their complexity. Generally speaking, they are two kinds: official and non-governmental. The number of non-governmental international organizations has increased to about 1500 in the 1960s. Their functions cover every field, every nook and corner of human endeavor, creating a cosmopolitan outlook. The primary form of official international organizations is the consular service and diplomatic system. In addition are international conferences, of which the number has increased at an accelerated pace, involving more and more nations and more and more subjects. Next are permanent international organizations, first in special fields such as the Universal Postal Union, International Bureau of Weights and Measures, International Institute of Agriculture, International Office of Public Health, and the International Labor Organization, then the general organizations: the League of Nations after the first World War and the United Nations after the second World War. Both are important experiments in history, but they were established from the past and not projected for the future. They were established as associations of nations with their member nations as the real masters. They set about to legalize, fortify and even strengthen the dominant position of their member nations in their Covenant or Charter by emphasizing such principles as "sovereign equality," "equal right and self-determination," "territorial integrity and political independence," "domestic jurisdiction," "self-defense" and "regional arrangements" with unanimous voting rule or veto power. These principles actually try to maintain a status quo and keep history standing still, and consequently they turn out to be obstacles to the building of one world.

As a special force in modern international developments, the socialist movement started to organize an international political party for a world revolution in the 1860s, later known as the First International. It was transformed into the Second International in 1889, and replaced by the Third International in 1919. The Third International was actually a disciplined unitary world Communist Party with a strongly centralized machinery. It claimed to be the general staff of world revolution with the aim of establishing a world government. However, it was crippled in the second World War and further disintegrated by nationalism reviving in the Communist world in recent decades.

7. The Nation Reviewed

The facts that both the United Nations and the socialist international movement have been seriously thwarted by nationalist forces, indicate that the nation as an independent group is still stalled on the way toward a single group for the whole world, even though all physical conditions have been ready for group expansion, and various endeavors have made great contributions to the building of one world. It is necessary therefore to make a fuller examination on the nation itself and the various important aspects concerning it or in relation to it.

Territorially, a nation is just a small part of the surface of the earth. The total surface of the earth is 196,950,769 square miles, of which 29% is land, the rest is covered by water. At the present time, the largest nation, the Soviet Union, has a territory of 8,649,489 square miles, about 15% of the land or 4.4% of the total surface. The smallest nation, the Maldives, has a territory of 115 square miles, only about 0.0002% of the land, or 0.00006% of the total surface. The average territory of the 135 nations in the United Nations in the early 1970s was approximately 300,000 square miles, about 0.52% of the land or 0.16% of the total surface.

The earth is a round ball, on which no nation is a center for others. In early times some places were regarded as the center, such as Jerusalem, China, because the knowledge about the world was greatly limited. Nowadays it would be ridiculous if someone believes that his nation is the center of the world.

The existence of the nation is not something permanent. It is just a step in the process of group expansion, or as Professor Harold J. Laski put it, "nothing more than an accident" in the long run of history. Actually the history of the nation has not been nearly as long as commonly thought. Crowded as the world is with nations today, it may be unbelievable that as late as four hundred years ago, only about one-fifth of the land surface of the earth was occupied by nations, and all the rest was scattered with smaller groups: tribes, clans, primitive communities, and early single families. It took a long time to explore the vast areas and to merge the various groups into nations. This is why most of the present nations are under two hundred years old, and many of them are much younger than the United Nations. There are indeed some senior nations, but their actual ages are always subject to guessing, because they usually include a long time of pre-nation history.

There are several elements that hold the nation together and not easily to turn loose. Important of them, generally speaking, are language, kinship, religion, history, and territory. But they are the same kind of elements that held together successively, the early single family, primitive community, clan, and tribe. They held the smaller groups together even much tighter than the nation, because the nation is usually too large to be tied up. Yet they were not able to hold these groups tight enough against the process of group expansion, and let them turn loose again and again. Can they hold up the nation and not let it turn loose for long?

In addition, national character and sentiment have been emphasized as important as the elements that hold the nation together. National character roughly means a certain mentality, traditions, habits and traits of a nation. Many attempts have been made to trace the origin of national character. In early times, natural influences were considered the main causes. Since the 19th century, however, with the increase of knowledge in geography and history, it has become clear that national character is made and modified by numerous factors. Among them, the dynamics of history constitute the main force, and the natural environment is only a relative condition. Since the dynamics of history are characterized by restless motion, it is obvious that national character is by no means unchangeable. For instance, "In the beginning of the 18th century, when the English were considered a nation most inclined to revolution and to change, while the French seemed a most stable and stolid nation. One hundred years later, just the opposite opinion about the English and French was generally held."

In respect to national sentiment, mutual sympathy was first regarded by John Stuart Mill as the essence of a nation. Others have stressed the consciousness, spirit, and even prejudices of a nation. Closely connected with national sentiment are national anthem and flag, and the use of a characteristic figure, animal, or plant as a national image. There are some people who have assumed that national sentiment is an instinct, and natural. However, if the definition of instinct excludes certain behaviors, such as impulse modified by customs, the imitation of the actions of a multitude, and response to public expectations, encouragements and pressures, its contribution to national sentiment would be insignificant, if any. It is more precise to say that national sentiment, to a great extent, is the product of education in the broad sense, received through school, the family, society, and especially the mass media. It is rather artificial.

Emphasized even more than national elements, character and sentiment, has been national sovereignty as a symbol of the independence of the nation. It has developed from very early times, and the first modern exponent was Jean Bodin. It was Thomas Hobbes who started to assume a social contract as its origin. In order to unite their nation through a strong central authority, both Bodin and Hobbes allocated sovereignty to the monarch. Consequently their theories merely served as a pretext for the rise of despotism. Then appeared a theory that the people as a whole were the sovereign, and thus the sovereignty resided in the nation. This was the main theme of the American and French Revolutions. Since the sovereignty belonged to the nation, it was not only unlimited, but also inalienable. So when adopted in international relations later, it changed in nature from an original principle of internal unity and order to a new doctrine of international separation and anarchy. It has become an ill omen rather than a noble emblem, and has been, as the political pluralists and some other scholars pointed out, incompatible with the interest of humanity and allegiance to the world.

As a symbol of independence, national sovereignty resembles ancient totemism. But totemism to primitive people was much more powerful than national sovereignty is to modern man, because the totem was something embodied, a deity of religion and an origin of blood relationship, whereas national sovereignty is merely an abstract hypothesis. It would be no more difficulty to get rid of the abstract hypothesis of sovereignty than to eliminate the embodied totemism.

Like national sovereignty, nationalism has also changed from a force of internal unity to a factor of international separation. It had certain roots with the renaissance and religious reform. Its first manifestation occurred in England during the Puritan revolution of the 17th century, followed by the American and French Revolution of the late 18th century. Since then, it has spread over the whole world. It has been viewed as the return of barbarism and tribalism along with the developing of modern intellectualism and irrationalism, and mingled with idealism and realism. Plainly "it is the soda water that mixes with all other drinks and makes them sparkle." For the very reason, it has become in modern times a dominating force which tends to be either too conservative to deal with new situations, such as political isolationism and economic protectionism, or too aggressive to be held in bounds, such as modern militarism and the most notorious imperialism. This is the primary reason for a bona fide nationalism to endure only temporarily anywhere. There are other ways through which nationalism has stirred the trouble water of the world: It connotes an utmost esteem of one's own nation, commands a paramount loyalty and duty to one's own nation, asserts the highest interest of one's own nation, and above all, supports the national independence as its agitator by all means.

It is necessary to note that the importance of the independence of the nation, the national sovereignty, and nationalism, stems from the assumption that the value of the nation is higher than anything else. This assumption is also the base for the efforts to magnify, glorify, perpetualize and divinize the position, nature, elements, character and sentiment of the nation. So based also is popular allegiance to the nation. The crucial problem, therefore, is what is the value of the nation as an independent group?

Basically the value of any independent group in group expansion from the early single family, primitive community, clan, tribe and the nation, lies in its size as a larger basis to extend more peace and promote more happiness. When its size

345

becomes smaller than the physical conditions can provide, its value diminishes. As regards the nation, its size as a basis for peace and happiness was larger than that of tribe, so its value has been recognized high for centuries. Now its size has become a basis too small for a world peace and the general happiness of mankind, and all physical conditions have been ready for merging all nations into a single group for the whole world, its value has been necessarily diminishing rapidly. Consequently there has been no room left for the independence of the nation, national sovereignty and nationalism to exist; the emphasis of the position, nature, elements, character and sentiment of the nation has not meant much more than blowing some air into a broken tire; and the popular allegiance to the nation has become merely a blind patriotism.

While the value of the nation as an independent group is diminishing rapidly and its ground is deteriorating in every aspect, it is remaining as the agent of its independence, sovereignty and nationalism:

—to be the organ of war with a built-in military establishment ready to fight anytime, to use best brains and high techniques to develop and produce weapons, to pour money, labor and resources into arsenals and arms races, to rely war as a foreign policy, and to permeate the poisons of spies everywhere;

—to limit the freedom of movement in migration and travel, to spread the drug abuse, to institute international terrorism, to hamper the efforts for the protection and improvement of global environment, to foster prejudice, suspicion, hatred and revenge toward other people, and to ignore humanity;

—to allow dictatorship in government, to strip liberties in life and property of the people, to interfere their daily life and to usurp their money, to maintain the arena for the power-hungry, greedy and paranoid leaders to play dirtist tricks and engage most feverish struggle for political power and dominant position, to keep their constant depredation and even to create the hell of civil wars; and

—to prevent people from enjoying the advantages of worldwide cooperation which the progress in modern science and technology has brought to the very door, to harbor economic egoism and antagonism, to engage in trade warfare, to erect tarriff barrier, to dump products, to issue hundreds of different currencies, and to induce the recurrent inflation, depression, and unemployment.

However, the nation may retain a bona fide position to do a good service in the long future, if and when its independence, sovereignty and nationalism were completely swept out.

8. World Commonwealth

When the process of group expansion merges all nations into a single group for the whole world, a world commonwealth will be spontaneously brought forth in a unitary or a federal form with a world government. Vested in the world government is a supreme authority derived from all peoples as a whole, and subordinated to the world government are the nations as autonomous local units or federal partners. Surely they cannot have independence, sovereignty and even nationalism anymore, nor to claim secession. Also they cannot engage in diplomatic business, enter into military alliances, produce and store arms, wage war, and impose tariffs. Nevertheless, they are regarded as self-ruled people. Their culture, economy, and government are respected as much as possible. They are encouraged to promote local business and social welfare. But they are not allowed to do anything against any law, policy or measure of the world government. Instead, they are obliged to carry them on by all means. Generally speaking, their status is similar to that of the state in the United States of America today.

Under the world government human rights and obligations will be well respected without any distinction as to race, sex, language or religion. Rights include: to life, liberty and security; to privacy, honor and reputation; to own property; to protect scientific, literary and artistic work; to free marriage and small family; to freedom of movement; to freedom of thought; to freedom of opinion; to freedom of assembly and association; to work and leisure; to economic and social security; to basic education; to participation in government; and to equal protection of the law. Obligations include: to humanity; to peace; to the general happiness; to care for the environment; to respect the rights and freedoms of others; and to obey the law.

The world government will consist of a world judiciary, a world administration, and a world council. The world judiciary is independent in nature, and will consist of a supreme court, regional courts and certain special courts. Its important judges are chosen by the world council. Going along with world judiciary is an enforcement system with an attorney general and regional attorneys, together with a small world police force. Important attorneys are also chosen by the world council. The enforcement system is subordinated to the world administration.

The world administration will consist of a board of directors under the leadership of a chairman, and a number of departments and agencies each headed by a director. The chairman and all directors are chosen by the world council and are responsible to it. The departments and agencies are service units, such as for population, food, health, energy, water, forest, housing, space, education, arts, athletics, finance, science and technology, commerce and industry, labor and management, transportation and communications, environment and conservation, social welfare, and natural calamities. There is no military unit, nor any unit for foreign affairs, because there is no other independent group to fight against and no foreign group to deal with anymore. Traditionally these two important units are where not only most of the money are spent, but also the dirtiest political tricks are played and feverish power struggles are engaged. Their omission means not only saving enormous expenses, but also stopping two evil sources of the government, and thus making it possible for the government to emphasize services rather than politics, and for experts rather than politicians to run the government.

For experts to run the government means not only to have all services performed by experts, but also to include their participation in lawmaking and policy decisions. It is for this reason that a house of experts is projected together with a house of commons to form a world council as the central organ of the world government. The house of experts will consist of a few hundred members, may be elected by worldwide academic, learned and professional associations on behalf of the people. They will select a chairman and will divide themselves into a number of committees under various subject headings to consider related proposals on law, policy, and assignment of important government jobs. Any proposal, either by the committees themselves, the world administration, the house of commons, or by other competent agencies, must first be deliberated by the related committee, then debated by the whole house, and finally forwarded to the house of commons for decision.

The house of commons will consist of members up to two times that of the house of experts. They will be elected by the people directly. If there is no other better way to allocate the seats for election, the nations as high level local units, can be used as basic electoral districts with a rational apportion according to population, such as one for a district with at least 1,000,000 (population); one for every 5,000,000 for the first addition of 50,000,000; one for every 25,000,000 for the second addition of 500,000,000: and one for every 125,000,000 for any further addition. A very large nation may divide into several high level local units, and neighboring very small nations may join into a high level local unit, with the approval of the world government.

The house of commons will select a chairman, and will take up any act forwarded from the house of experts for a general review rather than detailed discussions or minor modifications. If an act is favored by the house of experts, it can approve it by a simple majority, but cannot reject it without a two-thirds majority. If the act is not favored by the house of experts, it can reject it by a simple majority, but cannot approve it without a two-thirds majority. If it cannot either approve or reject, some solution may be worked out through a consultation with the house of experts, or decided by a majority of the world council.

The world council will be composed of all members of the two houses, each member with an equal vote. They will elect a president from the three candidates nominated by the house of experts. The president of the world council will also serve as the world president, with functions primarily in matters of official ceremony and formality.

The term of the president of the world council may be as long as to five years. The same is for the members of the house of commons, and double for the members of the house of experts. The longer terms for experts would make the government more stable for more regular business. There are four essences in the business of the world government: justice for the world judiciary, service for the world administration, knowledge for the experts and opinion for the commons. Since the commons are not obliged to spend as much time as the experts in the deliberation of legislation, they can pay more attention to looking over extensively any violation of laws and any neglect of duties by public officials. This kind of function is performed in some political systems by the public defender or ombudsmus.

It is the four essences of justice, service, knowledge and opinion that constitute a division of labor, in contrast to the traditional separation of three powers or balance and check, in the government. In order to make the division of labor working with high harmony, a world presidium will be established for coordination, consultation and reconciliation of the functions of the various branches of the government. The presidium will be composed of the world president, the chairmen of the world administration, the house of experts and the house of commons, and the chief justice of the world supreme court. Meetings will be called and presided over by the world president to discuss nothing more than certain cases in conflict.

Within the scheme of the world presidium, there will be a number of high offices, such as world budget bureau, world auditing bureau, world statistical bureau, world civil service commission, and world secretariat to assist the world president as an integrative organ.

The main purpose of the division of labor is to change the nature of the government from ruling the people to serving the people. This is in a positive way to apply the principles of democracy: of the people, by the people and for the people, based on the world law. The world law is a set of standard domestic rules for all functions of all governments and is to govern all individuals directly. It is superior to any local law, and leaves no room for the existence of international laws.

Of the world law, most important is a world constitution. With the fundamentals thus projected for the world government of the world commonwealth, a practical world constitution should be drafted for adoption as early as possible.

Along with the adoption of a world constitution, a suitable place should be chosen as the world capital, and perhaps several seats to be its regional centers. Also chosen is a common language for general as well as for official use, in addition to various native tongues. The metric system should be accepted as world standards for weights and measures. A world calendar should be perfected. A world zip code for mail and a world identification system for all individuals should be developed. Finally, it is necessary to adopt a world flag and a world anthem to promote supreme loyalty to all peoples through humanity.

There are two main objectives for the world government to achieve: permanent peace on earth and general happiness for mankind. The two objectives also are the ultimate goals of group expansion to reach eventually when all nations are merged into a single group. But time has been a most important factor now, because a nuclear war is threatening the whole world with a total destruction at any minute. Measures to prevent the catastrophe are urgently needed. They include to stand against any kind of war; to disband all armed forces except some police; to stop military conscription and training; to stop the making and developing any weapons, and to destroy all weapon stockpiles or to convert them for peaceful use. A world revolution is required to act for these measures right now, and the world government should finish the job and achieve a permanent peace on earth as its first objective.

In respect to the objective of general happiness, there are two requirements, two propositions, two themes, two priorities, and five important measures. The two requirements are:

351

the elimination of all war costs and the transfer of all money previously for military expenditures to finance the general happiness. The two propositions are: all natural resources of land, ocean, and space belong to mankind as a whole, and all existing economic systems are entitled to operate, compete and adjust by free will. The two themes are: advance through science and technology with humanity and ecosystems, and growth with balance; and the two priorities are: raising of the living standards in the poorer areas through the improvement and development of agriculture, industry, transportation and education, and control of the population to an optimum size in relation to food and other natural resources.

Finally come the five important measures: to save and develop energies, non-fuel minerals, forest products, and water; to improve and increase food production; to prevent and reduce natural calamities; to protect the environment with conservation by minimizing the destruction of natural resources, holding down pollutions, and relieving urban overcrowding with a pattern of small towns; and to to unify and equalize the economy with a world bank, world monetary system, universal income and inheritance taxes, and social security for all; by removing any barrier to trade and travel, and by stabilizing price and employment. Most of these measures need a world revolution to start actions too.

However, a world revolution is called primarily for a quick and complete sweep of the independence of the nation, national sovereignty, and nationalism, since they are the main stumbling blocks on the way of the group expansion to merge all nations into a single group. It is virtually a revolution in political ideology to wipe out traditional prejudice and superstition, and to free all peoples from the prison of the nation forever.

The call for a world revolution is very urgent, because a nuclear war may destroy the whole world at any minutes, and this threat can be avoided only by a quick and complete sweep of the main stumbling blocks to speed up the process of merging all nations into a single group. It should be done before it is too late and should be done right away by all means except violence. The world revolution does not rely upon violence.

352

The principle of non-violence distinguishes it from the conventional revolutions. Because of this, it may be not so sensational and so exciting. But reason will prevail. The support of the people will be the key to its success.

It is only through the success of the world revolution that all nations can be merged into a single group soon, only through the merging of all nations into a single group that a world commonwealth can be formed and an effective world government can be established, and only through the establishment of an effective world government that the two great objectives can be achieved. Since the support of the people is the key to the success of the world revolution, therefore, it is the people of the world who hold the key to their own permanent peace and general happiness.

Postlude

We mankind have come a long way from the same poor origin, have commenced our career at the bottom of the scale and found our way up from the savagery to build a civilization by hard works, and have accomplished a supremacy over the other creatures along rough roads.

The Planet Earth is our common home. It is nearly eternal. There is a great atmosphere to protect it, an immense water, agreeable air, vast land and beautiful forests to cover it, and a tremendous wealth of minerals to compose it. Thus our common home is actually a heaven with plenty of natural resources.

However, we have various troubles too, especially a cancer of war which has been threatening our civilization ever since, and its fever has been up and up in modern times. Since 1900, the nations have fought 207 wars in which 79 million people were killed, a 500% increase over the 19th century. Now a nuclear war may occur any minutes to destroy the whole world and annihilate all of us. There is no remedy for it and no way to escape from it except to abolish the war by merging all nations into a single group with a world government.

To merge all nations into a single group is the last step of the process of group expansion which we worked out and have applied step by step sucessfully for several million years. This process is a dynamic force of our history and the foundation of our civilization. It has enabled us to extend more and more peace, and to promote greater and greater happiness; and its last step would provide us with not only the only means to get rid of a nuclear holocaust but also the best chance to achieve a peace forever and a happiness everywhere.

Now modern science and technology have made all conditions ready for the last step of the group expansion to reach a world unity in which the nations, though merged into a single group, can still remain as autonomous local units under the world government. But their independence together with its symbol—national sovereignty and its agitator—nationalism must be completely swept out, because they are the main blocks on the last step to world unity.

Above all, war has deep roots in the independence of the nation, national sovereignty and nationalism, and war is legitimated and necessitated by them. They have made people cold-blooded to develop and produce weapons even for mass killing and total destruction, and professionally to plan and drill even for holocaust. They have made people to have no mercy to kill, no shame to destroy, and no fear even to doomsday. They have made people to ignore humanity, morality, commandment, law and order. They have made the whole world a vicious network of spy, and they have rendered all appeals for peace useless. Furthermore, they have made the nations to spend trillions of dollars every year to feed killing machines under the pretext of defense or pretending for peace, rather than to promote our livelihood and to save our environment. Yet, they are still defended, supported and worshipped in many ways, and even by those who are struggling for peace and world unity. This is a real danger, a danger to our existence.

Under the dangerous situation, let us remember the lesson of the great philosopher Albert Einstein that "A new type of thinking is essential if mankind is to survive and move to higher levels," and that "There is no salvation for civilization, or even the human race, other than the creation of a world government,"